Education, Pover Goals for Gender Equality

MW01030251

Drawing on case-study research that examined initiatives which engaged with global aspirations to advance gender equality in schooling in Kenya and South Africa, this book looks at how global frameworks on gender, education and poverty are interpreted in local settings and the politics of implementation. It discusses the forms of global agreements in particular contexts, and allows for an appraisal of how they have been understood by the people who implement them.

By using an innovative approach to comparative cross-country research, the book illuminates how ideas and actions connect and disconnect around particular meanings of poverty, education and gender in large systems and different settings. Its conclusions will allow assessments of the approach to the post-2015 agenda to be made, taking account of how policy and practice relating to global social justice are negotiated, sometimes negated, the forms in which they are affirmed and the actions that might help enhance them.

This book will be valuable for students, researchers, academics, senior teachers, senior government and inter-government officials and senior staff in NGOs working in the field of education and international development, gender, poverty reduction, and social development.

Elaine Unterhalter is Professor of Education and International Development at University College London, Institute of Education, London, UK.

Amy North is a Lecturer in Education and International Development, at University College London, Institute of Education London, UK.

Education, Poverty and International Development Series
Series Editors
Madeleine Arnot and Christopher Colclough
Centre for Education and International Development,
University of Cambridge, UK

This series of research-based monographs and edited collections contributes to global debates about how to achieve education for all. A major set of questions faced by national governments and education providers concerns how the contributions made by education to reducing global poverty, encouraging greater social stability and equity, and ensuring the development of individual capability and wellbeing can be strengthened. Focusing on the contributions that research can make to these global agendas, this series aims to provide new knowledge and new perspectives on the relationships between education, poverty and international development. It offers alternative theoretical and methodological frameworks for the study of developing-country education systems, in the context of national cultures and ambitious global agendas. It aims to identify the key policy challenges associated with addressing social inequalities, uneven social and economic development, and the opportunities to promote democratic and effective educational change.

The series brings together researchers from the fields of anthropology, economics, development studies, educational studies, politics, international relations and sociology. It includes work by some of the most distinguished writers in the fields of education and development, along with new authors working on important empirical projects. The series contributes significant insights on the linkages between education, economy and society, based on interdisciplinary, international and national studies.

Selected volumes will include critical syntheses of existing research and policy, work using innovative research methodologies, and in-depth evaluations of major policy developments. Some studies will address topics relevant to poverty alleviation, national and international policy-making and aid, while others will be anthropological or sociological investigations of how education functions within local communities, for households living in poverty or for particular socially marginalised groups. In particular, the series will feature sharp, critical studies that are intended to have a strategic influence on the thinking of academics and policy-makers.

Published titles

Education Outcomes and Poverty
A reassessment
Edited by Christopher Colclough

Teacher Education and the Challenge of Development
A global analysis
Edited by Bob Moon

Education Quality and Social Justice in the Global South
Challenges for policy, practice and research
Edited by Leon Tikly and Angeline Barrett

Learner-centred Education in International Perspective
Whose pedagogy for whose development?
Michele Schweisfurth

Professional Education, Capabilities and the Public Good
The role of universities in promoting human development
Melanie Walker and Monica McLean

Livelihoods and Learning
Education for All and the marginalisation of mobile pastoralists
Caroline Dyer

Gender Violence in Poverty Contexts
The educational challenge
Edited by Jenny Parkes

The 'Poor Child'
The cultural politics of education, development and childhood
Edited by Lucy Hopkins and Arathi Sriprakash

Educating Entrepreneurial Citizens
Neoliberalism and youth livelihoods in Tanzania
Joan DeJaeghere

Education, Poverty and Global Goals for Gender Equality
How people make policy happen
Elaine Unterhalter and Amy North

For more information on the series, please visit www.routledge.com/Education-Poverty-and-International-Development/book-series/EPID

Education, Poverty and Global Goals for Gender Equality

How People Make Policy Happen

Elaine Unterhalter and Amy North

Routledge
Taylor & Francis Group

LONDON AND NEW YORK

First published 2018 by Routledge

2 Park Square, Milton Park, Abingdon, Oxfordshire OX14 4RN
52 Vanderbilt Avenue, New York, NY 10017

Routledge is an imprint of the Taylor & Francis Group, an informa business

First issued in paperback 2018

British Library Cataloguing-in-Publication Data
A catalogue record for this book is available from the British Library

Library of Congress Cataloging-in-Publication Data
A catalog record for this book has been requested

ISBN: 978-0-415-82344-9 (hbk)
ISBN: 978-0-367-20379-5 (pbk)

Typeset in Galliard
by Apex CoVantage, LLC

In memory of Agnes Ndaba (28 Feb 1932–30 Jan 2017)
treasuring her life of love and hope

Contents

Tables

Acknowledgements

This book has been an inordinately long time in development and we are very grateful to the many people who have contributed along the way. The stepping off point for our analysis is the work we did together on the GEGPRI (Gender, education and global poverty reduction initiatives) research project between 2007 and 2011. GEGPRI was funded by an ESRC Award no. RES 167–25–260 under a partnership with DFID. The Institute of Education, University of London held the award and co-investigators were engaged in work for the project at the University of the Witwatersrand, University of KwaZulu-Natal and the Catholic University of Eastern Africa. We warmly acknowledge the financial and in -kind support from all these organisations.

We are very grateful for the contribution of participants in all the settings where we collected data in Kenya, South Africa, UK, USA and France. We recognise the time participants and members of our advisory committees gave to us, and the importance of their reflections, from which we have developed our analysis.

Our fellow members of the GEGPRI team were Veerle Dieltiens, Jenni Karlsson, Stu Letsasi, Herbert Makinda, Jane Onsongo and Chris Yates. Over the three years we worked together we learned a great deal and shared the pressures and pleasures of a cross-national collaboration, which involved fieldwork, and meetings in three countries, each going though different kinds of political change as the project unfolded. Our heartfelt thanks to all the members of the GEGPRI team for the work we did together, the discussions we had, and the insights we shared. Special thanks to Jenni Karlsson, who initially planned to be a co-author of this book, but had to withdraw because of changing work commitments. She made a substantial contribution to our thinking in shaping Chapter 5, and we are very grateful to her for helping with the beginnings of our book project. Chris Yates and Herbert Makinda have kept in touch with the project of writing the book, helpfully responding to our requests regarding sources and updating on developments. We hope this book, although somewhat different from some of our initial plans, stands as a record of our joint endeavour.

In addition to the core GEGPRI team many colleagues, students and friends have helped us by listening to ideas as we struggled to clarify them, reviewing some of the implications of the GEGPRI data, and alerting us to emerging scholarship on the themes of the book. It is difficult to name all the people on this long list, but we are most grateful for all these conversations. We have particularly appreciated invitations to present our emerging work at seminars, workshops, conferences and in policy discussions, all of which have helped us refine our insights. Side by side with acknowledging the professional climate which has nurtured some of our ideas, some special thanks are due. Firstly, these go to Jo Heslop, Jenny Parkes and Rosie Peppin Vaughan. Through our collaborative work on the MA in Education, Gender and International Development at the UCL Institute of Education, they have given us many opportunities to refine our thinking and reflect on our ideas with cohorts of students, who have asked wonderful and challenging questions. These interactions have kept returning us to the specifics of contexts and we want to acknowledge the insights we have gained from our colleagues and students with helping to unravel some of these processes. Secondly, a group of doctoral students, who, over the course of our work on this research project have crossed a boundary between being students and becoming colleagues and friends: Annette Braun, Emily Henderson, Helen Longlands, Tristan McCowan, Charley Nussey and Petya Ilieva-Tritchkova. They all generously gave time to talk about the hidden, difficult processes entailed in bringing a book to conclusion, linking this with the everyday work in a university. We very much appreciate their encouragement, and help with specific questions or problems, and the difficulties of the process. Thirdly, a group of critical friends have posed questions from the sidelines, prompting us to constantly examine our assumptions. Not all work on gender, education or poverty, but their sceptical questioning has kept us from falling into easy assumptions. Thanks to Sheila Aikman, Stephanie Allais, Saleem Badat, Leontine Bijleveld, Harry Brighouse, Bob Cowen, Ireen Dubel, Joan Dejaeghere, Ben Fine, Nora Fyles, Jasmine Gideon, Claudia Lapping, Thandi Lewin, Shirely Miske, Lebo Moletsane, Paul Morris, Rob Morrell, Gemma Moss, Moses Oketch, Louisa Polak, Ingrid Robeyns, Arathi Sriprakash, Sam Steel, Robbie van Niekerk, Jeff Waage and Melanie Walker for playing the valuable role of questioner.

This book has taken a very long time from the first outline, initially developed together with Jenni Karlsson in 2011, and then taking a circuitous path, to finalising the manuscript in early 2017. Without the sustained, constant and generous support of the Series Editors, Madeleine Arnot and Chris Colclough, we would have dropped the project because of many distractions that took us away from our initial ideas, and made it difficult to re-connect with the data after the GEGPRI project ended. Madeleine and Chris most generously encouraged us not to abandon the project. They were willing to read extremely preliminary drafts, comment with depth and insight, and help us as our ideas expanded from the initial commentary on the GEGPRI data, to more expansive reflections on the transition from the MDGs to the SDGs. They were always a wonderful mixture of rigour and encouragement. Our most sincere and heartfelt thanks to them for this substantial professional collaboration, going far beyond what we could have expected from editors. Without their encouragement, we would never have produced this book, and we have been immensely fortunate to work with their guidance and we are deeply grateful for all they have contributed.

In the last few months of preparing the manuscript Louise Wetheridge worked with us finalising the draft for copy editing. Her careful eye for detail, thoughtful pacing alongside us, and persistence to help us get the job done were immensely supportive. We thank her for her generosity with time, and all the work she has done, balancing our timetables against her own with good humour.

Our final big round of thanks go to members of our families who have seen close up some of the pressures of research, the difficulties of writing, and the uncertainties of projects which do not appear to finish. Over the long time of working on GEGPRI and this book four children were born into our immediate families, and four moved from school, through universities and into work. Our parents, partners, sisters, brothers, children and grandchildren have each in their own way given distraction, affection, support and love and we are immensely grateful to Ace, Beryl, David, Eli, Eloy, Hugo, Joe, Karrie, Oliver, Pau, Richard, Rosa, Sally, Sophie, Sophia and Tom.

Abbreviations

ANC	African National Congress
CBOs	Community Based Organisations
CEDAW	Convention on Elimination of Discrimination against Women
CRC	Convention on the Rights of the Child
CSOs	Civil Society Organisations
DFID	Department for International Development
EFA	Education for All
EFF	Economic Freedom Fighters
EPUs	Education Policy Units
ESRC	Economic and Social Research Council
FAWE	Forum on African Women's Education
FPE	Free primary education
FTI	Fast Track Initiative
GAD	Gender and Development
GCE	Global Campaign for Education
GEAR	Growth, Employment and Redistribution programme
GEGPRI	Gender, education and global poverty reduction initiatives
GEM	Girls' Education Movement
GETT	Gender Equity Task Team
GMR	Global Monitoring Report
GPE	Global Partnership for Education
IMF	International Monetary Fund
KESSP	Kenya Education Support Sector Programme
KNUT	Kenya National Union of Teachers
MDGs	Millennium Development Goals
NARC	National Rainbow Coalition
NGOs	Non Government Organisations
ODA	Overseas Development Assistance
RDP	Redistribution and Development Programme
SACMEQ	Southern and Eastern Africa Consortium for Monitoring Educational Quality
SADTU	South African Democratic Teachers Union
SAP	Structural Adjustment Programme

SDGs	Sustainable Development Goals
SMC	School Management Committee
SRGBV	School related gender based violence
UDHR	Universal Declaration of Human Rights
UN	United Nations
UNDP	United Nations Development Programme
UNESCO	United Nations Educational, Scientific and Cultural Organisation
UNGEI	United Nations Girls Education Initiative
UNICEF	United Nations International Children's Fund
USAID	United States Agency for International Development
WID	Women in Development
WIDE	World Inequality Database on Education

1   Introduction

As the new millennium dawned a chorus of voices asserted that linking policy and practice on gender, education and poverty might be, if not easy, largely a matter of political will and efficient planning.[1] As demonstrated in this book, analysis of practice indicates the frailty of this simple assertion. We examine some of the complex relationships entailed in the translation of global policy frameworks concerned with gender equality to national and local contexts, and whether, and on what terms, any authority is given to local actors. In charting the relationships entailed in taking global policy from a space of ideas, ideals and interpretations of experience, into action, we document how changed practice does and does not happen, and the ways in which people and the relationships they make are central to any process of change.

In September 2000 all the world's leaders gathered in New York for the Millennium Summit of the United Nations (UN). A decade of unprecedented collaboration in the afterglow of the fall of the Berlin Wall in 1989, and the end of the Cold War, had generated Declarations and cross-national working groups on pressing problems associated with poverty, climate change, inequalities, health, education, women's rights and many more. The importance of addressing the question of rights not just through states, transnational bodies and formal institutions, but through civil society and culture was widely acknowledged. The significance of gender in all the areas in which change was needed had been noted in many circles. The Beijing Declaration and Platform of Action from the World Conference on Women in 1995 had been agreed by virtually every government and a huge gathering of NGOs. High levels of economic growth in many countries meant there was no shortage of money for development assistance and the proliferation of information technologies pointed to a future where communication and information problems could be easily surmounted. It seemed there was a perfect alignment for addressing questions of gender, education and poverty and connecting policy and practice in these areas. A number of commentators remarked on the potential of this moment (Unterhalter, 2007; Kabeer, 2015; Mukhopadhyay, 2015).

In this climate, the Millennium Development Goals (MDGs) were agreed with a fifteen-year stretch to reaching targets which, in 2000, appeared achievable. The first three MDGs were concerned with poverty, education and gender

(Appendix 1). MDG2 on education, and elements of MDG3 on gender, echoed goals set out in the Dakar Framework on Education for All (EFA), which had been agreed in June 2000, also with an achievement date set for 2015 and with goals on addressing education access, quality and gender equality. The MDGs and EFA as policy frameworks were formulated to guide and accelerate processes that were already in train internationally, in the reformist agendas of many governments, and echoed some, but not all, of the demands of feminist activists. Gender and education had been centrepieces of global policy making for thirty years, while the expansion of schooling and strategies to engage with poverty had figured prominently in post-colonial policy discussions across the world since the end of World War 2. However, there were divided views amongst feminist activists and women's rights campaigners with regard to whether the location of gender equality reform in the MDG and EFA agenda was a good move, or, in the words of Peggy Antrobus, a most distracting gimmick (Antrobus, 2005). This book attempts to address this question, drawing on empirical data collected in Kenya, South Africa and in international organisations.

An unexamined assumption held by many, who agreed the MDGs and EFA, and went on to monitor and analyse them, was that policy rather than people made change happen in relation to gender equality. In this book, we question this. The argument we make shows that people, shaped by and shaping social relations under particular historical conditions, inside and outside government, take policy and re-make it through practice. The locations and relationships of people are an important part of how policy comes to be realised. The significance of this insight, long remarked in national studies of gender mainstreaming (Mkenda-Mugittu, 2003; Van Eerdewijk & Dubel, 2012; de Jong, 2016) is of particular salience when we need to understand gender equality policy and its transformation between global, national and local sites and the complexities of the relationships entailed. The settings, which comprise a mixture of physical, institutional and interpretative contexts, and the relationships of the people who inhabit these, have consequences for how policy is enacted as practice. People do not passively implement policy. They have views about the policy, even if they have not been directly involved in making it. Understanding the historically situated relationships of practices around gender equality policy is a key feature of understanding whether, or under what circumstances, global policy goals, like the MDGs, EFA and the current Sustainable Development Goals (SDGs) may be realised. An appreciation of these contexts can contribute to understanding how the critiques of these frameworks by feminist activists can chart some alternative ways forward. In this book we are concerned to trace these relationships and processes of enactment across the boundaries of what is deemed global, national and local. We look at how we can better understand the interconnection and separation of people, groups and organisations working in differently located sites of practice.

We focus on practices in what Chege and Arnot (2012) have called a gender, education and poverty nexus. Their framing joins sites of economic and gender inequalities with attempts to address these through education. They stress that through 'complex interactions' the three elements shape each other (2012, p. 196). Gender, education and poverty, the three areas of social development we are looking at, have all been the focus of scrutiny and debate regarding what they mean and the implications of different forms of understanding. Gender inequality in education and some aspects of poverty featured prominently in the planning for implementing the MDGs and EFA, for example, and they were monitored in the annual UNESCO EFA Global Monitoring Reports (e.g. UNESCO, 2004; UNESCO, 2010). However, gender is a term that encompasses many meanings (Connell, 2014; Henderson, 2014; Harcourt, 2016; Unterhalter, 2016) as is poverty (Chambers, 2006; Desai and Potter, 2013; Beneria, Berik and Floro, 2015) and while education is conventionally associated with schools, and the learning and teaching that takes place within them, the term itself has very wide connotations and many modalities that exceed this narrow setting (Brighouse, 2006; Cowen and Kazamias, 2009). The fluidity of meanings and the challenges entailed in building connections across areas of social development highlight some of the potential and some of the difficulties of engagements for gender equality reform.

In a key article, Grindle and Thomas (1991) defined the policy space as a site of process in which key decision-makers in government departments used choice, research, information and affiliation to take particular positions. They highlighted that a policy reform initiative may be altered by pressures and reactions from those who oppose it. 'Unlike the linear model, the interactive model views policy reform as a process, one in which interested parties can exert pressure for change at many points. . . . Understanding the location, strength and stakes involved in these attempts to promote, alter, or reverse policy reform initiatives is central to understanding the outcomes' (1991, p. 126). The work generated enormous attention to interactions around policy, and a number of studies looked at some of these in relation to education (Dyer, 1999; Riddell, 1999) or gender issues (Crichton, 2008; Walt et al., 2008; Moser, 2012). However, this work focuses on governments and institutions and we widen our scope in a number of directions: first to take account of global, national, and local processes; second to investigate relationships amongst particularly situated people within and beyond government concerning policy; and third to take account of the fluidity of the concepts under negotiation regarding gender, education and poverty policy, each of which is not just one 'thing'.

A prevalent feminist interpretation of the decade of the MDGs is that, for women's rights activists, it was a period of loss and diversion from the vision outlined at Beijing in 1995 (Sen and Mukherjee, 2014; Kabeer, 2015; Sandler, 2015). Our aim is to document whether this perception was shared by people working on gender equality, poverty and education issues in particular global, national and local settings. We investigate the practices and perspectives of reformers and those who refused change.

Central to our investigation and analysis is differentiating a number of overlapping terrains for gender equality reform, which we have identified as constituting *a middle space* and which stretches between a policy and its realisations. This space, positioned between the global and national/local is crucial for flows of ideas, and practices, which can facilitate or impede the realisation of international gender equality policy, and any appreciation of local contexts. We see this middle space as extensive. It stretches between two poles. One is constituted by a text, which articulates a policy, such as the list of MDG targets. The other comprises a series of finished actions signalled by the text such as enrolling girls and boys in school without discriminating on grounds of poverty or gender. The middle space is a large 'area' of institutions, intentions, opportunities, relationships and enactments, all of which shape gender equality reforms differently. We differentiate this space from particular sites of origin and realisation for policies. Sites of origin fix the relationships which ensure a policy text is agreed or money is allocated for implementation. Sites of realisation delineate the relationships when, in accordance with the policy aim, a child attends school, learns, is examined and awarded a qualification. Between these two are myriad settings for what Ball, Maguire and Braun (2012) call policy enactments. We argue that these enactments are all situated in a middle space, and that it is on this terrain that gender equality reform is worked out in practice. Practices take place in contexts where relationships are already set up by history, politics, economics or culture. But these can change, and how they do and in what directions is both a normative and an empirical question.

This middle space has a number of different contours and is occupied by diverse groups. This means that perspectives on gender equality are not just articulated in one terrain. The middle space comprises what Habermas (1989, 1996) and Taylor (1992) have called *the public sphere*. This is a fluid space of media, local public meetings and lectures in which public reasoning is aired. Seyla Benhabib (2011), in her writing on political philosophy and her theorisation of political membership, develops a notion of the public sphere that mediates some of the tensions between the universal and the particular, and which can be used to think about reflections on gender equality reform. She has also sought to theorise what she calls the challenge of *global constitutionalism*, that is the architecture of global policy frameworks. While these frameworks draw critiques both from theorists who stress the importance of state sovereignty and from those who highlight the significance of forms of communitarianism, Benhabib characterises a form of engagement with these processes that she terms *democratic iteration*. This is a process of public argument, deliberation and evaluation. It is Habermasian discourse ethics in action. While this is particularly appropriate to Habermas' idea of the public sphere, in Chapter 2 we develop an analysis that links democratic iteration with some of the ideas about the connection between different global and local spaces with regard to gender equality reform, and the practices of negotiating global policies.

A second terrain of this middle space is that of institutions, which frame, for example, the content and conduct of laws and regulations on gender equality, the organisation of a civil service, and assumptions about the exchange of money and services. A key perception of some of the work within national settings on gender mainstreaming, gender budgeting and getting institutions to respond to women and different facets of gender inequalities, had been that institutions were not sites where equality, rationality or efficiency could simply be imposed (Goetz, 1997; Moser and Moser, 2005; Waylen, 2007a). But the complexities of education institutions addressing gender inequalities across global, national and local boundaries have not been investigated very much, beyond documenting the difficulties of taking global gender equality policy into national settings (Greany, 2008; Manion, 2012; Russell, 2016). The ways that institutions concerned with gender reform may open or close down the terrain of the public sphere, and reflections from this terrain on gender and poverty, have not been much studied.

A third terrain of a middle space concerned with gender reform encompasses areas where institutions do not govern all aspects of social relationships. For example, relationships of professional conduct are sometimes regulated by official bodies. But they may also be guided by trade unions or more informal associations and by tacit codes of conduct. The relationships of professional associations most central to our investigation concern teachers, education officials, community workers and academic researchers, and hence we consider the extent to which gender equality was or was not part of their training, and practices of constitution, reflection and evaluation.

A fourth terrain of a middle space where gender equality reform is negotiated comprises other kinds of 'non-professional' relationships of sociability, such as the networks of friendship, the normative practices of NGOs around a common set of values or other types of association, for example as expressed by faith communities pursuing a particular set of normative beliefs or by community-based organisations (CBOs) promoting particular values of local belonging. Here, gender equality may be dealt with as a feature of formal employment practice, if a NGO has this in its work plan, or as an informal relationship of sociability. In some analyses, this is termed the terrain of civil society, and the ways in which gender equality is dealt with here are very nuanced in relation to context (Keck and Sikkink, 2014; van Leeuwen, 2016). Relationships may be animated by ties of legal contract or by affiliation, moral conviction and emotion. Inequalities and vulnerabilities, sometimes seen as illegitimate in the public sphere or in the realm of institutions or professional practice, may be given salience and consideration in the sphere of civil society.

We have analytically distinguished these four terrains of gender equality reform in a middle space that lies between global policy formulation and realisation because many analyses combine them. Indeed, as will be discussed in our data, in everyday lived experience these different terrains do intersect, and relationships criss-cross between them. However, the argument we make is that there are different terrains of gender equality in the middle space between policy formulation and realisation and all need attention, when working on gender, poverty and education, but in different ways. We can exemplify this analytical framework by looking at a well known example of a global gender equality policy, the Universal Declaration of Human Rights (UDHR) which moves across the arc of different terrains in this middle space between origin and realisation. In our illustrative example, we pay particular attention to how some of these dynamics play out in one country, South Africa.

In December 1948 UDHR was adopted by the United Nations General Assembly meeting in Paris. It contained a strong commitment to gender equality with regard to all humans having equal rights, regardless of race, sex or nationality. It detailed civil, political, economic, cultural and social rights. It included the right to free compulsory elementary education, general availability of technical, professional and higher education, and education dedicated to developing human personality. It enjoined an education that would inculcate respect for human rights and fundamental freedoms (Nickel, 1987; McCowan, 2013; Smith, 2016). As a legal instrument UDHR was accompanied by a number of Conventions that were agreed in subsequent decades. These included the Convention on the Elimination of Discrimination against Women (CEDAW), initially agreed in 1979, and the Convention on the Rights of the Child (CRC) formulated in 1989. These conventions were developed as instruments of international law, and then domesticated and adopted by national governments. This process marks the path we have referred to as the institutional terrain of a middle space on gender equality, and in this process we find international and national lawyers at work, and institutional structures being set up taking the form of national and international bureaucracies.

In our example it was noteworthy that South Africa, up until 1994, had a fraught relationship with texts like UDHR, was isolated internationally, and expelled from a number of bodies such as the Commonwealth and did not have a Constitution until after the end of apartheid. But, after that date, the national institutional terrain comprised laws on compulsory education, race and gender equality which echoed and expanded the UDHR and indeed made explicit reference formally and informally to a global architecture of human rights. Within the institutional terrain, there were relationships amongst civil servants who administered this system of education at national, provincial and district level. There was a Constitutional Court which adjudicated on problems and issues relating to gender equality, rights and education. The institutional terrain encompassed a process of reporting on progress to provincial assemblies and to the national parliament. In addition, the institutional terrain also faced towards international bodies, such as UNESCO, and the bodies the UN established to oversee CEDAW. South Africa reported formally to both. It can be seen that this institutional terrain of the middle space quite clearly demarcates areas that are international (for example concerned with CEDAW and UNESCO), areas that are national (laws, parliament, a Constitutional court), and areas that are local (provincial, district or circuit). The relationship between these is quite formally specified, with different areas of work identified and demarcated.

When we look at the public sphere there is a looser relationship between the global, the national and the local. Here, sections of UDHR on gender have elicited an enormous volume of commentary in media, scholarly publication, lectures, political interventions (for some examples and reviews see Steans, 2013; Otto, 2016). This work is not confined to a focus on one country or a particular locale but bears on conditions in over a hundred countries, and at the international and global level, and the similarities and contrasts between different local settings. Discussions in the public sphere include, for example, questions about whether rights to gender equality are normative and are to be adhered to because they are universal, or whether this vision imposes a particular world view from one part of the world on all others (Benhabib, 2011; Zwingel, 2012; Benería, Berik and Floro, 2015). In the terrain of the public sphere the discussion around gender equality and education is not sharply defined around boundaries of the global, the national and the local, although the salience of these boundaries is a key issue, as is the question of whether equalities can be transferred across borders. South Africa is sometimes exemplified in these commentaries because of its explicit engagement with a global architecture informing national constitution making (Waylen, 2007b; Langford et al., 2013). The public sphere in South Africa has some particular characteristics because of relatively large populations participating in discussions of gender through different forms of media, public gathering and educational reflection (Hassim, 2005; Fester, 2014; Gouws and Hassim, 2014; Walker, 2013). But these characteristics of the public sphere are not unique, and the kinds of debates in the public sphere in South Africa around gender reform have resonance with those in many other countries (Walsh, 2010; Paxton and Hughes, 2016).

In the terrain of professional association, a range of organised bodies of teachers, head teachers, social workers and education researchers, all have professional training, codes of conduct and approaches to learning about gender equality, human rights and education. While these bodies have national chapters, such as South African Democratic Teachers Union (SADTU), or South African National Association of Social Workers, they also are affiliated to international associations, such as Education International or International Federation of Social Workers. National professional bodies have local organisations and formal structures for reporting upwards and downwards in relation to how to take forward gender equality concerns. Thus in this terrain of gender equality reform there are bounded sites of professional activity, and looser international forums for exchanging ideas and building networks. While within SADTU, in the decade from 1994, there were tensions around gender equality, national and international affiliations, as Mannah's (2005) work highlights, forms of association around professional conduct shaped some of the ways in which these were negotiated.

In the terrain of civil society, there are a host of organisations with an interest in gender equality and education, ranging from international NGOs, like Amnesty, which has actively promoted UDHR, through to small service delivery organisations, linked to a particular place, person or project, such as Rape Crisis Cape Town or the Agenda media journal, which was initially a local publication of South African feminist researchers. Faith organisations have also been involved in work on gender, and many of these have transnational links, sometimes organised though large international organisations like CAFOD or World Vision. The long period of exile for people associated with the South African liberation movement meant that a shared vision of an aspect of equal rights, gender and education stretched across continents, ties of family, friendship and association. This is clearly evoked in a number of works of memoir and autobiography and has become the focus of some scholarly investigation (Bernstein, 1994; Morrow, Maaba and Pulumani, 2004; Suttner, 2003; Dalamba, 2008). It can be seen that this terrain of civil society working on gender, education and rights crosses nationally and/or locally defined spaces, and takes in ties of affiliation and belonging.

Thus in this example we can see that in all the four terrains of a middle space – the institutional, the public sphere, the professional and civil society – there have been different forms of engagement with a global policy like UDHR. Each of these engagements draw on different facets of education, but a concern with the formal setting of the school is common to all four terrains, although this appears in different guises. In virtually all contemporary states, the education system has developed in relation to institutions, but education provision is also shaped by the ideas, histories and relationships of professionals, discussions in the public sphere and the amorphous forms of civil society. This fluidity of education and perspectives on education is one of the features of the momentum of global gender policy we chart.

Conventional accounts of gender education policy transfer, borrowing or adaptation, consider only part of this terrain, generally looking at institutional or professional relationships. There is a considerable literature on attempts to transfer gender education policy from global bodies to national settings (Greany, 2008; Manion, 2012; Kendall and Kaunda, 2015; Stromquist, 2015). This shows how local interpretations do not connect well with global formulation. But there is little investigation as to why these disconnections might occur, and how ideas about gender in other areas might affect this process. Our aim in examining relationships and interpretation of gender reform in middle spaces, between policy formulation and implementation, is to try to understand what facilitates or impedes understanding flowing between differently situated groups. A feature of globalisation, and changing national and international strategies in education, is that in all four terrains we have delineated as facets of a middle space there is an overlap and intermixing between forms of association termed global, national and local. However, in different terrains this mixing takes different forms. Some may be formally demarcated institutionally, while others are very loosely intermixed. The term gender is deployed in relation to all four terrains but often suggests different kinds of concerns. In Chapter 2 we discuss some of the analytical issues this shape shifting raises.

The argument we set out in the book is that making an evaluation of global policy, like the MDGs or EFA, entails understanding the situations, responses and relationships of people in the different terrains of a middle space. Our specific focus is on how relationships in these terrains of a middle space work to form or fix practices in relation to gender equalities and inequalities, and gender equality policy. We give particular attention to education, and addressing poverty, themes given prominence in the MDGs and EFA, which echoed but reframed the vision of Beijing.

Researching global gender equality policy

Our rationale for researching global gender equality policy and how it was enacted needs clarifying in response to a number of implicit and explicit critiques of this aspiration. Firstly, there is a critique that global policy was clumsily framed, and would exacerbate, rather than undo gender inequalities. A number of commentators on the MDGs, and to a lesser extent EFA, raised concerns that the attenuated focus on limited targets, such as gender parity in education, would limit any success in implementation of wider gender equality goals, and that deeply ingrained sexism would inhibit the mobilisations needed to effect the necessary changes (Antrobus, 2005; Sen and Mukherjee, 2014; Vandenbeld, 2015). This critique points to the terrains of a middle space as sites where the direction of travel entails a *reproduction* of the gender inequalities of both global and national societies. This approach asks whether these terrains are able to offer locations for a set of processes or individual initiatives that might challenge these deeply entrenched inequalities. This analysis of reproduction suggests that global policy, which is not richly textured in demands for equalities, will provide no resources in the terrains of a middle space to shift these inequalities. Thus additional complementary policies to the MDGs and EFA are needed at the global and national level. The implication here is for better policy, and the assumption is that the terrains of a middle space are no different to that of global policy making, national or local implementation. Gender inequality is taken to be hardwired, and cannot be shifted without profound change. We have partly set out to examine the notion that all the terrains of a middle space work similarly to reproduce gender inequalities, and we also pose a question regarding what kinds of relationships and resources can help transform these same structures.

A second critique is not that the global gender and education policy is ineffective, but that it is too effective in the wrong areas and has had unintended consequences (Inoue and Oketch, 2008; Chisamya et al., 2012; Ngware et al., 2013). This argument, supported by a number of studies, shows that an effect of national governments responding to EFA and the MDGs meant that sites of poverty and gender inequality shifted from children out of school to those in school. Large numbers of children were enrolled in poorly equipped and supported schools, where teachers understood little about gender equality. Global policy, therefore, rather than transforming relations of inequality, merely relocated these. The implication of this analysis was that groups situated in the terrains of a middle space uncritically advocated these changes, without thinking about the contextual consequences. Expanding access to school in programmes for Free Primary Education (FPE) did not pay enough attention to new challenges emerging about quality or equality. The implication here was a need for better practice, largely at local and national level. But this analysis does not comment on how or whether different and more gender equitable forms of practice at the global level were appropriate for addressing gender inequalities nationally and locally, and what kinds of connections in the terrains of a middle space – institutions, the public sphere, professional practice or civil society – were most effective.

A third comment (DeJaeghere and Wiger, 2013; Moon, 2013; Baily and Holmardotir, 2015) was that there was insufficient capacity to realise the global gender equality policy frameworks in national and local settings. This was most evident in the inadequate numbers of teachers in post in some countries, which meant there were high pupil–teacher ratios as more children enrolled in schools. But gaps were also noted in the limited expertise in gender and poverty in teacher training courses, in NGOs and governments (DeJaeghere and Wiger, 2013; Bustelo, Ferguson and Forest, 2016). The critique here was that neither more policy, not better practice, would emerge without better understanding. However, what kind of understandings were needed to build capacity in the different terrains of a middle space were not well specified. Capacity development associated with gender mainstreaming, building institutions that could support women's rights, or undo cultures of patriarchy, were acknowledged to be difficult in an academic literature, though were sometimes discussed by practitioners as a technical issue requiring resources or training (Daly, 2005; van Staveren, 2008; Davids, Driel and Parren, 2014). While evaluators noted that more context sensitive policy and practice did not simply flow from technical training, narrowly understood, there was limited discussion of how to build capacity to engage in connecting work on gender, poverty and education across all terrains of a middle space.

We identify institutional, professional and ideational settings of a middle space as situated in locales between the global gatherings that decide on policy, like the MDGs and EFA, and the places where policy is implemented in schools. These comprise, for example, offices of multilateral and bilateral agencies, and NGOs, the work places of civil servants engaged with administering gender, education and poverty policy, and the meeting places of professional organisations, trade unions or local-level organisations. A range of relationships are also significant in the terrains of the middle space shaped by employment, affiliation, obligation or social division. In our analysis we attempt to trace the ways that relationships, histories and locales shape these terrains, and some of the consequences of this for how we understand negotiations with regard to global policy frameworks. Our concern is primarily with what practitioners in terrains of a middle space can learn from the experience of working with gender, poverty and education framed by the MDGs and EFA for the upcoming round of engagements with global policy making linked with the SDGs. We are also concerned to document whether opportunities were opened up or closed down for engagements with the wider vision of gender equality and women's rights formulated at Beijing in 1995.[2]

Drawing on empirical data we have collected from two national settings we suggest what such engagements look like, how and why discussion resolves in particular directions, and what additional resources of time, education and experience might be needed to deepen these reflections by groups differently situated in a middle space. We also consider whether particular kinds of negotiations are associated with specific forms of gender practice. We thus seek to draw out how the interface between the global, the national and the local textures the forms of democratic iteration that have occurred with regard to gender, poverty and education. In effect, our analysis looks at how global frameworks on gender, education and poverty are interpreted in a range of locales, and are subject to democratic dialogues, which take many forms and involve many actors in a middle space. Drawing on our findings by the end (Chapter 9) we attempt to theorise further the nature of the terrains of a middle space, the groups which occupy these spaces, and some implications for the SDG project.

Researching global gender policy across the terrains of a middle space

Our research on these themes has not been a simple matter. Our project collected and analysed data in a three and a half year collaborative research project, *Gender, education and global poverty reduction initiatives* (GEGPRI). This was funded by the UK Economic and Social Research Council (ESRC) between 2007 and 2011.[3] The project aimed to examine empirically initiatives which engaged with global aspirations to advance gender equality in and through schooling in contexts of poverty. Kenya and South Africa were selected as the research settings because both countries had put in place policies to address poverty reduction, the expansion of education provision and gender equality. Both countries were therefore active players in relation to the global policy frameworks in these areas. However, there were suggestive differences between the countries in relation to the histories of their engagement with global gender policy, pathways to democratic politics and their forms of the state. We thus considered that the similarities and the differences had potential to yield rich insight into variations in relationships in a middle space.

Our research aim was to explore, using a comparative approach in two countries, how the global gender frameworks of the MDGs and EFA were understood by people who were involved with negotiating and facilitating implementation. We looked at a range of sites which constituted a middle space between policy adoption and action. The sites were selected to examine the effects of particular histories of connection and disconnection to the global and the local. We wanted to investigate institutional, as well as personal, positioning in terrains of a middle space and how this played out in interpretations and practices regarding linkages between gender, poverty and education.

Three major research sites allowed for a set of nested comparisons. We chose these settings because all three were sites where there were active groups concerned with poverty, gender and education working in state and non-state settings. We expected to find in all three sites some form of engagement with the global–national–local dynamic. However, we were also concerned to understand how different settings in a middle space, and different relationships to the global, the national and the local, might form different actions of gender reform or refusal around education and poverty. Thus we aimed to select a number of different research settings within each large research site, so that we could examine similarities, differences, shifts and transformations regarding practices in a middle space.

We used a number of complementary qualitative research strategies to understand these processes in depth. We researched a number of state and non-state settings between 2008 and 2011. This strategy was designed to understand organisations and institutions in a key phase of activity around the MDG and EFA project. Two forms of comparison shaped the selection of research sites. Firstly, we were interested in vertical comparisons, considering differences between organisations that operated at the level of the global, the national and the local. Thus, we investigated different interpretations of the MDG policy regarding gender, education and poverty articulated by and in multilateral and bilateral bodies and global NGOs, comparing this with interpretations made at the national to the local level. Secondly, we were interested in horizontal comparison between state and non-state bodies at different levels (global, national and local). We investigated whether there were similarities and differences with regard to interpretation made in state and non-state organisations working at international, national and local level.

Key sites for data collection were global organisations, that is multilateral bodies, like UNESCO and UNICEF, bilateral organisations, such as DFID and USAID, and global NGOs like Oxfam and Save the Children. All had offices in capital cities in G8 countries. We conducted interviews with key members of staff in organisations of this type engaged in taking forward policy on gender, education and poverty. We discussed their views of the form and process of global agreements, how they considered these agreements were being put into effect, and the relationships they were forming with governments and NGOs. In these discussions we did not limit observations to reflections on relationships with Kenya and South Africa but ranged very widely over the different areas in which global organisations were engaged.

Our first strategy for the vertical comparisons in each country was to document the work on gender education and poverty of the national education department (the Department of Education in South Africa and the Ministry of Education in Kenya). In both, we anticipated there was likely to be a strong engagement with a national project of education expansion to address poverty, given concerns with transforming the relationships of apartheid in South Africa, and implementing the Free Primary Education (FPE) policy in Kenya. We also anticipated that here we would find discussion of gender and education, as this had been an issue highlighted at Ministerial level in both countries when the study was being designed (Kenya, 2005; South Africa, 2007). However, we anticipated there would be national differences. This was partly because of the prominence and influence of the viewpoints of the development assistance community in Kenya. At the time of the data collection, aid was flowing to the Ministry of Education in Kenya after many years of suspension amid concerns at corruption and poor governance. By contrast, South Africa was not so closely interlinked with overseas development assistance (ODA) for basic education provision. In joining the G20 in 2008 and taking a seat on the Security Council, South Africa was becoming a powerful global player, both in Africa and at the UN. Thus, we considered the national departments of education in each country, while engaged with gender and poverty, would provide different portrayals of sites in a middle space in relation to global politics.

We also anticipated that the form of institutional arrangement from the national centre to local education departments would be different in each country, providing further examples of variations of relationships in a middle space. In each country we made a study of a provincial department of education in a region with a large, predominantly rural population with high levels of poverty, according to a range of indicators. We looked at work on gender, poverty and education at district level in urban, peri-urban and rural districts in this province/ region in each country.

The level of institutional autonomy at provincial level was different in each country. In South Africa, a substantial part of local decision-making and education policy implementation rests with elected provincial assemblies. The national Department oversees co-ordination and provides policy leadership, rather than directing every detail of policy orientation and day-to-day administration. In Kenya, by contrast, at the time of data collection, the national Ministry of Education was an apex organisation through which all decision-making passed and there was no devolution of decisions around policy or practice to local assemblies. (Our data collection took place before the formation of counties in Kenya in 2012). Thus since the organisational form in each country was different, we were concerned to examine how different institutional forms shaped engagements with global gender equality policy.

We also anticipated we would find different kinds of national perspectives on gender equality. In South Africa, key figures from the women's movement had gone into government in the 1990s (Hassim, 2005), while in Kenya women's organisations stood at some distance to government (Tripp, 2001). We wanted to examine how these different positions might affect approaches to gender mainstreaming and gender policy negotiation in the national government department. We anticipated that the politics of ethnicity in Kenya, and race in South Africa, might shape local level engagements with gender and poverty, articulated by government officials, but we did not know how historically nuanced relationships of race and ethnicity might play out in relation to interpretations of global policy frameworks regarding gender, education and poverty.

The last setting for our vertical comparison was a qualitative investigation in one school in each country in a matched neighbourhood on the edge of a large city serving a poor population. The arrangements for school-level governance in South Africa give somewhat more decision-making power to governing bodies, compared to Kenya (Sayed and Soudien, 2005) and key responsibilities are associated with language and teacher employment. We wanted to explore whether this might expand into concerns with poverty and gender equality, and whether more limited local-level responsibility in Kenya might shape different kinds of views on social division.

Our horizontal comparisons between state and non-state organisations looked at these in terms of global-national and local levels of engagement with gender, education and poverty policy in each country. From the 1990s, NGOs had been key players taking forward arguments around expanding education rights, and engaging with gender equality (Mundy and Murphy, 2001; Robertson, Mundy and Verger, 2012; Macpherson, 2016). NGOs take many forms, with some in a position to nominate key players to take part in global decision-making fora, while others work close to the grassroots. Some education NGOs have close relationships with government and others are fierce critics (DeJaeghere, Parkes and Unterhalter, 2013; Macpherson, 2016). Thus the NGO sector offered a range of different ways to look at the relationships in a middle space. In each country qualitative data was collected from an NGO working on questions of poverty, gender and schooling in a rural setting. This gave opportunities to look at relationships in a middle space close to experiences of poverty and inequality. We also conducted research in each country in an NGO working at the national level on gender and poverty. These were engaged in discussions with global networks, as well as work at a national and local level. We hoped this research strategy would allow us to document relationships on terrains of a middle space associated with civil society and the public sphere, in addition to institutions and professional associations.

To sum up our research design and the different sites of data collection Table 1.1 shows both the levels of vertical comparison (from global, through national to local), and the horizontal comparisons between state and non-state organisations.

In collecting and analysing data across these different sites we set out to disentangle forms of relationship, terrains of a middle space, and contestations over meanings with regards to global policy. A multi-country research team (Appendix 2) collected the data. The instruments for data collection were developed through a process of consultation and review that involved research team meetings, country advisory committees, ethics review committees at universities in the UK and South Africa and the Ministry of Education in Kenya. Pilot interviews were conducted in all the research sites. Thereafter, in each research site

Table 1.1 Horizontal and vertical comparisons: sites of data collection

Vertical comparisons	*Horizontal comparison*	
	State	*Non-state*
Global level	Multilateral and bilateral organisations	Global NGOs
National level	Ministry of Education Kenya & Department of Education South Africa	Global NGO operating in Kenya & South Africa
Provincial & district level	Provincial & District level offices of Ministry of Education (Kenya) and Department of Education (South Africa)	Provincial and district level projects of global NGO in Kenya and South Africa
Local level	School in peri-urban area in Kenya & South Africa	Local NGO working on rural poverty & education in Kenya & South Africa

we conducted in depth semi-structured interviews with key stakeholders engaged in aspects of policy enactment in relation to the gender, education and poverty nexus and collected observation data in offices and meetings, as well as analysing key documents. In a series of report back meetings on preliminary findings in each research site, we shared our emerging analysis with research participants, and listened to their reflections on this.

Table 1.2 lists all the data collected and analysed for the study. Each chapter in Part 2 of this book draws on data from all the research settings,[4] and indicates the similarities and differences between how issues emerged and were negotiated by diverse kind of groups in the terrains of a middle space, which had different contours in each country.

In interpreting the data we drew on skills of the multi-country team, with different kinds of connection to the issues being researched and the locales in which the negotiation of global policy frameworks took place. Social location, processes of negotiating relationships with data collection and analysis and the shifting hierarchies between the global, national and the local played a particular

Table 1.2 Data collected and analysed for the study

	Phase One	*Phase Two*
MoE/DoE Kenya South Africa	Feb 2007–Apr 2009: Interviews, informal discussions, focus group discussions, observations, document analysis, report back discussions	Oct 2008–Aug 2010: Interviews, group discussions, focus group discussions, report back and exit interviews
Province/district Kenya South Africa	Feb–Aug 2009: Interviews, focus group discussions, observations, document analysis, report back discussion	Oct–Nov 2010: Interview; report back and exit interview
School Kenya South Africa	Mar–Jun 2008: Interviews, focus group discussion, observations, community mapping, document analysis, report back discussion	Jul–Dec 2010: Interviews, group discussions, report back and exit interview
Local NGO Kenya South Africa	Jun–Aug 2009: Interviews, focus group discussions, observations, document analysis, report back discussion (Feb 2010)	Mar 2010: Interviews, focus group discussions, report back and exit interview (Nov 2010)
National/global NGO Kenya South Africa	Mar–Aug 2009: Interviews, focus group discussions, observations, document analysis, report back discussion	Aug–Dec 2010: Interviews, focus group discussions
International organisations	Jul 2007 – Nov 2010 Interviews with key informants, observations, document analysis	

part. These themes were not just as the area for investigation, but also shaped the professional biographies of the research team. Two members, Elaine Unterhalter, who co-ordinated the research project, and Amy North, who was the Research Officer based in London, have worked since 2000 on aspects of gender, education and poverty reduction with different kinds of global organisations. They have participated in meetings of multilateral and bilateral organisations, have been part of NGO networks and from 2003, when Elaine Unterhalter had set up the *Beyond Access* project with Sheila Aikman. They have worked to promote and co-ordinate discussion among policy makers, practitioners and researchers on the gender and education MDGs (MDG2 and 3). During the fieldwork phase of GEGPRI, Elaine Unterhalter was also involved in a number of NGO-led research projects on gender and education, and, since the end of the GEGPRI project, has maintained links with a number of NGOs concerned with gender, education and poverty, as well as some of the key multilateral organisations. Amy North had inside knowledge of one large global NGO and civil society networks, having worked for Oxfam for two years. Elaine Unterhalter had discussed some of the ideas GEGPRI set out to examine empirically in her largely theoretical book *Gender, schooling and global social justice* (Unterhalter, 2007), which was partly a reflection on the experience of *Beyond Access*. In designing the project and collecting data she was able to draw on her experience of growing up and studying in South Africa, her work on education and gender with the ANC in exile in London to 1991, and her participation with many South Africans in the development of a post-apartheid education system and discussions within a number of global organisations.

Research in Kenya and South Africa required particular knowledge of local contexts which ranged from the national Department/Ministry of Education, through provincial departments, down to a school and a rural NGO. In South Africa, Jenni Karlsson and Veerle Dieltiens both had long experience of working with the Education Policy Units (EPUs) at the University of KwaZulu Natal and Witwatersrand respectively. The EPUs, initially set up in the late 1980s to support the mass democratic movement against apartheid with research, transformed with the establishment of the new government into centres for research, critique and analysis. Although by the time the GEGPRI research took place Jenni Karlsson had left the EPU and was a Senior Lecturer at the University of KwaZuluNatal (UKZN), the network of contacts she and Veerle Dieltiens could draw on in national and provincial government as well as the NGO community was a significant resource for the project. They were assisted in field work by two project officers, Setungoane Lestatsi and Nomanesi Madiye, who had recently completed Masters degrees and thus had insight into some of the conceptual themes we were examining. Amongst this research team there were language skills to enable interviews to take place in languages in which informants were comfortable.

In Kenya, the fieldwork was conducted by a team of three. Jane Onsongo had experience of qualitative research in education and involvement with gender activism. She had to resign from the project before its conclusion because of her appointment to the Anti Corruption Commission in 2010. Herbert Makinda, who had been the project officer, took over and completed the field work and analysis building on his knowledge of local communities. Chris Yates from the Institute of Education, University of London, led on some of the interviews with the national Ministry of Education and the global NGO. Access to the Ministry of Education was facilitated partly because of Chris Yates' work over fifteen years with staff in the Ministry on teacher development projects and a number of large evaluations for DFID. Support from members of the project Advisory Committee in Kenya (Appendix 3) were also crucial in helping to gain access to research sites. It can thus be seen that the social location of the research team helped facilitate access to the research sites, and shaped features of the analysis that developed. We return to further reflection on this theme in Chapters 3–6.

In all the research sites, the research design involved report back meetings and reflections on the emerging findings. Thus a critical perspective on location and the process of negotiating between the different levels in the global–national–local nexus was a key reflexive theme throughout the project. The members of the Kenya and South Africa advisory committees, set up by members of the research team (Appendix 3) were a crucial resource in helping to plan these report back meetings and make sense of the discussions that emerged. It can thus be seen that particular skills concerned with networking, local knowledge, personal history and political engagement have been an important resource for the conduct of this study.

Many researchers were associated with the GEGPRI project and the ethos of work on the project stressed collaboration and discussion. In developing the analysis of data from that project for this book, we were committed to continue this process, but aware that it is impossible for many people to co-author and share responsibility equally. We thus took a decision as a team that there would be two lead authors (Elaine Unterhalter, Amy North) who put the book together developing its overall argument, updating the analysis to take account of the events that had taken place since the original phase of data collection, ensuring coherence, and seeing the manuscript through publication.[5]

The structure of the book

The chapters that follow take up a number of themes that illuminate the politics of policy negotiation and transformation, and the practices used by different kinds of groups in a middle space. We analyse forms of engagement around different locales and terrains of a middle space, some of which connect and some of which divide policy flows on gender, education and poverty. We explore these to consider the translation of global policy frames into local contexts. We look both at enabling pathways that suggest deepening insights into rights and equalities and also settings that attenuate or disorient these processes. The themes we consider are concerned with the relationship between global principles and obligation and local policy and practice, when neither is static and untouched by the complexities of history and the instability of the shifting form of groups located in a middle space. The key line of investigation in the book concerns the nature of the MDG and EFA projects in relation to gender equality reform in education. We examine how these were interpreted in different locales, and struggles over meaning and action that ensued.

The chapter structure has been organised to build up different perspectives on this issue. We begin in Chapter 2 to discuss some of the key contentions around defining gender, equality, poverty and global policy flow. This provides some of the theoretical and conceptual background to the scholarly investigation, to which our discussion aims to contribute.

In Part 1 we provide background on the research settings, looking at the global level in Chapter 3, the country context in Kenya (Chapter 4), and in South Africa (Chapter 5). These chapters also provide some detail of our approach to data collection and the range of perspectives participants in each setting formulated on the MDGs. Chapter 3 outlines the first research settings, analysing the international policy frameworks which provided the context for some of the key global policy actors we spoke to. It outlines some of the perspectives of key informants on how they saw the global–national–local relationships in which gender and education policy was being negotiated. Chapter 4 gives a background history on Kenya, the second research setting, from 1960 to approximately 2012, and the policy context concerning gender, education and poverty. It details our research in different sites in state and non-state settings for work on gender, education and poverty, and presents some engagements of key informants with global gender equality policy. Chapter 5 provides a similar context for the South African phase of the research.

In Part 2 we look across the various research sites and consider how particular facets of global policy on gender, education and poverty were negotiated, interpreted and enacted. Chapter 6 looks at the meanings of gender equity in play in a range of locales, and the processes by which richer and more complex meanings tended to be silenced or reduced to essentialised features of girls and school performance, and some of the reasons for this. Chapter 7 presents data on how blame and disconnection from the lives of the poor feature in a nexus of ideas and actions about implementing global policy. Chapter 8 investigates gender mainstreaming and how the distinctions Unterhalter (2007) suggested between interventions, institutions and interactions might illuminate different approaches to adopting this. The conclusion (Chapter 9) considers some of the implications of the analysis for the upcoming engagement with the SDGs, and discusses some of the additional work needed both conceptually and empirically to understand the terrains of a middle space in relation to policy on gender equality, poverty and education. We point to the need for adequate resources, and structures for co-ordination and in-depth education, including teacher development and training for civil servants, particularly at district level, and NGO workers. We conclude on the importance of reflexive engagements with theory and practice as part of the process of democratic iteration, and more engaged practice on women's rights, gender and other equalities, education and approaches to address poverty, so that in building to support the SDGs some of the difficulties associated with the history with the MDGs and EFA can be acknowledged and transformed.

Notes

1 This was a widespread belief expressed in speeches by leading political figures, such as Kofi Annan, the directors of large global NGOs, civil servants and researchers. Some of the detail of these assertions are assembled in Aikman and Unterhalter, 2005; Aikman and Unterhalter, 2007; Monkman and Hoffman, 2013.
2 UN Women (1995). Fourth World Conference on Women Beijing Declaration [online]. Available at www.un.org/womenwatch/daw/beijing/platform/declar.htm
3 The project *Gender, education and global poverty reduction initiatives* was funded by the UK Economic and Social Research Council (ESRC) Award no. RES 167–25–260 under a partnership with the UK Department for International Development (DFID). The project began in September 2007 and was completed in March 2011. The Institute of Education, University of London held the award and co-investigators were engaged in work for the project at the University of the Witwatersrand, University of KwaZulu Natal, and the Catholic University of Eastern Africa. Appendix 3 lists all the people who contributed to the work of the project.
4 A report (Unterhalter et al., 2011) based on a first analysis of the data from all the case studies was prepared for dissemination meetings which took place in Nairobi, Johannesburg and London in 2011. The full data set of transcribed interviews, discussions and field notes is available from the UK Data Archive at Essex University at https://reshare.ukdataservice.ac.uk/cgi/users/home?screen=EPrint%3A%3AView&eprintid=852640. A number of journal articles, book chapters, conference papers and discussions for professional publications have been prepared exploring aspects of this data.
5 All the people listed in Appendices 3 and 4 made contributions to elements of the research project from which this book has developed Jenni Karlsson was initially a member of the team working on the book, and researched some of the material which was incorporated into Chapters 3 and 5. However, changing work circumstances meant she was not able to participate in the formulation of the argument and analysis for the book which stepped off from the GEGPRI project. Herbert Makinda and Chris Yates were valuable interlocutors as we revised the material for Chapter 4.

References

Aikman, S., & Unterhalter, E. (2005). *Beyond Access: Transforming Policy and Practice for Gender Equality in Education*. Oxford: Oxfam, GB & Practical Action Publishing.
Aikman, S., & Unterhalter, E. (Eds.). (2007). *Practicing Gender Equality in Education*. Oxford: Oxfam GB & Practical Action Publishing.
Antrobus, P. (2005). MDGs: Most distracting gimmicks? *Convergence*, 38(3), pp. 49–52.
Baily, S., & Holmarsdottir, H. B. (2015). The quality of equity? Reframing gender, development and education in the post-2020 landscape. *Gender and Education*, 27(7), pp. 828–845.
Ball, S., Maguire, M., & Braun, A. (2012). *How Schools Do Policy: Policy Enactments in Secondary Schools*. Abingdon: Routledge.

Benería, L., Berik, G., & Floro, M. (2015). *Gender, development and globalization: economics as if all people mattered.* London: Routledge.

Benhabib, S. (2011). *Dignity in Adversity: Human Rights in Troubled Times.* Cambridge: Polity Press.

Bernstein, H. (1994). *The rift: The exile experience of South Africans.* London: Random House.

Brighouse, H. (2006). *On Education.* London: Routledge.

Bustelo, M., Ferguson, L., & Forest, M. (Eds.). (2016). *The Politics of Feminist Knowledge Transfer: Gender Training and Gender Expertise.* London: Palgrave Macmillan.

Chambers, R. (2006). What is Poverty? Who asks? Who answers? *Poverty in Focus,* pp. 3–4 [online]. Available at https://opendocs.ids.ac.uk/opendocs/bitstream/handle/123456789/120/rc145.pdf?sequence=2&isAllowed=y.

Chege, F. N., & Arnot, M. (2012). The gender–education–poverty nexus: Kenyan youth's perspective on being young, gendered and poor. *Comparative Education,* 48(2), pp. 195–209.

Chisamya, G., DeJaeghere, J., Kendall, N., & Aziz Khan, M. (2012). Gender and Education for All: Progress and problems in achieving gender equity. *International Journal of Educational Development,* 32(6), pp. 743–755.

Connell, R. W. (2014). *Gender and Power: Society, the Person and Sexual Politics.* London: John Wiley.

Cowen, R., & Kazamias, A. (2009). *International Handbook of Comparative Education.* Dordrecht: Springer.

Crichton, J. (2008). Changing fortunes: analysis of fluctuating policy space for family planning in Kenya. *Health Policy and Planning,* 23(5), pp. 339–350.

Dalamba, L. (2008). Storing and storying lives: the biographical illusion in three musicians' autobiographies. *SAMUS – South African Music Studies,* 28(1), pp. 55–72.

Daly, M. (2005). Gender mainstreaming in theory and practice. *Social Politics,* 12(3), pp. 433–450.

Davids, T., van Driel, F., & Parren, F. (2014). Feminist Change Revisited: Gender Mainstreaming as Slow Revolution. *Journal of International Development,* 26(3), pp. 396–408.

DeJaeghere, J., Parkes, J. & Unterhalter, E. (2013). Gender justice and education: Linking theory, policy and practice. *International Journal of Educational Development,* 33(6), pp. 539–545.

DeJaeghere, J., & Wiger, N. (2013). Gender discourses in an NGO education project: Openings for transformation toward gender equality in Bangladesh. *International Journal of Educational Development,* 33(6), pp. 557–565.

de Jong, S. (2016). Mainstream (ing) has never run clean, perhaps never can: Gender in the main/stream of development. In Harcourt W. ed. *The Palgrave Handbook of Gender and Development.* London: Palgrave Macmillan, pp. 92–105.

Desai, V., & Potter, R. B. (2013). *The Companion to Development Studies.* Abingdon: Routledge.

Dyer, C. (1999). Researching the implementation of educational policy: a backward mapping approach. *Comparative Education,* 35(1), pp. 45–61.

Fester, G. (2014). South Africa: Revolution protracted or postponed? In Nazneen, S. & Sultan, M. eds. *Voicing Demands: Feminist Activism in Transitional Contexts.* London: ZED Books.

Goetz, A. M. (1997). *Getting Institutions Right for Women in Development.* London: ZED Books.

Gouws, A., & Hassim, S. (2014). Who's afraid of feminism? South African Democracy at 20: An Introduction. *Agenda*, 28(2), pp. 4–6.

Greany, K. (2008). Rhetoric versus reality: Exploring the rights-based approach to girls' education in rural Niger. *Compare: A Journal of Comparative and International Education*, 38(5), pp. 555–568.

Grindle, M. S., & Thomas, J. W. (1991). *Public Choices and Policy Change: The Political Economy of Reform in Developing Countries.*Baltimore: Johns Hopkins University Press.

Habermas, J. (1989). *The Structural Transformation of the Public Sphere.* Cambridge: Polity Press.

Habermas, J. (1996). *Between Facts and Norms: Contributions to a Discourse Theory of Law and Democracy.* London: The MIT Press.

Harcourt, W. (2016). Gender dilemmas in international development studies. *European Journal of Development Research*, 28(2), pp. 167–174.

Henderson, E. F. (2014). *Gender Pedagogy: Teaching, Learning and Tracing Gender in Higher Education.* London: Palgrave.

Inoue, K., & Oketch, M. (2008). Implementing Free Primary Education Policy in Malawi and Ghana: Equity and Efficiency Analysis. *Peabody Journal of Education*, 83(1), pp. 41–70.

Kabeer, N. (2015). Tracking the gender politics of the Millennium Development Goals: struggles for interpretive power in the international development agenda. *Third World Quarterly*, 36(2), pp. 377–395.

Keck, M. & Sikkink, K. (2014). *Activists Beyond Borders: Advocacy Networks in International Politics.* Ithaca: Cornell University Press.

Kendall, N., & Kaunda, Z. (2015). Girls, schooling, and reproductive realities in Malawi. In *Educating Adolescent Girls Around the Globe: Challenges and Opportunities.* Abingdon: Routledge, pp. 23–39.

Kenya, Ministry of Education Science and Technology (2005). Kenya Education Sector Support Programme Nairobi: Ministry of Education, Science and Technology.

Langford, M., Cousins, J. & Madlingozi, T., eds. (2013). *Socio-economic Rights in South Africa: Symbols or Substance?* Cambridge: Cambridge University Press.

Macpherson, I. (2016). An Analysis of Power in Transnational Advocacy Networks in Education. In Mundy, K., Green, A., Lingard, B., & Verger, A. eds. *The Handbook of Global Education Policy.* Chichester: Wiley-Blackwell, pp. 401–415.

Manion, C. (2012). Power, knowledge and politics: Exploring the contested terrain of girl-focused interventions at the national launch of the United Nations girls' education initiative in the Gambia. *Theory and Research in Education*, 10, pp. 229–252.

Mannah, S. (2005). The state of mobilisation of women teachers in the South African Democratic Teachers' Union. In Chisholm, L. and September, eds. *Gender Equity in South African Education 1994–2004: Perspectives from Research, Government and Unions: Conference Proceedings.* Pretoria: HSRC Press, pp. 146–155.

McCowan, T. (2013). *Education as a Human Right: Principles for a Universal Entitlement to Learning.* London: Bloomsbury Academic.

Mkenda-Mugittu, V. (2003). Measuring the invisibles: Gender mainstreaming and monitoring experience from a dairy development project in Tanzania. *Development in Practice*, 13(5), pp. 459–473.

Monkman, K., & Hoffman, L. (2013). Girls' education: The power of policy discourse. *Theory and Research in Education*, 11(1), pp. 63–84.

Morrow, S., Maaba, B. & Pulumani, L. (2004). *Education in Exile: SOMAFCO, the African National Congress School in Tanzania, 1978 to 1992.* Cape Town: HSRC Press.

Moser, C. (2012). *Gender Planning and Development: Theory, Practice and Training.* London: Routledge.

Moser, C., & Moser, A. (2005). Gender mainstreaming since Beijing: A review of success and limitations in international institutions. *Gender & Development*, 13(2), pp. 11–22.

Mukhopadhyay, M. (2015). Gender citizenship in the postcolony. In Baksh, R., & Harcourt, W. eds. *The Oxford Handbook of Transnational Feminist Movements.* New York: Oxford University Press, pp. 607–625.

Mundy, K., & Murphy, L. (2001). Transnational advocacy, global civil society? Emerging evidence from the field of education. *Comparative Education Review*, 45(1), pp. 85–126.

Ngware, M., Oketch, M., Ezeh, A.C., & Mutisya, M. (2013). The effect of free primary education policy on late school entry in urban primary schools in Kenya. *International Review of Education*, 59(5), pp. 603–625.

Nickel, J. W. (1987). *Making Sense of Human Rights: Philosophical Reflections on the Universal Declaration of Human Rights.* London: University of California Press.

Otto, D. (2016). Gender and Sexual Diversity: A Question of Humanity? *Melbourne Journal of International Law*, 17, pp. 477–488.

Paxton, P. & Hughes, M. (2016). *Women, Politics and Power: A Global Perspective.* Third edition. USA: CQ Press.

Riddell, A. R. (1999). The need for a multidisciplinary framework for analysing educational reform in developing countries. *International Journal of Educational Development*, 19(3), pp. 207–217.

Robertson, S., Mundy, K., Verger, A., & Menashy, F., eds. (2012). Public Private Partnerships in Education: *New Actors and Modes of Governance in a Globalizing World.* Cheltenham: Edward Elgar Publishing.

Russell, S. G. (2016). Global gender discourses in education: evidence from postgenocide Rwanda. *Comparative Education*, 52(4), pp. 492–515.

Sandler, J. (2015). The "Warriors Within": How feminists change bureaucracies and bureaucracies change feminists. In Baksh, R. and Harcourt, W. eds. *The Oxford Handbook of Transnational Feminist Movements.* Oxford: Oxford University Press, pp. 188–214.

Sayed, Y., & Soudien, C. (2005). Decentralisation and the construction of inclusion education policy in South Africa. *Compare*, 35(2), pp. 115–125.

Sen, G., & Mukherjee, A. (2014). No empowerment without rights, no rights without politics: Gender equality, MDGs and the post-2015 development agenda. *Journal of Human Development and Capabilities*, 15(2–3), pp. 188–202.

Smith, R. K. M. (2016). *Textbook on international human rights.* Seventh edition. Oxford: Oxford University Press.

South Africa, Department of Basic Education (2007). *Progress Report to the Minister of Education Mrs GNM Pandor, M.P. Ministerial Committee on Learner Retention in the South African Schooling System.* Pretoria: Department of Education.

Steans, J. (2013). *Gender and International Relations.* Third edition. Cambridge: Polity Press.

Stromquist, N. (2015). Gender structure and women's agency: toward greater theoretical understanding of education for transformation. *International Journal of Lifelong Education*, 34(1), pp. 59–75.

Suttner, R. (2003). Culture(s) of the African National Congress of South Africa: Imprint of Exile Experiences. *Journal of Contemporary African Studies*, 21(2), pp. 303–320.

Taylor, C. (1992). *Modernity and the Rise of the Public Sphere. The Tanner lectures on human values*. Stanford: Stanford University Press.

Tripp, A. M. (2001). Women's Movements and Challenges to Neopatrimonial Rule: Preliminary Observations from Africa. *Development and Change*, 32(1), pp. 33–54.

UNESCO (2004). *Education for All: The Quality Imperative*. Paris: UNESCO.

UNESCO (2010). *Education for All: Reaching the Marginalized*. Paris: UNESCO.

Unterhalter, E. (2007). *Gender, Schooling and Global Social Justice*. Abingdon: Routledge.

Unterhalter, E. (2016). Gender and education in the global polity. In Mundy, K., Green, A., Lingard, B. and Verger, A. eds. *The Handbook of Global Education Policy*. Oxford: John Wiley, pp. 111–127.

Unterhalter, E., Dieltiens, V., Karlsson, J., Onsongo, J., North, A., Makinda, H., & Yates, C. (2011). *Gender, Education & Global Poverty Reduction Initiatives: Report on comparative case studies in Kenya, South Africa & selected global organisations*. London: Institute of Education.

Vandenbeld, A. (2015). International Trends in Women's Political Participation and Representation. In Baksh, R., & Harcourt, W. eds. *The Oxford Handbook of Transnational Feminist Movements*. Oxford: Oxford University Press, pp. 215–248.

Van Eerdewijk, A., & Dubel, I. (2012). Substantive gender mainstreaming and the missing middle: a view from Dutch development agencies. *Gender & Development*, 20(3), pp. 491–504.

Van Leeuwen, M. (2016). *Partners in Peace: Discourses and Practices of Civil-Society Peacebuilding*. Abingdon: Routledge.

Van Staveren, I. (2008). The gender bias of the poverty reduction strategy framework. *Review of International Political Economy*, 15(2), pp. 289–313.

Walker, C. (2013). Uneasy relations: Women, gender equality and tradition. *Thesis Eleven*, 115(1), pp. 00. Available online at http://journals.sagepub.com/doi/abs/10.1177/0725513612470535

Walsh, D.M. (2010). *Women's Rights in Democratizing States: Just Debate and Gender Justice in the Public Sphere*. New York: Cambridge University Press.

Walt, G., Shiffman, J., Schneider, H., Murray, S. F., Brugha, R., & Gilson, L. (2008). 'Doing' health policy analysis: methodological and conceptual reflections and challenges. *Health policy and planning*, 23(5), pp. 308–317.

Waylen, G. (2007a). *Engendering Transitions: Women's Mobilisation, Institutions and Gender Outcomes*. Oxford: Oxford University Press.

Waylen, G. (2007b). Women's mobilisation and gender outcomes in transitions to democracy: The case of South Africa. *Comparative Political Studies*, 40(5), pp. 521–546.

Zwingel, S. (2012). How do norms travel? Theorizing international women's rights in transnational perspective. *International Studies Quarterly*, 56(1), pp. 115–12.

2 Contested meanings of gender equality in education

Our focus in this book is global gender equality policy and related practice through education to address poverty. However, one of the themes we chart is how many interpretations exist of what this comprises. All these terms – global, gender equality, education and poverty – have a wide range of meanings, which entail particular kinds of actions. These shifting delineations have implications for how the relationships in the terrains of a middle space we have identified shape engagement with global policy formulation and realisation. In this chapter we set out some of the main discussions around these issues, looking first at different ways of understanding the relationship of global, national and local, and then exploring some contentions around meanings of gender equality in education. We consider how these line up with different views of poverty. In concluding we consider some of the implications of these diverse meanings for the relationships between people that propel policies across an arc from global through national to local.

Global–national–local connections to policy

An everyday meaning of 'global' in relation to global policy negotiations implies that the global stands above, outside, or beyond, spheres defined as national or local. Much literature over the last twenty years has charted how top-down processes of global policy formation either fail to appreciate or actively undermine bottom-up processes of engagement, critique and reflection on context (Mundy, et al., 2016; Verger, Novelli and Altinyelken, 2012). This global view is associated with international organisations, often linked to the UN. This perspective on the global is also often articulated by powerful governments invoking old hierarchies of colonialism or new relationships of neoliberalism, which seek to impose particular kinds of arrangements for finance, trade or aid. A notion of the global standing outside the national is also voiced by multi-national corporations, which may use a Foundation or partnerships with the public sector to develop the conditions for expanding business. But this notion of global policy, standing outside and being imposed on a national or local formation, is challenged by other ways of viewing the relationship of global, national and local as not so sharply differentiated from each other. In Chapter 1 we exemplified different contours of terrains of a middle space concerned with global gender equality policy. We described these as lying between policy formulation on a global instrument, like UDHR, and national and local realisation in the context of South Africa. In each of these terrains for engagement with UDHR – the institutional, the public sphere, the professional association and civil society – there was a different configuration of what was deemed global, national and local. Let us now try to unpack further some assumptions about what global policy is, how it relates to national and local sites of realisation, and what this suggests about the different terrains of the middle space we have been mapping.

Some metaphors are helpful in trying to sort out different perspectives on this issue. From one perspective we can think of this relationship in terms of a ladder, where the top steps constitute the site of global policy formation, steps in the middle comprise the national level, and the lowest rungs comprise the local level. Thus, on the top step would be the formulation of the gender equality education text of the MDGs or the SDGs, on the middle step would be their interpretation by national governments, and on the lowest steps their implementation in particular schools.

This is a standard view of global policy formation and adoption in international relations, comparative and international education (Cowen and Kazamias, 2009; Phillips and Schweisfurth, 2014; Yeates, 2014). The form of relationship from global, through national to local is delineated in terms of the institutional relationships of states articulating with international and subnational structures. Interpretations of global policy are either shared or contested, and it is the fit or lack of fit between these that helps account for what is implemented in the form of policy transfer or borrowing, selective appropriations, and the ways in which local contexts transform or reconfigure global policies that move (Steiner-Khamsi, 2004; Cowen, 2009; Phillips and Schweisfurth, 2014). In some of the debates in political philosophy, for example, sorting out positions on cosmopolitanism, one strand of discussion concerns differentiating sites that are global, national and in-between. Clarifying and critiquing the basis of these relationships can help with discussions of regulation and negotiation in attempts to investigate fair institutions (Ben-Porath and Smith, 2012; Rovisco and Nowicka 2012; Brock 2013). Good planning, well thought-out institutions, clear formulations and communication, and adequate and appropriate resources are frequently identified so that the steps of the ladder can lead unproblematically up or down. But the legacies of histories and the contours of contexts may mean that these processes are not realised in the ways intended.

Although, as is discussed in detail below, gender is a problematic concept, many of the difficulties about definition are ignored in the approach outlined above, which centres on the idea of a ladder, for understanding the relationship of the global with the national and the local. In this framework it is accepted that state-level institutions form the laws which direct gender relations in public and some private places, organise the provision of formal education and regulate the economy and forms of social protection to address poverty. These state institutions articulate with multilateral bodies formally through treaties, conventions and other legal instruments. In addition, there is a shared engagement by national and international bodies, with the soft law relating to global policy declarations concerning gender equality or Education for All. This shared engagement might take the form of relationships around aid, education exchanges between governments and other public sector bodies, or participation in global gatherings, like the UNESCO General Council, or the Commission on the Status of Women (CSW) held annually at the UN New York.

In delineating different terrains of a middle space where gender equality policy is negotiated, we specified one as an institutional space (Chapter 1). Institutions are bounded by particular laws, work relationships and levels of responsibility within a formal organisational structure. This institutional terrain of a middle space seeks to delimit clearly which spheres of work are global, falling within the remit of multilateral organisations or bilateral agreements. Institutions acknowledge the scope of national laws as they apply to a single country. Institutions will also define the local very specifically in terms of the areas of association those laws regulate. This institutional terrain of a middle space maps easily onto seeing engagements with global gender equality policy as a ladder. The MDGs concerned with gender equality, education and poverty, according to this interpretation, are developed as a global policy text by an international body like the UN. They are then interpreted by national governments, like that of South Africa and Kenya, which review their policies, and hand down to provincial or district levels of administration guidance, which is then enacted in local sites, such as schools.

The metaphor of a ladder connecting the local, national and global, also works well to capture relationships within a professional association. Thus, the global policy message of EFA or the MDGs is taken, for example, by an international association of education workers, like *Education International*.[1] It guides general strategy, engagement with national affiliates, and these in turn communicate the key ideas downward to local teachers' trade union branches. The ladder also connects a professional association, for example of social workers, or education researchers, from the local to the global, so that local branches can send their perspectives on gender equality issues to a national organisation, which, in turn, sends delegates to an international body. This formulates broad policy direction, which the national affiliate seeks to implement. Within teacher organisations or other professional associations, compared to that of state institutions, there may be more or less dynamic traffic up and down the ladder from the lower rungs to the global level. But the image prevails of steps connecting professional concerns with education though levels of discussion between the local, the national and the global.

But the metaphor of a ladder is much less clear when it comes to explaining the other terrains of a middle space which we have distinguished – the public sphere and civil society. We need different metaphors to think about their connections with policy, where the spaces of action and forms of relationship are less clearly distinguished from each other. A second possible metaphor that could help us think about the relationship of global gender equality policy to sites which are deemed national and local uses the analogy of weather systems which comprise areas of low or high air pressure. These areas move across land masses and the seas resulting in fine weather, rain or wind. Key to this metaphor is the notion that high and low pressure areas are not one thing (in contrast to a rung on a ladder), but are made up of a combination of the temperature of land or sea masses and bands of air pressure interacting with each other. A number of authors writing about the global seek to decentre a privileging of the institutions of the nation state and the policy centres of bodies associated with the UN or the EU. They characterised the global as a volatile terrain of mobilities associated with different mixtures of the global and the local in a series of policyscapes (Appadurai, 1996; Carney, 2011; Dale and Robertson, 2014). These fluidities can be partially fixed at certain historical moments, but there is an intermixing and interweaving of what is global, what is national or local, and none of these are stable. It is to capture this sense of flux and intermingling that a metaphor of shifting bands of high or low pressure, associated with winds, storms or sunshine has been chosen.

Global gender equality education policies flowing between contexts can be understood as examples of bands of high or low pressure moving across different sites. They comprise ideas mixed from different contexts, possibly human rights, basic needs, capabilities, different meanings of gender. The policies are discourses, practices, power relations, depending on the context, and the global, national and local are jumbled together in how they are interpreted. Vavrus and Bartlett (2009) have outlined a methodology to studying this fluidity which they call the *vertical case study* (VCS) approach. This attempts methodologically to engage with the manifestation and transformation of global education policies, processes and discourses in local spaces taking account of networks and articulations which problematise the institutional authority of the nation state. Through a number of multi-sited ethnographies, they chart the sociocultural dynamics of actors' relationships with education policy, noting the mutability of policyscapes where assemblages of ideas flow through different settings. Significant terrains include those formed by discourse, agency, networks, processes of contestation and engagements with experience.

A number of writers have documented the shape of gender equality policy shifting between different sites or articulation, be this transnational or local (Verloo and Lombardo, 2007; Walby, 2011; Tickner and Sjoberg, 2013). Sylvia Walby (2009) usefully employs the term intersectionality to denote features of social formations where inequalities overlap. Drawing on complexity theory she seeks to analyse the mutablities of social polities, which negotiate global policy. She shows how the flow of these negotiations happen alongside many other relationships. In this process, she suggests, the institutions of the nation state may or may not provide appropriate forms to distribute resource or enable participation and reflection, but will themselves be stretched and reformed through the agency of networks and individuals who demand this.

This depiction of global policy as gusts of wind flowing between different sites considered global, national or local, where it is hard to say which is the most significant at any moment, has resonance with some of the terrains of a middle space we have sketched out. With regard to the public sphere as an area of debate, contestation and evaluation, there is considerable intermixture of views that flow from within and beyond national contexts. Here, voices or points of view mix, a bit like the wind or areas of pressure. Just as in weather systems it is not a foregone conclusion that areas of high or low pressure will move in a particular direction or be experienced as heavy rain or low drizzle in a particular town, so, in relation to the public sphere. It is not a foregone conclusion that discussions about rights, or gender equality, or Education for All will resolve in a particular direction or be understood in a particular way in a given location. Many structural formations, processes and intermixtures of ideas bear on this.

The notion of democratic iteration developed by Seyla Benhabib (2004, 2011) may provide a useful way to understand this. When Benhabib argues that a cosmopolitan theory of justice needs to be established she emphasises not only abstract rules or principles, but also practices, which enact just political membership of polities. These are 'non-discriminatory in scope, transparent in formulation and execution, and justiciable when violated by states and other state-like organisations' (Benhabib, 2004, p. 4). Democratic iteration is the notion she develops as a form of discourse ethics to show how this process of political membership is put into practice. Democratic iteration entails complex processes of deliberation and learning through which universal rights claims are addressed. In expanding the concept of democratic iteration, Benhabib explains that it encompasses 'how the unity and diversity of human rights is enacted and re-enacted in strong and weak public spheres, not only in legislatures and courts, but often more effectively by social movements, civil society actors, and transnational organisations working across borders' (Benhabib, 2011, p. 112). We interpret this definition as an attempt to hold together engagements with human rights that are *both* juridical and socially contextualised. Benhabib attempts to sketch settings that are institutional and informal. She evokes human rights not just through laws and formal institutional structures, but as articulated through everyday practices in speaking, listening, reflecting, connecting and acting. This process of democratic iteration in the public sphere is a bit like both trying to understand the science behind the weather charts shown on television each night and discussing how the weather forecast will affect every day plans about going on a picnic or taking an umbrella to work. The global, national and local intermix, but this is not random, unconsidered or without some expert assessments.

The metaphor of global, national and local intermixing like weather systems can also capture the diverse ways in which the relationships of civil society engage with global policy flows. NGOs, faith or ethnic organisations, may take their remit from a global policy framework like CRC or CEDAW because it accords with their values, regardless of whether the government within the country in which they are located is or is not implementing this. These organisations may connect with each other across transnational networks which sometimes recognise international rights frameworks as having higher authority than those at national level, or use international frameworks to hold national systems to account.

The two metaphors of a ladder and a weather system we have used to think about the relationship of global education policy to national and local settings are relatively impersonal. However, although global gender equality policy may be impersonal and institutional (as these metaphors evoke), it may also be highly personal, affecting how an individual feels about herself, her most intimate relationships and how she chooses to live. In a number of personal memoirs and autobiographies, women who experience discrimination, abuse, oppression or violence recount how much hearing about a right to education formulated globally (in a number of different senses) meant to them personally (e.g. Kartini, 1920; Magona, 1990; Angelou, 1997). Similar accounts of the personal significance of global policy formulations on gender and education emerge from the life stories of women's rights activists (Schaffer and Smith, 2004; Dames fan 'e Riege, 2016). To render this personal dimension of significance and inspiration associated with global gender equality policy we need a third metaphor. We have selected that of a letter or a message, posted in one part of the world and received in another. The institutional ladder might affect whether the letter is posted and received efficiently, and the gusts of wind around policyscapes might explain the language the letter is written in, the ideas that are shared and the networks invoked. But what the letter means to the person who writes it and the person who reads it is not captured by either of those metaphors. We therefore want to use the idea of global gender equality policy as a personal letter of aspiration or affiliation to delineate a slightly different feature of policy flow that goes beyond that evoked by institutions or networks. Discussions of development ethics stress the importance of needs, rights and capabilities being articulated taking account of local authorship, assessment and participatory processes (Goulet, 1995; Gaspar, 2004; Sen, 2004). While it is possible to understand these processes in terms of rungs of a ladder or the gusts of air associated with the movement of ideas, what is important to the ethical frame is a notion of a person as an end, not a means, and the local claims as personally significant, articulating values. It is this ethical appreciation of an individual that is part of the notion we want to capture with the image of global policy on gender as a message. In this guise it has personal meaning associated with values for particularly situated individuals. This process of personal meaning making, is not simply global, national or local, but always a mixture.

The three metaphors we have selected for understanding the relationship of the global, national and local with regard to policy flows distil different kinds of movements. The metaphor of the ladder signals relationships that are planned, organised and amenable to measurement and evaluation. Policy is a bundle of discrete goods to be distributed. The metaphor of the weather systems depicts relationships that are more freeform, complex and intermixed. Policy is a set of ideas and actions that expresses this. The metaphor of the letter signals the importance of noting personal values, connections and compassion as a component of the relationships, and acknowledging that these values may not always be rational, or formed by available discourses. Policy here signals something of personal significance to particularly situated individuals. Just as these global–national–local relations can be interpreted in a number of guises, so too can meanings of gender equality, education and poverty. We now turn to look at some of these mutations and mixtures in the categorisations of gender equality, poverty and education.

Gender equality, poverty and education

There are a very wide range of academic and political positions on how to understand gender, gender equality policy and what the implications of these different perceptions are for work on education and poverty. A continuum moves from thinking at one end about gender as a socialised version of sex, conceptualised only along one binary division of male/female, moving through multifaceted structural relationships and mutable performances and intermixtures of sex, sexuality and gender, to at the other end an ideal, ethical or aspirational version of gender equality that dissolves or recognises particular forms of similarity or difference, and is more or less interested in how ideas are realised in practice. There are a number of positions in between and various permutations that combine elements along this continuum and mix gender with other social relations. Below we set out how different meanings of gender cluster with different approaches to defining the nature of gender inequalities, poverty, and the policies and practices associated with gender equality in education.

Those approaches that view gender as particular kinds of constructed, but more or less fixed, socialised relationships for girls and boys, women and men, which become part of each individual's particular attributes. Some earlier work (Unterhalter, 2007, 2012, 2016a) has characterised this as a view which entails seeing gender as a noun. Gender is a 'thing', a set of categories, which can be described and distinguished, and from which certain kinds of relationships can be inferred. Although this view of gender is widely criticised by theorists of structure, agency, performance, discourse and heteronormativity as discussed below, it is the view of gender that is most commonly used in policy texts like the MDGs, and frequently underpins the programmes of large multilateral and bilateral donors, such as the World Bank or DFID (DeJaeghere, 2015; Unterhalter, 2016a). Central to this view of gender is the methodological assumption that counting the numbers of girls, boys, women, men, in various areas of education gives an accurate description of gender equalities and inequalities. Thus, as has been shown (Unterhalter 2005, 2012), gender equality comes to be understood as entailing equal numbers of girls and boys enrolled or completing school. Internationally comparative indicators have been developed to establish to what extent for any particular country or sub-category, there is a measure of gender parity, that is girls as a proportion of boys (UNESCO, 2016, p. 495). Gender parity in enrolment and completion rates for various phases of education was one of the key indicators in the MDG framework (See Appendix 1).

From this perspective, achieving gender equality often entails removing barriers which prevent girls enrolling or progressing in school, studying or achieving in the same fields as boys. Thus, gender inequalities are often linked with resource deficits, of money, safe water or sanitation, or transport. Poverty, understood as a lack of income, is one such barrier. Calculations of poverty in terms earning less than $1 a day underpinned the MDG framework and UNESCO calculations of poverty have been based on income quintiles (WIDE database).[2]

However, in addition, barriers are understood to comprise institutional gaps, such as lack of definite policy or training for adequate numbers of teachers

(Tembon and Fort, 2008). Barriers are also linked with socially constructed attitudes largely of parents or ethnically defined communities, which keep girls from school (King and Hill, 1991; Lewis and Lockheed, 2007; Lewis and Lockheed, 2008; Unterhalter, 2016b). These barriers to gender equality in education may or may not lead to women working as the equals of men, earning the same amounts or exercising authority in the same domains, usually the public sphere. But the relationships of levels of gender equality or inequality in school to barriers to gender equality beyond school, is not well understood or documented from this perspective (Unterhalter et al., 2014).

This conception of gender as a biological or social category, links with a framework known as women in development (WID). WID, as a policy framework, links together a number of ideas about modernisation, economic growth and efficiency (Beneria et al., 2016). In the WID framework gender equality in education is both the presence of girls/women in adequate numbers in education institutions, political institutions and well paid jobs *and* the removal of barriers to access, progression and achievement of girls in education. This minimal view of gender equality in education often links the presence of girls in school with benefits that data indicate flow from this, including limiting population growth, improving productivity and economic growth, enhancing the ties of social capital and improving inter-generational outcomes in health, income and environmental protection (Tembon and Fort, 2008; Kabeer and Natali, 2013; Lutz and Kumar, 2013; Stacki and Baily, 2015). In the policy and practice that derives from this view of gender equality in education it has been argued that the presence of girls and women in education, regardless of the form of relationships, is sometimes portrayed as instrumental to other benefits (Unterhalter, 2016a). In some more recent articulations, getting girls into school is seen to stand as a placemarker for undertaking all the other work around international development in health, work, economic, social and environmental relations, that it is argued flows from this.

This stance on equality, which comprises only equal numbers or the removal of barriers, is generally not accompanied by reflection on issues around women's rights, particularly reproductive rights, addressing violence (except insofar as this may keep girls out of school) and understanding forms of discrimination and injustice, both within and beyond education. As Kabeer and Natali (2013) note, while there is a clear association from many studies between an expansion of education for girls and economic growth, there is not such a clear association between economic growth and gender equality. The complexities of gender and poverty that touch on, but also go well beyond, lack of income are not addressed in this approach to equality (Kabeer, 2015; Campbell and Gillespie, 2016). Achieving gender equality, from this perspective, can be simply practice oriented with a stress on interventions which work to get girls into school and maintain their progression (Sperling and Winthrop, 2016). Policy may be an intervention but is valued only if it works. Interventions which are considered to work often focus on allocating financial or other physical resources. Some examples, detailed by Sperling and Winthrop (2016) comprise making education free, providing cash transfers or running special programmes in subjects in which girls are often under-represented like STEM (science, technology, engineering and maths).

Some programmes support the recruitment and training of women teachers, as much literature points to a possible contribution between the employment of women teachers and the attainment of girls at school, although there is not complete consensus on the causal links (Glick, 2008; Unterhalter et al., 2014; Sperling and Winthrop, 2016). The view of gender equality here rests on the assumption that the presence of girls in school, women in employment or decision making will help undo policies and practices of gender inequality, which tend to be linked with the establishment of barriers – resource constraints or neglectful attitudes. Many critics question this rather limited understanding of addressing poverty, inequality and gender injustice (Beneria et al., 2016; Harcourt, 2016).

It has been suggested (Unterhalter, 2016a) that the WID or 'get girls into school' approach to gender equality may comprise a necessary step, but is not sufficient to undo the many structural, material, normative, symbolic and emotional relationships that form gender inequalities and the multidimensionality of poverty. An important gap in this view of gender equality in education is that it does not question what is taught or learned, how education is conducted or what its purpose is. By focussing an approach to poverty primarily on income it fails to consider the many structural, political and inter-generational relationships that constitute poverty. Understanding gender, equality, education and poverty in this bounded way fits well with viewing global policy as a 'thing' which can be moved rationally up and down a ladder of organisational connections from the global to the national and the local, or in the opposite direction. However, there are other ways to think about gender equality, education and poverty.

Midway along a continuum to understand different approaches to the mobile concept of gender equality in education, we can position a cluster of views about gender that are concerned not with what gender is, or is assumed to be, as signalled by the notion of gender as a noun discussed above. This cluster concerns what gender does both as a set of relationships between individuals, groups and institutions. It is also concerned with what Henderson (2016) has distinguished as the concept of gender, and what this does as a discursive practice in relation to pedagogies, research and forms of action. This cluster of analyses looks at what gender and the concept of gender *does* in shaping institutions, structural relationships, aspirations, actions and discourses. These include a wide range of views on the nature of poverty as structural, discursive and experiential (Farmer, 2004; Gornick and Boeri, 2016).

A number of earlier works (Unterhalter, 2007, 2012, 2016a) have identified instances of what gender does in work on education, which can be seen to operate on systems of relationships as an adjective, a verb and a gerund do within language constructions. Seeing gender as an adjective, it has been shown, entails assumptions about gender relationships, structures of power and identities associated with hierarchies, exclusions or forms of exploitation. These gendered formations are evident, for example, in a curriculum or textbooks, which assemble and distil knowledge relating to the power and authority between men and women. These relationships can also be structured into the distribution of resources, or employment conditions, for example what arrangements are made to cover women teachers' maternity leave of promotion. Thus one facet of what gender does in education is that it structures hierarchies concerning what women and men do in an institutional form, and inscribes these in everyday discourses.

A second facet of what gender does, makes and unmakes these structural relationships. This process has been depicted (Unterhalter 2007, 2012, 2016a) as 'gender as a verb', drawing on Butler's notion of performance, and various ideas about agency (Butler, 1990; McNay, 2000). Thus each and every living person will do gender, sex and sexuality differently. For some individuals, there will be dramatic changes in these forms of agency over the course of a lifetime, and for some very marked changes even in the space of a day. Post-colonial writers draw attention to how there are profound struggles about whether one does gender in ways that confirm the gaze of the coloniser, or affirm the aspirations of the colonised (Spivak, 1988; Mohanty, 2013; Gerrard and Sriprakash, 2015). Thus, a focus on what gender does in education notes that it is both fixed in structures and discourses, and changed in practices and relationships, which are themselves situated and mutable.

These historically and contextually located processes document gender, linked with other kinds of social division, working *through* education, rather than education working mechanically for girls, as is asserted in the framework which sees gender as a noun and draws on WID forms of analysis. In defining gender relationally to other social divisions, rather than as a thing, we see constructed and multi-faceted forms of gender working structurally, discursively or performatively to constrain opportunities for differently situated groups and to shape particular kinds of institutional and distributional relationships. This understanding of how gender works in education, draws from the framework often referred to as GAD (Gender and Development) (Kabeer, 2004; Beneria et al., 2015), which gives analytical primacy to structures of political economy. GAD emerged in the 1970s, with much of the key analysis initiated by feminist economics who charted the uneven forms of capitalist development, the incorporation of women into wage labour and the ways in which state institutions for social welfare and protection sometimes established hierarchies around gender, class, race and ethnicity. Many GAD writers were critical of the ways in which a WID approach singled out gender equality, excluding other kinds of equalities and the debates associated with these (Beneria et al., 2016). However, generally, GAD theorists, because of their disciplinary roots in economics did not analyse many of the more fluid kinds of identities people work with around sex, gender and sexuality and their interconnections. These have been the concern of post-structural, post-colonial and queer theorists, who map mutabilities, and the ways that different discourses, texts or interactions in education seek to fix these (Squires, 1999; Hey, 2006; Jolly, 2011). How these processes of fixing are delineated, accepted, challenged or undone is a key area of investigation in relation to undoing gender inequalities.

One example theorising these mutabilities is the sociologist Floya Anthias' idea of translocational positionality (Anthias, 2008). This maps out a multiplicity of gendered practices that are only semi-fixed by relationships of the global, national and local. The notion of tranlocational positionality aims to capture aspects of identity, belonging, structure, agency and hybridity. The idea of translocations draws out how individuals and groups occupy multiple locations, and the fractured and connected form of their relationships. For Anthias:

> A translocational positionality is one structured by the interplay of different locations relating to gender, ethnicity, race and class (amongst others), and their at times contradictory effects. Positionality combines a reference to social position (as a set of effectivities: as outcome) and social positioning (as a set of practices, actions and meanings: as process). That is, positionality is the space at the intersection of structure (social position/social effects) and agency (social positioning/meaning and practice). The notion of 'location' recognises the importance of context, the situated nature of claims and attributions and their production in complex and shifting locales. It also recognises variability with some processes leading to more complex, contradictory and at times dialogical positionalities than others.
>
> (Anthias, 2008, p. 15)

This analysis suggests gender inequalities are aspects of translocational positionality and thus at different points and for different groups are more or less substantively disentangled through forms of education. From this perspective, global gender and education policy might encode structures of inequality, or only partially confront the exploitative of unjust relationships around education and gender that exist. Practices engaging with this policy might perform gender confirming relationships of inequality or trying to undo them. We can thus see all three metaphors we have used to depict the global–national–local positioning of policy as various formations of translocation.

This nexus of ideas which is concerned with what gender or the concept of gender does to the contextualised analysis of structure and agency in relation to education and poverty often does not have a clearly defined normative position on what gender equality entails. Sometimes writers working with this position invoke frameworks of women's rights, human rights, social justice or acknowledge the importance of care, vulnerability, empowerment or affiliation (Batliwala, 2015; Bradley, 2015; Case, 2016). These values are often invoked in context, rather than abstractly *outside* particular lived experiences. Writers, like Anthias, suggest gender equality is a process of making meanings and taking actions that moves attention away from inequalities, and relations of poverty, recognising them or trying to change them. Some formulations depict gender equality in education as a refashioning of institutions associated with gender inequalities and resetting them so that the institutions drive towards equalities (Goetz, 1997; Branisa, Klasen and Ziegler, 2013; Campbell and Gillespie, 2016). Gender mainstreaming was a key strategy, advocated in the Beijing Declaration of 1995, and promoted as a means to make institutions reflexive about gender hierarchies, and responsive to address inequalities (Moser and Moser, 2005; Porter and Sweetman, 2005). Unterhalter and North (2010) summarised some of the critiques of gender mainstreaming in education, where it was seen to be limited to a number of techniques, rather than to challenging the structural basis of gender inequalities. Similarly, Lombardo, Meier and Verloo (2016) point out the many ways in which gender mainstreaming came to be adapted, often losing sight of the aspirations of the feminist activists who had promoted it. Stromquist (2015) looks at the way the US state and many mainstream development organisations frame gender equality exclusively in terms of non-discriminatory practices or limited forms of equal opportunities. This falls short of fostering changes in gender attitudes and identities in educational institutions in the US and globally. Unterhalter (2016a) identifies the practices of large international organisations doing gender, claiming to move in the direction of gender equality, but not undoing other inequalities, as using gender as a gerund, playing with the mutablility of the term.

To sum up, at this point on the conceptual continuum we have been sketching it appears to us that writers who make an analysis of the complex intersections associated with gender do not always concern themselves with normative questions about gender equality. Many focus primarily on analysis of what relationships associated with gender do, and not on a normative orientation, around what might be right or good, and how to establish this. For those who do depict some normative direction, they tend not to stress this as an abstract process. They emphasise instead the context in which gender equality or work against poverty are negotiated and realised as lived processes in particular contexts. Batliwala's book (2015), which comprises a personally inflected history of work in India since the 1970s around the notion of women's empowerment exemplifies this approach. We can apply all three metaphors we have developed to the kind of analysis of what gender does that she, and writers like her, develop. Thus global gender equality policy appears in these accounts as handed up or down a ladder of institutions, as mixing the global and the local in unpredictable gusts, like a wind, and as articulating sincerely expressed aspirations as a letter might do.

At the far end of the conceptual continuum we are sketching is a cluster of gender equality formulations which regard gender equality in education both abstractly and substantively, partly enmeshed in the detail of the kind of negotiations Batliwala depicts and partly formulated though other somewhat more abstract processes that push against some of the tensions of the general and the particular, the abstractly formulated, and the concretely experienced. These have been grouped together in terms of what gender and women's rights activists dream about (Unterhalter, 2015). These ideas draw on formulations from feminism, human rights, the capability approach, empowerment and gender justice. However, there are some quite sharp differences of view regarding these gender equality aspirations. One group of writers set out to depict gender equality in education as a set of normative propositions. Some writers (Subrahmanian, 2005) and policy interventions, like the UNESCO Global Monitoring Report of 2004 (UNESCO, 2004) derive these largely from the existence of UN declarations specifying rights to, in and through education, all of which invoke gender equality as an aspiration. For example the concept of equality between men and women, boys and girls, was set out in UDHR, elaborated in CEDAW, CRC and the Beijing Platform for Action in 1995 (see Chapter 3 for further discussion). All contain sections that deal with education and poverty that go beyond the absence of income, and link gender inequalities with a range of public and private settings. The UN Security Council Resolution 1325 in 2000 on women, peace and security also contains a formulation of gender equality and education. This view of gender equality dreams articulated in UN documents works well with a notion of global policy stretching as a ladder, in which this version of the dream is realised at different levels as appropriate even down to the household.

A different approach to formulating the aspiration associated with gender equality in education does not start with the text of a declaration, but with some assertions about justice and equality. Martha Nussbaum (2001, 2006, 2011), for example, develops one such normative vision of gender equality in education from a particular set of propositions. She suggests ab initio that gender equality in education is not just one thing. Welding together thinking about national and global forms of social justice, her analysis outlines a substantive floor of central capabilities (which includes education) that all states owe their citizens. For this list of capabilities to constitute sufficient conditions for social justice they must be ensured by a formal social contract, which is complemented by forms of formal and informal political engagement with ethical issues of equality and social justice. Such engagements need to be addressed by non-state actors positioned locally, nationally and globally. The practices of both formal and non-formal education represent key threads in these political–ethical actions which entail groups building understanding, affiliation and developing emotional insights for work on justice that are not only parochial, but also national and global. These engagements encompass issues that are socio-economic and also resonate with arts, humanities and the many facets of culture. In their global reach these actions do not lose the timbre of local or national reflection. The terrains of a middle space we have outlined could be one area of engagement around these reflections.

How normative positions on gender equality and rights to education are reflected on in local settings is a key issue under debate for a number of writers. For Onora O'Neill, terms such as cosmopolitan duties, associated with gender equality in education, are more minimal than those outlined by Nussbaum, but nonetheless establish substantial obligations. She writes that, in designing policies and practices, we must ask whether the 'arrangements that structure vulnerable lives are ones that could have been refused or renegotiated by those they constrain' (O'Neill, 2000, p. 163). The notion of global duties O'Neill develops does not accord cultural recognition in particular local sites the status of a principle, but she highlights the importance of participation in reviewing the process of refusal and renegotiation of the conditions that structure vulnerable lives. In later work O'Neill points out that economic or material justice cannot be achieved 'without avoiding institutionalized as well as individual forms of coercion' and that understanding this and how to minimise the coercion is a key aspect of work on equality (2008, p. 153). She starts with a Kantian principle 'human obligations are obligations never to act in ways in which others in principle cannot also act' (O'Neill, 2008, p. 150). With regard to obligations of justice, these entail relationships which are non-coercive, particularly on the poor. We thus need to look critically at actions we take through institutions which do to people things we consider are for their own good, but which involve coercion. Because of poverty, poor people can be treated in ways in which they are made offers they cannot refuse. This, O'Neill argues, raises ethical problems. 'What might be genuine offers among equals, which others can respect or reject, can be threatening and unrefusable for the needy and the vulnerable (O'Neill, 2008, p. 151). The implications are that an important dimension of global social justice is building the institutional conditions through which poverty and these coercive forms can be eliminated. Addressing gender equality in education as a principle cannot be asserted without taking account of such a process. Thus the form of the ladder from global to national needs to take account of 'personal letters' sent by the poor, what it is they value and their perspectives.

Iris Marion Young's (2006, 2011) view entails another perspective on what gender equality in education under conditions of widespread poverty entails. She does not see national or local forms of belonging as key to outlining gender equality dreams. Instead she depicts lines of association which stretch from local to global linked with power and powerlessness. Individuals and organisations are unequally placed within this network of associations. This recalls our metaphors of the weather systems and the ladder. Young (2006) advances an argument about social connection and the responsibility this entails to address obligations that exist across historically constructed lines of violence and exclusion. Structural injustices and inequalities, including those associated with gender inequalities in education, form global social relations. In these systems some benefit and some fail to thrive out of all proportions to any actions they take. This poses serious questions about responsibility in the face on injustices. We are involved, but we are not individually to be blamed to the same degree. Nonetheless, such injustices are perpetuated through our participation, in market relations or other kinds of connections between global, national and local (Young, 2011). Young's interactionist account of responsibility brings out both the ways in which groups working on terrains of a middle space may share in the perpetuation of injustices, and suggests that changing understandings and actions at all the points across a global–national–local continuum will build forms of agency and responsibility for global justice, which will entail some formulation of gender equality in education.

In contrast to those analyses which distil the meaning of gender equality from abstract principles, a group of writers stress the importance of local negotiation and process in formulating what gender equality in education is. Their work proceeds by documenting the aspirations of what young women in schools or higher education living in contexts of poverty want or value for themselves and the field of study and work (Walker, 2007; Murphy-Graham, 2012; DeJaeghere and Wiger, 2013; Unterhalter et al., 2013; Loots and Walker, 2015). These studies generally do not seek to generalise from the particular settings in which these views were collected, but they raise questions as to how a formulation of what gender equality is connects local voices with top-down frameworks of addressing rights.

There are thus many facets to understanding what gender equality dreams comprise. The normative work regarding gender equality in education can, thus, be defined though policy texts, through ideas of social contract, obligation, affiliation or voice. Some of these positions are exclusive of others; for example, the stress on abstract principles does not sit easily with a position that stresses local negotiation and voice. To date there has not been much synthesising work analytically attempting to bring these formulations of normative aspiration together with the more sociological work on what gender does. In Part 2, we try to bring these threads together in our analysis of empirical data on how gender policy on education was interpreted.

It can be seen that when gender is defined as a 'thing', a relationship or process, or a feature of a normative aspiration, gender equality and addressing poverty come to be understood differently. These positions along a definitional continuum regarding the concept of gender and poverty also mean that education is either narrowly linked with schooling, or very substantively merged with other relationships, institutional formations or processes of political and ethical reflection. The different ways of viewing the global–national–local arc all have a bearing on the relationships that are made and the negotiations that ensue. In the next chapter, we provide an overview history of the key global policy instruments concerned with gender equality, education and poverty from the end of World War 2, and sketch some of the terrains of a middle space associated with the formation of the global.

Notes

1 *Education International* is a federation of organisations of teachers and other education employees, with representation from across the world. It represents around thirty-two million education employees in about four hundred organisations in one hundred and seventy countries.
2 World Inequality Database on Education (WIDE). [online]. Available at www.education-inequalities.org/. [Accessed 12 February 2017].

References

Angelou, M. (1997). *I Know Why the Caged Bird Sings*. New York: Bantam Books.
Anthias, F. (2008). Thinking through the lens of translocational positionality: An intersectionality frame for understanding identity and belonging. *Translocations: Migration and Social Change*, 4(1), pp. 5–20.
Appadurai, A. (1996). *Modernity at Large: Cutural Dimensions in Globalisation*. Minniapolis: University of Minnesota.
Bartlett, L., & Vavrus, F. (2014). Transversing the vertical case study: A methodological approach to studies of educational policy as practice. *Anthropology and Education Quarterly*, 45(2), pp. 131–147.
Batliwala, S. (2015). *Engaging with Empowerment: An Intellectual and Experiential Journey*. New Delhi: Women Unlimited.
Beneria, L., Berik, G., & Floro, M. S. (2015). *Gender, Development, and Globalization: Economics as If All People Mattered*. 2nd ed. Cambridge: Routledge.

Benhabib, S. (2004). *The Rights of Others: Aliens, Residents, and Citizens.* Cambridge: Cambridge University Press.

Benhabib, S. (2011). *Dignity in Adversity: Human Rights in Troubled Times.* Cambridge: Polity Press.

Ben-Porath, S. R., & Smith, R. M. (Eds.). (2012). *Varieties of Sovereignty and Citizenship.* Philadelphia: University of Pennsylvania Press.

Bradley, H. (2015). *Fractured Identities: Changing Patterns of Inequality.* 2nd ed. Cambridge: Polity Press.

Branisa, B., Klasen, S., & Ziegler, M. (2013). Gender inequality in social institutions and gendered development outcomes. *World Development*, 45, pp. 252–226.

Brock, G. (2013). Contemporary Cosmopolitanism: Some current issues. *Philosophy Compass*, 8(8), pp. 689–698.

Butler, J. (1990). *Gender Trouble: Feminism and the Subversion of Identity.* New York: Routledge.

Campbell, J., & Gillespie, M. (Eds.). (2016). *Feminist Economics and Public Policy.* Abingdon: Routledge.

Carney, S. (2011). Imagining globalization: Educational policyscapes. In *World Yearbook of Education 2012.* Abingdon: Routledge.

Case, K. (2016). *Intersectional Pedagogy.* Abingdon: Routledge.

Cowen, R. (2009). The transfer, translation and transformation of educational processes: And their shape-shifting? *Comparative Education*, 45(3), pp. 315–327.

Cowen, R., & Kazamias, A. M. (Eds.). (2009). *International Handbook of Comparative Education.* Dordrecht: Springer.

Dale, R., & Robertson, S. (2014). Global education policies. In Yeates, N. ed. *Understanding Global Social Policy*, Bristol: Policy Press, pp. 209–236.

Dames fan 'e Riege (2016). *Report on the Seminar Gender, Women and Development 1980–2015.* The Hague: Institute of Social Studies. Pingjum: Dames fan 'e Riege.

DeJaeghere, J. (2015). Reframing gender and education for the post-2015 agenda. In McGrath, S. and Gu, C. eds. *Routledge Handbook of International Education and Development*, Abingdon: Routledge, pp. 63–77.

DeJaeghere, J., & Wiger, N. (2013). Gender discourses in an NGO education project: Openings for transformation toward gender equality in Bangladesh. *International Journal of Educational Development*, 33(6), pp. 557–565.

Farmer, P. (2004). *Pathologies of Power: Health, Human Rights, and the New War on the Poor.* Berkley: University of California Press.

Gaspar, D. (2004). *The Ethics of Development.* Edinburgh: Edinburgh University Press.

Gerrard, J., & Sriprakash, A. (2015). Gender, postcolonialism, and education. In Peters, M. A. ed. *Encyclopaedia of Educational Philosophy and Theory.* Singapore: Springer, pp. 1–6.

Glick, P. (2008). What policies will reduce gender schooling gaps in developing countries: Evidence and interpretation. *World Development*, 36(9), pp. 1623–1646.

Goetz, A. M. (1997). *Getting Institutions Right for Women in Development.* New York: Zed Books.

Gornick, J. C., & Boeri, N. (2016). Gender and poverty. In Brady, D. and Burton, L. eds. *The Oxford Handbook of the Social Science of Poverty.* Oxford: Oxford University Press, pp. 221–246.

Goulet, D. (1995). *Development Ethics: A Guide to Theory and Practice.* Lanham, MD: Rowman & Littlefield.

Harcourt, W. (2016). Introduction: Dilemmas, dialogues, debates. In *The Palgrave Handbook of Gender and Development*. London: Palgrave Macmillan, pp. 1–10.

Henderson, E. F. (2016). *Eventful Gender: An Ethnographic Exploration of Gender Knowledge Production at International Academic Conferences*. Doctoral dissertation, UCL (University College London).

Hey, V. (2006). The politics of performative resignification: Translating Judith Butler's theoretical discourse and its potential for a sociology of education. *British Journal of Sociology of Education*, 27(4), pp. 439–457.

Jolly, S. (2011). Why is development work so straight? Heteronormativity in the international development industry. *Development in Practice*, 21(1), pp. 18–28.

Kabeer, N. (2004). *Reversed Realities: Gender Hierarchies in Development Thought*. London: Verso.

Kabeer, N. (2015). Gender, poverty, and inequality: A brief history of feminist contributions in the field of international development. *Gender & Development*, 23(2), pp. 189–205.

Kabeer, N., & Natali, L. (2013). Gender equality and economic growth: Is there a win win? *IDS Working Papers, 2013*, 417, pp. 1–58.

Kartini, R. A. (1920). *Letters of a Javanese Princess*. New York: CPSIA.

King, E., & Hill, M. (1991). *Women's Education in Developing Countries: Barriers, Benefits and Policy*. John Hopkins University Press for The World Bank.

Lewis, M., & Lockheed, M. (2007). *Exclusion, Gender and Education: Case Studies from the Developing World*. Washington, DC: Center for Global Development.

Lewis, M., & Lockheed, M. (2008). *Social Exclusion and the Gender Gap in Education*. Washington, DC: World Bank.

Lombardo, E., Meier, P., & Verloo, M. (2016). Policymaking from a gender + equality perspective. *Journal of Women, Politics & Policy*, pp. 1–19.

Loots, S., & Walker, M. (2015). Shaping a gender equality policy in higher education: Which human capabilities matter? *Gender and Education*, 27(4), pp. 361–375.

Lutz, W., & Kumar S. K. (2013). *Demography and Human Development: Education and Population Projections*. UNDP-HDRO Occasional Papers.

Magona, S. (1990). *To My Children's Children*. Cape Town: David Philip Publishers.

McNay, L. (2000). *Gender and Agency: Reconfiguring the Subject in Feminist and Social Theory*. Cambridge: Polity Press.

Mohanty, C. T. (2013). Transnational feminist crossings: On neoliberalism and radical critique. *Signs*, 38(4), pp. 967–991.

Moser, C., & Moser, A. (2005). Gender mainstreaming since Beijing: A review of success and limitations in international institutions. *Gender & Development*, 13(2), pp. 11–22.

Mundy, K., Green, A., Lingard, B., & Verger, A. (Eds.). (2016). *Handbook of Global Education Policy*. Oxford: John Wiley & Sons.

Murphy-Graham, E. (2012). *Opening Minds, Improving Lives: Education and Women's Empowerment in Honduras*. Nashville: Vanderbilt University Press.

Nussbaum, M. C. (2001). *Women and Human Development: The Capabilities Approach*. Cambridge: Cambridge University Press.

Nussbaum, M. C. (2006). Education and democratic citizenship: Capabilities and quality education. *Journal of Human Development*, 7(3), pp. 385–395.

Nussbaum, M. C. (2011). *Creating Capabilities*. Cambridge, MA: Harvard University Press.

O'Neill, O. (2000). *Bounds of Justice*. Cambridge: Cambridge University Press.

O'Neill, O. (2008). *Rights, Obligations and World Hunger*. In Pogge, T. and Horton, K. eds. *Global Ethics: Seminal Essays*. St Paul MN: Paragon House, pp. 139–155.

Phillips, D., & Schweisfurth, M. (2014). *Comparative and International Education: An Introduction to Theory, Method and Practice*. 2nd ed. London: Bloomsbury Academic.

Porter, F., & Sweetman, C. (2005). *Mainstreaming Gender in Development: A Critical Review*. Oxford: Oxfam GB.

Rovisco, M., & Nowicka, M. (2012). *Cosmopolitanism in Practice*. Ashgate.

Schaffer, K., & Smith, S. (2004). *Human Rights and Narrated Lives: The Ethics of Recognition*. Dordrecht: Springer.

Sen, A. (2004). Capabilities, lists, and public reason: Continuing the conversation. *Feminist Economics*, 10(3), pp. 77–80.

Sperling, G., & Winthrop, R. (2016). *What Works in Girls Education: Evidence for the World's Best Investment*. Washington DC: Brookings Institution Press.

Spivak, G. C. (1988). Can the subaltern speak? In Nelson, C. and Grossbery, L. eds. *Marxism and the Interpretation of Culture*. Urbana: University of Illinois Press, pp. 271–313.

Squires, J. (1999). *Gender in Political Theory*. Oxford: John Wiley.

Stacki, S. L., & Baily, S. (Eds.). (2015). *Educating Adolescent Girls Around the Globe: Challenges and Opportunities*. Abingdon: Routledge.

Steiner-Khamsi, G. (2004). *The Global Politics of Educational Borrowing and Lending*. New York: Teachers College Press.

Stromquist, N. (2015). Gender structure and women's agency: Toward greater theoretical understanding of education for transformation. *International Journal of Lifelong Education*, 34(1), pp. 59–75.

Subrahmanian, R. (2005). Gender equality in education: Definitions and measurements. *International Journal of Educational Development*, 25(4), pp. 395–407.

Tembon, M., & Fort, L. (2008). *Girls' Education in the 21st Century: Gender Equality, Empowerment and Economic Growth*. Washington, DC: The World Bank.

Tickner, J. A., & Sjoberg, L. (Eds.). (2013). *Feminism and International Relations: Conversations about the Past, Present and Future*. Abingdon: Routledge.

UNESCO (2004). *Education for All: The Quality Imperative*. Paris: UNESCO.

UNESCO (2016). *Education for People and Planet: Creating Sustainable Futures for All*. Paris: UNESCO.

Unterhalter, E. (2005). Fragmented frameworks? Researching women, gender, education and development. In Aikman, S. and Unterhalter, E. eds. *Beyond Access: Transforming Policy and Practice for Gender Equality in Education*. Oxford: Oxfam, pp. 15–35.

Unterhalter, E. (2007). *Gender, Schooling, and Global Social Justice*. Abingdon: Routledge.

Unterhalter, E. (2012). Mutable meanings: Gender equality in education and international rights frameworks. *Equal Rights Review*, 8, pp. 67–84.

Unterhalter, E. (2015). Thinking backwards to the future: Some reflections on gender, women and development' in Dames fan 'e Riege. In *Report on the Seminar Gender, Women and Development, 1980–2015*. The Hague: Institute of Social Studies, pp. 23–29.

Unterhalter, E. (2016a). Gender and education in the global polity. In Mundy, K., Green, A., Lingard, B. and Verger, A. eds. *The Handbook of Global Education Policy*. Oxford: Wiley Blackwell, pp. 111–127.

Unterhalter, E. (2016b). *Literature Review on Girls' Education, Marginalisation, Gender Inequalities and Interventions for Equality.* Review prepared for ICAI, London.

Unterhalter, E., et al. (2014). Interventions to enhance girls' education and gender equality. *Education Rigorous Literature Review.* London: Department for International Development Research for Development.

Unterhalter, E., Heslop, J., & Mamedu, A. (2013). Girls claiming education rights: Reflections on distribution, empowerment and gender justice in Northern Tanzania and Northern Nigeria. *International Journal of Educational Development,* 33(6), pp. 566–575.

Unterhalter, E., & North, A. (2010). Assessing gender mainstreaming in the education sector: Depoliticised technique of a step towards women's rights and gender equality? *Compare: A Journal of Comparative and International Education,* 40(4), pp. 389–404.

Vavrus, F., & Bartlett, L. (2009). *Critical Approaches to Comparative Education: Vertical Case Studies from Africa, Europe, the Middle East and the Americas.* New York: Palgrave Macmillan.

Verger, A., Novelli, M., & Altinyelken, H. K. (2012). *Global Education Policy and International Development: New Agendas, Issues and Policies.* London: Bloomsbury Academic.

Verloo, M., & Lombardo, E. (2007). Contested gender equality and policy variety in Europe: Introducing a Critical Frame Analysis approach. In *Multiple Meanings of Gender Equality: A Critical Frame Analysis of Gender Policies in Europe.* Budapest-New York: CPS Books, p. 309.

Walker, M. (2007). Selecting capabilities for gender equality in education. In Walker, M. and Unterhalter, E. eds. *Amartya Sen's Capability Approach and Social Justice in Education.* London: Palgrave Macmillan, pp. 177–195.

Walby, S. (2009). *Globalization and Inequalities: Complexity and Contested Modernities.* London: Sage Publications Ltd.

Walby, S. (2011). *The Future of Feminism.* Cambridge: Polity Press.

Yeates, N. (Ed.). (2014). *Understanding Global Social Policy.* Bristol: Policy Press.

Young, I. M. (2011). *Justice and the Politics of Difference.* Princeton: Princeton University Press.

Young, I. M. (2006). Responsibility and global justice: A social connection model. *Social Philosophy and Policy,* 23(1), pp. 102–130.

Part 1

3   Ladders in the wind
Global policy on gender and education

In 1995, when the Beijing World Conference on Women agreed a wide-ranging Platform for Action on women's rights and gender equality, education and poverty featured prominently. The dynamics of the conference put multilateral organisations, national governments and a large NGO/civil society community into dialogue. These discussions, while often robust, coming from different perspectives seemed to promise a great deal for future connections and joint actions. They signalled processes which would engage at multiple levels across diverse interests, purposively linking from the site of global policy declaration through diverse networks to multiple sites of realisation involving individuals, institutions and organisations to challenge gender inequalities associated with or amplified by poverty and exclusions from education.

Our aim in this chapter is partly to map some features of this global terrain and the ways in which connections were made from this space to various sites of national and local policy realisation, considering the ways in which the terrains of a middle space were viewed. In order to do this we first provide a brief introductory review of the historical background to the Beijing Conference of 1995, and discuss the experience of global convening and connecting on gender and women's rights movements this represented. We then take this story forward from 1995, outlining the international policy declarations and key gatherings that framed the MDGs and EFA in 2000, and the reviews that took place up to 2015, thus setting the scene for the SDGs, which replaced the MDG framework. This global policy landscape from 1995 forms a backdrop to the practices associated with the terrains of a middle space, which we will discuss through background histories of Kenya and South Africa in Chapters 4 and 5, and then through detailed exploration of data from our research study in Part 2. At the end of this chapter we will attempt to characterise some features of this global policy area and some of the ways in which relationships formed with the terrains of a middle space we examine.

We are interested here in exploring ways to think about the kinds of connections between different groups forged at the Beijing Conference and sustained or undermined in the decades that followed. We look, for example, at the connection between differently situated constituencies, and some of the ways the links between poverty, gender and education were made within these groups. We pose questions about the kinds of practices associated with the four terrains of a middle space we have mapped. In developing this discussion in this chapter we draw on data that we collected through interviews conducted with key participants working on gender and education within ten multilateral and bilateral agencies, global education partnerships and coalitions, and large international NGOs between 2007 and 2011. The majority of these interviews took place face-to-face in the offices of the organisations working at a global level, whilst a few were conducted by telephone. Many of the participants in these interviews were known to each other and to the interviewers through their participation in a number of events concerned with building support for EFA, issues of gender and women's rights.

As we discuss in detail below, the practices invoked by the gatherings at the Beijing Conference were associated with a self-proclaimed politics of transformation, which combined ideas about what gender does with formulations of what gender activists dreamed about and aspired to realise. This politics recognised the institutional remit of states and multilateral bodies working with structures and relationships that could be described using the ladder metaphor connecting global with national and local, as outlined in the previous chapter. In this stream of analysis and action the global terrain was largely institutional, and worked to realise gender equality aspirations through institutions and organisations that worked with the rational planning frameworks the ladder metaphor seeks to delineate.

In addition, however, the transformational politics articulated at the Beijing Conference also portrayed the global terrain in terms of the intersectional and translocational positioning of a diverse women's movement, which made links with other organisations concerned with social justice. This was neither entirely and only global or local, moving between the two, taking in some guises the form of the metaphor associated with weather systems. In this stream of analysis the global terrain was partly institutional, but was also more amorphous, shape shifting around the networks, and relationships of women's organisations. Here the terrains of a middle space associated with civil society and the public sphere complemented those of state institutions and the formal structures of professional organisations.

A third feature of the politics of the Beijing Conference was the way in which the conference documents, and the experiences of those who contributed to drafting these, formulated specific ethical obligations of individuals and groups to engage in action to eradicate poverty, build equalities and affirm women's diverse identities. From this perspective the global terrain of policy making is one that formulates ethical connections and directions, which reverberate in different ways with the terrains of a middle space we have identified. The personal statements associated with these actions resonate with the metaphor of the letter or personal message of global promise that we explored in the previous chapter.

Although these three different ways of understanding the global terrain of gender and education policy making were distilled at the Beijing Conference and re-interpreted in the decades after 1995, a major focus of this chapter is the way the policy ladders were set up, and then affected intermixtures of processes associated with the global, national and local. At the end of the chapter we reflect on some ways of understanding the global landscape of gender equality policy, relationships with terrains of a middle space and different ways of connecting global, national and local.

As global relationships around gender and women's rights were being constituted in the 1990s occupying the formal terrain of institutions and establishing relationships with NGOs, a complementary policy process in education was also taking place linked to Education for All (EFA), and also establishing formal institutional relationships. EFA envisaged connections from global to local primarily in terms of the rungs of a ladder working through the institutional structures of state education systems. In this chapter we draw out some of the differences between EFA and the women's movement, with its range of different engagements with global policy making and terrains of a middle space. Drawing on key documents and data from interviews, we highlight how the assumptions of those working on EFA in global policy bodies saw the links between gender, poverty and education. These were somewhat differently framed to the perspectives of those associated with the women's rights movements which had gathered at the Beijing Conference in 1995. We describe the nature of the institutions and the global NGOs as examples of terrains of a middle space where global policy frameworks concerning gender equality and education were reviewed by differently situated actors. Our empirical data documents the period up to around 2010. However, our analysis offers insights into the global policy landscape put in place after our fieldwork concluded, which is intended to frame policy post-2015. We thus assess some of the meanings of gender, poverty and education being proffered and the forms of global relationship invoked as a result of engagements with the agendas of the Beijing Conference and EFA. On the basis of this analysis we suggest some ways of understanding the global terrain of gender equality policy making, themes we return to in our Conclusion (Chapter 9).

Global frameworks on gender, education and poverty: the Beijing Platform for Action

The 1995 Platform for Action adopted at the Beijing Conference outlines many areas of social action to support gender equality and the advancement of women. Under Strategic Objective 2, detailed attention is given to education, gender equality and women's rights. Access, progression and completion of different levels of schooling have some prominence, but so do other sites of education, including adult learning. The objective outlines a comprehensive engagement with gender equality and the quality of education provision, particularly stressing the content and organisation of what is taught in school. It points to the need to address inequities through monitoring and research, building lifelong learning pathways and enhancing women's participation in leadership and decision-making. Access to information, participation in sport, artistic and cultural arenas are highlighted as important areas of education, which in this articulation, entails more than simple enrolment in school. It thus maps connections between sites of realisation – schools, classrooms, education projects – and many spaces of a middle terrain – institutional, professional, civil society and the public sphere – where gender equalities and women's rights could be reflected on and planned.

Strategic Objective 1 of the Platform of Action identified the high numbers of women worldwide living in poverty. Poverty, the document notes, has many guises:

> including lack of income and productive resources sufficient to ensure a sustainable livelihood; hunger and malnutrition; ill health; limited or lack of access to education and other basic services; increasing morbidity and mortality from illness; homelessness and inadequate housing; unsafe environments; and social discrimination and exclusion.
>
> (Beijing Declaration and Platform of Action, 1995, p. 19)

It can be seen how these definitions of poverty are linked with inadequate education and forms of discrimination. The Platform for Action argued that ending poverty would not be achieved by anti-poverty programmes on their own. The comprehensive nature of poverty and disadvantage required substantive changes including 'democratic participation and changes in economic structures in order to ensure access for all women to resources, opportunities and public services' (Beijing Declaration and Platform of Action, 1995, p. 19).

In the Platform of Action education is woven into programmes to address poverty. Actions outlined to address the Strategic Objective on poverty concern changes in macro-economic policies, laws, financial products and research. This invokes the institutional terrains of a middle space and the idea of a public sphere.

The last Strategic Objective in the Platform for Action brings together policies on 'the girl child' and the need to address 'negative cultural attitudes and practices against girls' (Beijing Declaration and Platform of Action, 1995, p. 113). There is a stress on the need to enhance girls' access to education, skills development and training. Actions are proposed to enhance girls' health and nutrition, eliminate the economic exploitation of child labour, eradicate violence against girls and promote their social, economic and political participation and awareness. All these actions invoke spaces associated with terrains of middle space, in particular institutions, professional, civil society and public engagements for social change.

Gender mainstreaming was a key technique identified at the Beijing Conference for advancing change at global, national and local levels. It was outlined in its own strategic objective and identified as a key practice to effect transformation. Gender mainstreaming was defined here as 'mechanisms for promoting the advancement of women'. It required:

> . . ., Governments and other actors . . . [to] promote an active and visible policy of mainstreaming a gender perspective into all policies and programmes, so that, before decisions are taken, an analysis is made of the effects on women and men, respectively.
>
> (Beijing Declaration and Platform of Action, 1995, p. 27)

The stress on gender mainstreaming as a key 'mechanism' to effect change in diverse organisations was consonant with the political vision of the Beijing Platform, which stresses multiple sites for realising women's rights and gender equality. The ground is therefore prepared for gender mainstreaming to happen in any of the terrains of a middle space we have identified. In subsequent decades, the extent to which the approach was able to effect changes in institutions became a major area of investigation (Jahan, 1996; Moser and Moser, 2005; Porter and Sweetman, 2005). As we shall see in Chapter 8, how the relationships between global, national and local affected forms of gender mainstreaming needs some careful unravelling.

The historic gathering at the Beijing Conference was attended by virtually all governments, Inter-Government organisations, and representatives of 2,600 NGOs and civil society organisations. At the time it was criticised for not engaging incisively enough with the complexities of gender inequalities and the multiplicities of approaches to supporting women's rights (Baden and Goetz, 1998; Charlesworth, 2005). However, looking backwards across the space of twenty years, many of the affirmations and associations made at Beijing were detailed and complex discussions of rights and equality which laid out different ways of connecting in and through the four terrains of a middle space, utilising a range of varied practices (Baksh and Harcourt, 2015). Some of these practices were sustained, while in some areas the policy vision of Beijing came to be diluted, precipitating different actions (Kennett and Payne, 2014; Termine and Percic, 2015). To understand these processes it is useful to set the Beijing Conference in the context, firstly, of the history of global convening around women's rights and gender equality and to contrast this with the somewhat different history concerning global education policy making. This parallel discussion will enable us to see the ways in which understandings of the global policy landscape and the terrains and relationships of a middle space were somewhat different in the two processes.

A history of global convening on women's rights and gender equality

The Beijing Conference was part of a long process of global convening on many aspects of gender equality and women's rights, which gave particular prominence to poverty and education and which mapped terrains of a middle space between policy formulation and implementation as a central area of political and social engagement. Unterhalter's (2016a) recent review of a history of discussions and meetings on women's rights, poverty and education shows that these reach back to the late 18th century. Her identification of three distinct phases in the history of concerns with gender and girls' education in the global polity can be extended to include consideration of forms of connection between global, national and local spaces and some of the engagements with the four terrains of a middle space we have outlined.

The first and longest phase Unterhalter's analysis identifies is associated with rights. From the late 18th century ideas were initially formulated bottom up by small groups of women and some men arguing for expanded education, partly to facilitate women's participation in the public sphere, and partly to steer women away from what were portrayed as narrow-minded concerns, which, it was believed, undermined their claims to moral, political, economic and social equality. While the movement was initially not closely engaged with aspects of poverty, the widening ambit of participation in this informal network of commentators brought in activists who were very centrally concerned with poverty, slavery, exploitative work and legal forms of economic discrimination. This initial bottom-up, often informal engagement ebbed and flowed like weather systems, and was often very literally expressed through handwritten letters posted between friends. It exemplified the notion of the public sphere and many key ideas were articulated in meetings. But it also exhibited many features of civil society as it was sustained by personal networks of friendships across diverse locations, and commitments to ethical responsibilities. Up until the late 19th century states were not sites to facilitate the expansion of education or establish institutional frameworks to build gender equality or address poverty. The only supra-national bodies in this first phase were religious, mercantile or ethnic and were blown on the winds of different kinds of affiliation these invoked. Thus the terrains of a middle space connected across horizontal networks, rather than institutional hierarchies or ladders. Because of the absence of inclusive governments and states concerned with equalities, the moral arguments about responsibility for gender equality, providing education or addressing poverty, are made with some conviction and somewhat less doubt about legalities or the efficiency of bureaucracies. Democratic iterations in the public sphere often take the form of critique, and are not yet able to reflect on the outcomes of research or practice.

Unterhalter (2016a) shows how with the end of World War 2 the focus of the work of women's rights activists moved from the informal bottom-up networks of the early 19th and 20th centuries to attempting to engage with the more formal institutional realm of Constitutions, law making, national governments and global policy. The shift to trying to work top down was accompanied by an attempt to 'establish ladders' of formal consultation and engagement with decision making which could connect formally to ascertain the views of those located in spaces far from what had been established centres of power. Thus forms of local government, social survey, devolved management and consultation with trade unions all evolved in this period, opening up some space for voicing concerns on women's rights and gender equality. The more fluid types of mobilising, associated with ideas and aspirations, blowing with the wind of global networks connecting with local mobilisations, was not abandoned. However, this became more segmented, with distinct areas of work on reproductive rights, indigenous rights, land ownership or education emerging. The need to build ladders of connection from central institutions down to grass roots was acknowledged, but not always achieved. Work on poverty and education together, as expressed in many of the engagements with the public sphere or civil society of the earlier period, was not always taken forward. However a number of international policy declarations were adopted that dealt with these areas. The most notable for this discussion were the International Covenant on Economic, Social and Cultural Rights (ICESCR) adopted by the UN General Assembly in 1966, and brought into force from 1976, the Convention on the Elimination of Discrimination against Women (CEDAW) adopted at the UN in 1979, and the Convention on the Rights of the Child (CRC) adopted in 1989. The world conferences on women in Mexico City (1980), Nariobi (1985) and Beijing (1995) were partly organised to help build connections between the formal realms of developing global legal frameworks, and the multiple sites of practice to realise women's rights and gender equality (Wetzel, 1993; Arat, 2015; Sandler, 2015). What was significant about Beijing was the extensive presence of governments, inter-government organisations and the ways in which NGOs emerged to articulate some of the aspirations of women's rights advocates. This kind of alliance and identification of multiple connections top-down, bottom-up and through multiple sites of a middle space was itself an outcome of the international collaborations of the post-Cold War era, sometimes remarked on as the growth of a global civil society (Kaldor, 2013) and the Beijing Declaration was a key example of this.

In reviewing the key meetings and policy declarations in relation to women's rights and gender equality that have taken place since 1945 two different kinds of dynamics associated with connecting from global through national to local are apparent. The first is directed through laws and institution building, as expressed for example in CEDAW or CRC and exemplified by our metaphor of the ladder. The second is associated with the global women's movement, linked with grassroots mobilising from the bottom up, building networks, and working the intersections of translocations, which could be seen, for example, at the Women's conferences that took place in Mexico and Nairobi in 1980 and 1985. These exemplify the metaphor of weather systems moving like the wind. However, both of these approaches change in the period after 1990. A series of policy declarations – for example those associated with the International Conference on Population and Development (ICPD) in 1994 and the World Summit on Social Development, held in Copenhagen in 1995 – invoked both changing institutions and building forms of participation and social action through the terrains of a middle space as articulated at the Beijing Conference. They suggest a blending, and an amalgamation of two of our metaphors, distilled through the notion of ladders in the wind. This metaphor combines two kinds of approach to working with notions of the global, national and local, that is the structured form of relationship signalled by the institutions or organisational forms evoked by the notion of the ladder, and the more uneven and unpredictable kind of mixture of global, national and local captured by the metaphor of the weather and wind. The MDGs, while presented as a form of institutional change or a particular kind of ladder, because of their stress on results based management, considerably shifted the way in which institutions were to be viewed and attempted to situate the mixture of global, national and local associated with older formations of the women's movement in a relationship to service the narrow focus the MDGs delineated.

Global education policy making: EFA and the MDGs

In contrast to global policy making around women's rights, the global policy landscape in education conformed much more to the metaphor of a ladder than that of a weather system. The terrains of a middle space were, in contrast to those associated with gender and women's rights, more contoured around institutional frameworks and professional organisations. Only from the late 1990s did organisations of civil society begin to play some role, largely articulated through global NGOs, and often having close links with the institutional forms of states and the global architecture of aid.

The World Education Forum at Dakar, held in 2000, at which the Dakar Platform for Action was agreed, is often seen as a particularly significant moment for the forms of global mobilisation and networking around education (Mundy and Murphy, 2001; Colclough, 2005; Unterhalter, 2014). It came ten years after an earlier meeting of governments and some NGOs held in Jomtien in 1990, at which the Education for All (EFA) framework was initially formulated (Dakar, 2000). The Dakar EFA Programme of Action, did not have a specific concern with poverty reduction, but it did implicitly address a number of poverty and gender issues in the education sphere. In this text there is an 'education first' approach to poverty, so that the focus is on areas in which poverty has kept children out of school, for example because of fees, and where lack of literacy has diminished earnings, but it does not give particular attention to the gender dimensions of poverty or to addressing the causes and consequences of poverty. However, implicitly the Dakar Programme provides policy attention to a range of sites of gender inequality associated with schooling, ranging from lack of provision of early childhood education, low levels of adult literacy and the nature of learning. The specific gender goal (goal 5) 'aimed at eliminating gender disparities in primary and secondary education by 2005 and achieving gender equality in education by 2015, with a focus on ensuring girls' full and equal access to and achievement in basic education of good quality'. Although this was often to be interpreted narrowly in terms of gender parity (equal numbers of girls and boys) in primary and secondary education, it also gave scope for interpretation in terms of establishing school environments free from discrimination, offering equal opportunities to girls and boys (UNESCO, 2014, p. 5). When, in the same year, the Millennium Development Goals (MDGs) were agreed, MDG2 and MDG 3 drew directly from the more expansive set of six education goals agreed at Dakar, but limited the focus on gender simply to ensuring gender parity.

Dakar holds particular significance for the global education community in terms of representing a developing global consensus around education and its place within the broader development agenda. It was also associated with the emergence of new forms of partnership, donor coordination and the engagement of new actors in the EFA movement. Following the Dakar forum, UNESCO continued to take on the role of official coordinator of the EFA initiative – a role that it had occupied since the 1960s – although both the World Bank and UNICEF took more prominent roles from 1990 onwards. The annual Global

Monitoring Reports (GMR), which analysed data regarding progress towards the EFA goals on education from 204 countries around the world, have been published by UNESCO and from 2003–4 gave considerable space to engaging with the question of gender, and from 2010 to thinking about poverty and marginalisation. Other agencies and actors also stepped forward to take on new roles and lead on different aspects of the implementation of the EFA global agenda.

The 2003/4 GMR provided an analysis which took a very broad definition of gender equality, linked to ideas about rights (UNESCO, 2003) and drew on analysis of sites outside schools associated with inequality, notably labour markets and household relations (Colclough et al., 2003). These early volumes of the GMR suggested more fundamental social and economic reforms would be necessary, not just increasing enrolments. The 2005 GMR report on education quality, noted good quality in education was impossible if gender inequality persisted in school processes and outcomes (UNESCO, 2005, p. 31). But this wide angle view of gender and schooling lost focus in some later volumes of the Report, although by 2015 the gender work of the Report had become an in-depth analysis.

Two examples show how policy relationships linked with EFA were generally structured in the forms of a ladder connecting the global to the local. The Fast Track Initiative (FTI), which became the Global Partnership for Education in 2011, was launched immediately following Dakar as a mechanism designed to leverage additional resources for education from the donor community. The FTI emerged specifically as a response to the commitment made in Dakar to a Global Initiative, which was initiated by NGOs and supported by UNESCO, 'with the aim of holding donors to account with respect to mobilisation of additional technical and financial resources needed to accelerate progress towards the Education for All (EFA) goals' (Rose, 2005, p. 381). In particular it aimed to ensure that donors were held to the commitment they made at the World Education Forum in 2000 that '"No countries seriously committed to Education for All will be thwarted in their achievement of this goal by a lack of resources"' (Rose, 2005, p. 381). Thus states positioned in the middle of the ladder stretching between global and national levels were to pass requests relating to the need for resources upward to global organisations and downwards to local sites of delivery.

The FTI was coordinated by the World Bank due to concerns that UNESCO lacked the capacity to lead such a global financing initiative. Representing a partnership of multilateral and bilateral agencies and regional development banks, it sought to mobilise external resources to provide long-term education financing to countries with 'credible' education plans and a Poverty Reduction Strategy Paper. Despite this, it is notable that the original version of the FTI initially did not include any specific attention to gender. However, as the fund developed, a limited concern with gender was apparent in its activities and some gender disaggregated indicators were developed, working with the notion of gender as a noun and measuring levels of gender parity. In 2016 the Global Partnership for Education (GPE), as FTI was now renamed, adopted a gender equality policy and strategy that made gender responsiveness a core priority for its work, noting issues of gender inequality within and beyond schools, and claiming a leadership role for itself in relation to advancing the SDG gender and education agenda (Global Partnership for Education, 2016).

The second example of a multi-agency initiative emerging from the Dakar Forum was more explicitly aimed at accelerating progress on gender equality in education, and did not have the conventional ladder relationship between global and local evident in the FTI. The UN Girls Education Initiative (UNGEI) was launched in Dakar by then United Nations Secretary-General Kofi Annan as a multi-stakeholder partnership which aimed to raise the profile of girls' education and contribute to achieving the EFA goals relating to gender equality. UNGEI is coordinated by a secretariat located in the UNICEF headquarters in New York and guided by a Global Advisory Committee. Advisory committee members include representatives from multilateral agencies, bilateral donors and civil society organisations including INGOs. In contrast to the FTI, whose main purpose was the mobilisation of resources and coordination of aid, UNGEI's focus has been on providing leadership and coordination to policy dialogue, advocacy, knowledge exchange and capacity development, with a specific focus on girls' education and gender equality globally, and, through working with regional and local networks, at regional, national and sub-national levels. UNGEI partly exemplifies the relationships portrayed through the image of the ladder, although because it is not primarily dispensing funds through the institutions of the state, like the FTI/GPE, it has the potential to be more responsive to some of the gusts of wind associated with the global–national–local waves of ideas linked to the women's movement or civil society.

Recent assessments of the UNGEI's impact have highlighted achievements in providing global leadership on girls' education through its networking among multilateral and bilateral donors. For example, in the 2015 Global Monitoring Report, the link between UNGEI and other global organisations is stressed, rather than its responsiveness to women's rights mobilisation:

> The most visible of all global mechanisms associated with gender equality has been the United Nations Girls' Education Initiative (UNGEI), a multi-stakeholder partnership established in Dakar in 2000. [. . .] An evaluation of UNGEI particularly acknowledged its contribution in global policy dialogue and advocacy. . . . Recognizing the challenge of translating globally agreed priorities into country-level activities, UNGEI has created stronger links with the GPE. The evaluation also praised UNGEI's role in coordination and priority-setting among its members.
>
> (UNESCO, 2015, p. 36)

However, while initial progress made by UNGEI after the Dakar Forum was slow and the initiative was criticised for lacking a clear agenda (Rose, 2005; Smyth and Rao, 2005), from 2010, with many donor agencies and NGOs giving girls' education prominence, UNGEI came to play a more dynamic role, engaging with national projects international policy debate, and from 2014 making presentations at the annual meeting of CSW in New York. In 2015, UNGEI led some of the discussions on gender equality in education, helping to negotiate the Incheon Declaration on Education for All and some of the gender equality content of SDG 4. Since 2013 UNGEI has been active in mobilising discussion around school-related gender-based violence (SRGBV), teacher education and employment, indicators and the measurement of gender equality in education in the context of these new global frameworks. It has made some key connections to work with education unions on SRGBV (UNGEI, 2015; Global Working Group to end SRGBV, 2016). Thus, although initially conceived to connect the global and the local, in the somewhat conventional form of a ladder, UNGEI has often been responsive to some of the discussions of terrains of a middle space associated with professional organisations, civil society and the public sphere, and has acknowledged some of the dynamics of the intermixture of global, national and local that the metaphor of weather system seeks to capture.

The example of UNGEI indicates how the connections concerning global gender policy between global, national and local did not only take the form of a ladder connecting national state institutions with UN structures. From the late 1990s the area of global education policy discussion generated its own version of the networks of civil society working like the formations of a weather system, with some similarities with the forms of the transnational women's movement. The Global Campaign for Education (GCE) emerged as a wide ranging coalition of NGOs, teacher unions and other civil society organisations working at national, regional and global levels to advance demands around EFA. GCE was formed in 1999 at a meeting hosted by Oxfam, ActionAid International, Education International and the Global March against Child Labour. It was initially conceived of as a short-term campaign focused on the Dakar forum, and aimed to ensure that gathering would result in "concrete commitments and viable policies to implement the Education for All (EFA) goals" (GCE Constitution, 2001; Mundy, 2012). It provided a focus for coordinated civil society action around Dakar in 2000 (Mundy and Murphy, 2001; Gaventa and Mayo, 2009). The presence of NGOs and civil society voices had been limited in global education policy fora pre-Dakar. The Dakar process itself, and the presence of a coordinated civil society coalition in the form of GCE was therefore significant in enabling civil society actors to take a part in the push towards achieving Education for All (Sivasubramaniam, 2008). Organisations of GCE played a key role in mobilising popular participation in the framing of the SDGs (Naidoo and Seim, 2013; Tikly, 2017). Since 2000, GCE has thus represented a significant civil society voice on EFA. Its mixture of global NGOs, like ActionAid, Oxfam and Save the Children, working with local national civil society networks, exemplifies gusts of wind. These have blown with a focus on gender equality and women's rights sometimes given prominence, but sometimes muted.

Thus, while the form of global, national and local connections within the women's movement and the education movement were somewhat different, there were also some hybrid forms in each. In the next section we draw on some of the perspectives of people we interviewed working in a number of global organisations to consider the ways in which they saw links being made between gender, education and poverty, and the ways in which they understood the flows between different sites of policy engagement.

Framing global gender policy: actors' perspectives

People employed in organisations that defined themselves as working at a global level, placed considerable emphasis on building this area and establishing transnational institutions and networks that would sustain global initiatives. These global organisations were sometimes viewed as settings for discussions of accountability with regard to global policy, and sometimes as places where negotiations on what was to be funded took place. The significance of new spaces emerging at the global level, and the need to develop coordination and connections between bilateral and multilateral agencies and representatives of civil society in order to take forward the EFA agenda was emphasised by many of the participants we interviewed. For many, building hybrid organisations across multilateral, bilateral and large non-government organisations was an important site of opportunity. Although the FTI or UNGEI were seen as imperfect, and sometimes criticised for lacking focus, engaging with them was a key area of effort. One staff member from an international civil society network, while expressing concerns about the limitations of global processes and the need for work at the local level, explained:

> We are going to continue to be heavily engaged with the global processes [such as the FTI]. I think if anything we want to kind of take our ambition a bit higher and be more involved in global processes – well, not involved in, influential of – global processes like EU, G8, G20, IMF and World Bank and so on.
>
> (International civil society organisation 1, staff member, 23/12/2008)

A similar perspective on the potential of the FTI, particularly for leveraging action on girls' education, was articulated by staff members we interviewed working in bilateral organisations. For example:

> The FTI appraisal process with its guidelines which are, I mean I know the indicative framework is contested in a few other areas, . . ., but as a tool for coalescing donors around financing education at a country level and identifying the two or three areas which need to be unblocked within the education sector in order to make progress I found it very helpful and useful. I mean the appraisal we did certainly did have a section on girls' education, largely around differentials in learning outcomes.
>
> (Bilateral agency, staff member 2, February 2009)

A representative from one of the multilateral organisations acknowledged that the resources going to the FTI were small compared with those for health, but they helped mobilise support for the MDGs by national governments:

> Another way to think about is that in spite of the fact that the Fast Track Initiative isn't huge, and isn't only a funding agency by the way, . . . and yet

if you look at the averages across the world by region you see big increases in education at least with respect to the MDGs, right? That must mean that the national resources have actually gone to education. Not perfectly, and not as much as we would want, certainly in some countries, but it must mean that there is some buy-in into this goal of educating more kids.

(Multilateral agency 1, staff member, 18/06/2010)

Although the results of the UNGEI partnership were viewed by some, at the time of interview in 2009, with disappointment with regard to its overall achievements, a number recognised that there were challenges, but stressed its value in catalysing action and bringing different stakeholders together. For example:

I think the thing is that there are always going to be limitations with mecha-nisms like this [UNGEI]. But I do think though that something like UNGEI, and the way that we've seen it . . . , building on from the last point about the MDGs providing a framework for accountability, a vehicle like UNGEI does then create the platform or the opportunity to use that framework of accountability and really to be creating a space in which different kinds of organisations – UN, Donors, Civil Society – are coming together to examine the MDGs and what the kinds of obligations and goals should be together as partnership together to achieve this, and what kinds of calls we should be making on our respective partner governments to actually achieve those. So I think from that perspective it does provide a vital space to be able to use those MDGs.

(International civil society organisation 2, staff member, 09/01/2009)

An employee of a donor agency also noted some doubts about what UNGEI could achieve, but saw that even modest gains around enhancing information flow were important to building a global coalition:

. . . I think you always have to critically assess how valuable international networks are and especially when you haven't got much time and also the resources. . . . But my experience at the moment and I still hold on to it is that I think we need to keep gender and education there in these interna-tional forums and that's where I see that they play a key role really . . . . So I think that's their [UNGEI's] role really, to keep it up on the agenda. And also they're useful in terms of sharing information and you know and mak-ing, and the technical side to a certain extent.

(Bilateral agency, staff member 1, 28/01/2009)

However there were concerns among some participants – particularly those from global civil society organisations – that global initiatives such as UNGEI, as well as other initiatives for global convening, such as the UNESCO EFA high-level group, had not been effective in providing the leadership needed on gender equality and education. One staff member from a global NGO suggested there was a need for civil society groups to call for stronger leadership on gender equality issues on the global stage and should ask:

> why UNGEI is not as effective as everybody would want it to be, because for me it is a disgrace that a UN agency like that is unstructured.
>
> (International civil society organisation 3, staff member, 07/12/2007)

Another staff member, from a different NGO, explained that their organisation was "very disappointed with UNGEI", though recognised that the lack of early engagement with UNGEI by civil society groups may have helped "undermine it further" (International civil society organisation 4, staff member, 13/03/2008). This participant questioned the decision to house UNGEI within UNICEF rather than in UNESCO as the lead agency on EFA more generally, raising issues around ownership and international leadership.

What is striking here is the assumption amongst a section of the education NGO community that global leadership or co-ordination by a UN body was an important gain. They were disappointed that UNGEI was not providing this. Their concern with the need for this from a UN organisation contrasts with the more fluid views of multiple organisations that characterised some the networks taking forward the Beijing process. In that constituency there were concerns of a different stamp, that UN leadership undermined, rather than enhanced the authenticity and radicalism of women's rights demands (Sandler, 2015).

Linking gender, education and poverty

The meetings that took place in Dakar and New York were not only significant for the ways in which they opened up new forms of global connection, but also in the ways in which ideas around gender, education and poverty were articulated within the agreements and policy frameworks. While the six goals agreed at Dakar represented a relatively expansive vision of education, which included concerns with educational quality, adult literacy and vocational skills as well as access to primary and secondary schooling, the goal that was taken up in the MDG framework (MDG2) was much narrower, with the focus limited to the achievement of universal primary education. Addressing gender inequality in schooling (MDG 3) meanwhile required ensuring all girls complete at least primary school by 2015 and there are equal numbers of boys and girls in each phase of education (Appendix 1). Addressing poverty was associated with reducing the proportions of the world's population who have minimal income and food and lack decent work. This approach may be thought of as ensuring a certain level of sufficiency or crossing a line of minimum income, calorie intake, employment status or school completion for girls and boys. Gender in this framework is largely about equal numbers of boys and girls.

In the wording of the international policy frameworks of 2000 (The Dakar EFA Programme and the MDGs) the focus shifted from earlier phases of policy, which had primarily concerned themselves with rights and aspects of equality.

Gore (2010) describes the MDG shift as moving from a 'procedural conception' of international society with a 'common respect for a set of rules, norms and standard practices' such as those associated with the Universal Declaration of Human Rights or the Beijing Declaration on Women and Gender, to a 'purposive conception', where the stress is on a 'co-operative venture to promote common ends'. For Gore, a procedural conception entails a maximalist view of development. Here aspects of equality and flourishing are goals for rich and poor countries. The proceduralist conception may also be taken to entail multi-dimensional perspectives on poverty and gender inequality, and integrated or connected approaches to addressing this. A purposive conception, by contrast, is associated with a minimalist view, which ensures the most deprived cross a threshold of adequate provision in some, but not all, areas of development. This might mean earning a dollar a day or completing a primary cycle of schooling.

However, by implication both the procedural and the purposive approach face a problem relating to the nature of the social contract that underpins them. The more demanding the social justice content of the procedural approach, the more difficult it becomes to secure, full human rights or gender equality through agreements at all levels, from multinational conventions, to national governments, down to local assemblies. There are particular problems for groups, like refugees, who stand outside official state structures. The more minimal the purposive agreement, the easier it might be for governments to sign up, but the more fragile the range of what can be achieved and the more elusive the promise of the integrated agenda. Even governments committed only to purposive agreements may not be able to implement these fully.

To a large extent these purposive framings of education, gender and poverty can be associated with what has been described as 'the get girls in school approach', which dates back to the 1960s (Unterhalter, 2016a). This policy approach, which was led from the health sector and was associated with fears of what was viewed as a population 'explosion', identified the links between education, poverty and gender differently to those associated with the long histories of campaigning around women's rights. In the 'get girls into school', which by the 1990s had come to be linked with strategies to address poverty, there was a stress on flow diagrams of efficiency. Access to school is conceived somewhat like access to contraceptives, and the fluidities, moral reflections and political mobilisations associated with women's rights, were replaced by a technical stress on building schools, training teachers and rolling out specialist projects.

This work, largely led by multilateral organisations, drawing on research evidence put together by the World Bank (King and Hill, 1991), had a very limited engagement with poverty as a site of multiple oppressions and violations. It tended to define poverty in terms of income, and sometimes features of marginality associated with location or ethnicity (Tembon and Fort, 2008). The multilateral organisations who had advanced arguments to 'get girls in school' were active at the Beijing Conference, but had also run a number of complementary conferences earlier in the decade, such as the EFA and UNICEF conferences in 1990. While they acknowledged the importance of the Beijing Conference, they did not take their agenda from it. The more limited vision of education,

poverty and gender they advanced had much more money and political influence behind it than that articulated through the Beijing Conference Platform of
Action (Unterhalter, 2007; Sen and Mukherjee, 2014). Thus one set of meanings
linked with poverty, education and gender puts a stress on technical delivery, gender as a noun, equality as parity and education as school, the smooth connection
up and down a ladder of organisations running from global to local. The other
set of meanings represents the more fluid hybrid mixing of ideas from multiple
sites and perspectives on gender, education and equality, in which the global,
national, local and translocational intersect like weather.

These two perspectives were evident in the interviews we conducted, sometimes articulated very clearly linked to the remit of a particular organisation, but
sometimes being negotiated by the same individual within a global organisation,
which was moving between positions.

For staff in the bilateral and multilateral organisations, the Dakar platform
and the MDGs were influential in giving direction in determining the way in
which they operationalised concerns with gender equality, education and poverty
through their programmes. They saw these texts as helping them, prioritise, focus
on measurable outputs and outcomes,

> I think that the experience of the MDGs is a good one, its correct for us to be
> much more aware of the indicators, because if we don't measure these things
> we don't focus, right. It's crazy that we didn't do this 50 years ago . . . . The
> disadvantage is that we get so focused on the numbers . . ., to give ourselves
> a benchmark to some extent. At the same time as 2015 approaches we get so
> wrapped up in the numbers, well what, it seems to be its a test of how do we
> get though numbers rather than looking at the policies.
> (Multilateral agency 1, staff member, 18/06/2010)

> this goes back to the issue of the MDGs, girls' education and parity in enrol-
> ment has kind of sunk in, I think, it's important to recognise that there's
> been some usefulness about that. And you know, we've got some examples
> of how having a really really clear message and something that's measurable
> and all the rest of it can make a difference.
> (Bilateral agency, staff member 2, February 2009)

> I believe that by having a target that this helps countries and other actors to
> focus their efforts, to prioritise, and this is particularly where the EFA goals
> and the MDGs also are useful.
> (Multilateral agency 2, staff member, 26/07/2008)

This positive view of the MDGs and the way in which they had limited the
meaning of gender went together with a view that the MDGs had helped enhance
the status of education in relation to development:

> I think they've [the MDGs]) been incredibly useful. . . . And I think actu-
> ally the difference between the MDGs and the EFA goals is interesting. The

MDGs are fewer in number, they're prioritised and they are very easy to measure. And I think as a result of those the things and the fact that they have been nested into a broader set of goals, they're not just about education has been really important in galvanising this international level of support. People can talk MDG language across the board and you've got non education people talking about education.

(Bilateral agency, staff member 2, February 2009)

For staff in the global NGOs, the MDGs were also seen to provide a framework for holding governments and multilateral organisations to account:

I think for us the Millennium Development Goals, while there are questions around how achievable, how committed people are to them, I think it does provide that framework of accountability in the context of girls' education and the urgency for this generation. It's for us I think the most useful and tangible framework to be able to do that. And . . . particularly in the context of UNGEI, to be able to have some kind of frame of reference to be able to have a dialogue . . . others around these kind of issues. We're all signed up and we're all in the same space. I think it does put us in the same space in a way that some of the other frameworks haven't necessarily done.

(International civil society organisation 2, staff member, 09/01/2009)

Many participants, including those working in bilateral and multilateral agencies and those from civil society, were, however, critical of the narrow framing of gender equality and education within the MDGs. Nonetheless, within these organisations there was a view that the frameworks could be drawn on strategically: the policies were seen to have leverage, to widen the scope of work on gender. MDG 3 was seen by staff in bilateral, multilateral and NGOs as providing an advocacy tool, which could be used for pushing action on gender by other agencies and within the international community:

I think because of the MDGs, actually – ironically – although we all know, I'm certainly not a fundamentalist when it comes to the MDGs – but, you know because gender is there and quite strong – that's really where it comes into the MDGs is in education – that means it has necessitated it being monitored at country level. In, you know, very quantitative ways, but it is there. So I think without that it might drop off, it could drop off.

(Bilateral agency, staff member 1, 28/01/2009)

So in that sense the MDGs is a weaker document for women and for the women's agenda. It's not agenda for women, that's clear with the MDGS and it's never claimed to be so. But unfortunately, but the good thing about the MDGs and the declaration is that it put gender, it brought it into the mainstream. That gender is one among eight goals, whereas Beijing is a stand alone agenda for women and those who are working for women had something that they could rally around and could push for, but it wasn't necessarily on the agenda of those who were out of Beijing and once Beijing died down it was only being carried by the women's movement. Whereas MDGs is something that's being, it's on everybody's lips . . . it's part of a movement that has definitely made it possible, to finally consider that gender equality should be right up there among, as a global goal, fundamental to the progress of societies. I don't like giving too much importance to the MDGs (laughs), its serves a lot of other purposes.

(Multilateral agency 3, staff member, 06/09/2010)

For other participants, the 'gets girls in school' approach associated with the MDG target was seen as much more problematic. A number of global civil society participants expressed concerns regarding the way in which the presence of the MDGs on the global stage had captured "language and territory" associated with wider concerns around gender and education linked to ideas of equality and empowerment, contained within the Dakar EFA and the Beijing platforms. They argued that global spaces such as the FTI, by focusing exclusively on the MDG targets and primary enrolment, had 'contributed to this narrowing of frames of reference' (International civil society organisation 1, staff member, 23/12/2008). One global civil society participant recognised that, as a result, their own organisation's work in education and gender had often become narrowly focused on enrolment figures and gender parity, to the neglect of a deeper engagement with other issues of importance to the broader EFA framework:

I definitely think that . . . we fell into the trap of thinking that MDGs 2 and 3 . . . were like the low hanging fruit and we'd pluck those off and it was just a sequencing thing. And now I suddenly understand the [EFA] goals are so much more interrelated and mutually reinforcing and that going off down one route has actually regressed progress in the others.

(International civil society organisation 1, staff member, 23/12/2008)

Another said:

So I do think that the MDGs framework almost actively undermines Beijing and EFA. And I see that again and again and again. It is for example, going back to what I was just saying, in the EFA Fast Track Initiative, which is about making aid to education, is called the Education For All Fast Track Initiative, but decided to only focus on the MDG of getting all children into primary school. But because they occupy the EFA language and territory, there was no prospect of any parallel initiative being created which would bring all the donors together in order to support adult literacy or early childhood education or the other goals, they occupied that entire space.

(International civil society organisation 4, staff member, 13/03/2008)

Amongst donor agency participants, while there were fewer criticisms of the MDGs as a narrow policy framework, some participants particularly those with a long history of working on gender raised similar concerns:

> MDG3 as you know relates to gender equality and women's empowerment but it has a target related to gender parity in primary, secondary and eventually all levels of schooling. And therein lies the rub in terms of some of the challenges that we have seen with regard to gender because in fact a number of countries and a number of actors have chosen to interpret the MDG3 target in a very narrow fashion. Um, we have attained gender parity in education in our country at all levels and so therefore we do not have a gender problem.
>
> (Multilateral agency 2, staff member, 27/06/2008)

These critical voices, which were much more apparent in organisations with long histories of work on women's rights and gender equality, to some extent appear to reflect what has been identified as a concern in global policy making on gender and girls' schooling moving 'beyond access' (Unterhalter (2016a). This phase exhibits some of the features Kantola and Squires (2012) have identified with a new equality agenda, moving from concerns with redistribution, to aspects of identity and participation.) This beyond access phase in education also emerged partly as a critique of the limited focus on enrolment and attendance in the policy discussion and actions which followed the setting of the targets for MDG2 and MDG3 in 2000 (Unterhalter, 2016a).

One strand of work in the beyond access phase has been associated with increasing attention to defining and addressing school-related gender-based violence (Parkes, 2015). This issue first surfaced in global policy making in the UNGEI Declaration of 2010 (UNGEI, 2010; Unterhalter and North, 2011), where it, together with poverty and quality, were seen as major challenges relating to gender and girls' schooling in the next decade. Another strand of beyond access work discussed aspects of education quality and learning outcomes, particularly how these were measured, and what the results of various tests in reading, writing and numeracy showed with regard, partly, to the differences between girls and boys. Poverty, largely defined in terms of income, was, together with rurality and gender, a significant variable in these studies (UNESCO, 2015).

It can be seen that in taking forward agendas to address poverty, gender and education in the era of EFA and the MDGs, there was some narrowing of the meanings of gender to mean primarily girls and boys, poverty to mean primarily income level, and education to be centred largely on school. Practices associated with terrains of a middle space entailed establishing the rungs of an institutional ladder from global to local to support this focus. A range of critical voices offering other meaning of gender, poverty and education had less resonance with powerful bodies. Many global NGOs or civil society organisations, although sympathetic to these critical perspectives, were also concerned to engage with the global politics of the multilateral organisations, and the MDG framework. This was, Gore (2010) argues, a Faustian bargain, in which as much was lost as was gained. In Part 2 we trace these processes through different sites of engagement with this bargain.

The post-2015 agenda

In 2010 when the UN General Assembly and many civil society organisations and commentators reviewed progress on the MDGs and EFA the mood was far less optimistic than in 2000. Large numbers of the poorest children were still out of school and gender inequality remained a feature of much education provision (UNESCO, 2010). In discussions there appeared to be two stances. Either, the argument went, the glass was half full, and more had been achieved than could have been hoped through the bringing together of international aid and global and national policy communities around the MDG and EFA frameworks. Thus a significant premium was associated with global co-ordination, shared development assistance agendas, and efficiencies in monitoring. Others, however, proposed the glass was half empty, the targets inappropriate, achievement unlikely, and the process of global convening was a flawed exercise in which powerful nations dictated to the powerless, located in national and local spaces, diverting attention away from concentrations of military might, unjust economic power, hypocritical support for dictators and very limited engagements with gender, poverty or substantive aspects of education (Verger, Novelli and Altinyelken, 2012).

Extensive discussion evaluating the MDGs and EFA in terms of outputs took place from 2010 to 2015, when the SDGs were adopted (Benavot et al., 2016; Lingard, Martino and Stelar, 2015; Sayed et al., 2013). In May 2014, government ministers, representatives from bilateral and multilateral agencies and civil society organisations gathered in Muscat, Oman, and agreed a draft set of seven goals for a post-2015 global education agenda, which, they argued should be 'rights – based and reflect a perspective based on equity and inclusion, with particular attention to gender equality and to overcoming all forms of discrimination in and through education' (UNESCO, 2013). However, within the goals themselves a concern with gender was limited to referencing 'boys and girls' and to a focus on gender equality in relation to skills training for adults and youth. The Muscat meeting was followed by the World Education Forum, held in Incheon, Republic of Korea. Delegates in Incheon set out a vision for 'a single, renewed education agenda' (UNESCO, 2015b). While no targets were agreed at Incheon, delegates instead committing themselves to the targets being agreed for SDG 4 in a parallel process, the Incheon Declaration contained an explicit commitment to the promotion of gender equality that went beyond that articulated in Muscat. This included attention to the process of achieving gender equality in education, including a commitment to support 'gender-sensitive policies, planning and learning environments; mainstreaming gender issues in teacher training and curricula; and eliminating gender-based discrimination and violence in schools' (UNESCO, 2015b, p. 7).

After 2010 UNGEI became a leading voice for expanding the focus of work on gender and education so that it would be wider than a narrow focus on girls. In a series of commissioned studies, reviews of literature and network-building initiatives it set out to deepen discussion of gender equality and girls' education, contribute substantial analysis to the annual UNESCO Global Monitoring Reports and lobby within national and international organisations around the positioning of gender in the post-2015 agenda (King and Winthrop, 2015; UNGEI, 2015).

In September 2015, the UN general assembly adopted 17 Sustainable Development Goals (SDGs), which superseded the MDGs. SDG 4 "Ensure inclusive and equitable quality education and promote lifelong learning opportunities for all" was linked to seven targets and three means of implementation. These carried forward some of the 'education first' concerns set out in Dakar with achieving quality basic education for all, and the elimination of gender disparities, but also emphasised the acquisition of 'the knowledge and skills needed to promote sustainable development', including gender equality (SDG 4.7). SDG 5 meanwhile set out a broader agenda for the achievement gender equality and the empowerment of women and girls, with targets concerned with the elimination of violence and trafficking, harmful practices such as early marriage and genital mutilation, the recognition of unpaid care work, political participation and leadership, reproductive rights, access to economic resources, the use of technology and gender equality legislation.

One of the institutional actors involved in the negotiations regarding SDG 5 was UN Women, which was established in July 2010 by the UN General Assembly as part of the UN reform agenda. As a new UN entity, UN Women brought together the work of four previous UN bodies – the Division for the Advancement of Women (DAW), the International Research and Training Institute for the Advancement of Women (INSTRAW), the Office of the Special Adviser on Gender Issues and Advancement of Women (OSAGI) and the United Nations Development Fund for Women (UNIFEM). It was set up in order to bring the resources and mandates of these previously distinct bodies together to accelerate work on gender equality and women's empowerment. It seeks to do this through engaging in political negotiations around globally agreed standards for gender equality, and supporting UN member states to implement these at national level.[1] The establishment of UN Women was controversial in the international women's movement, as it was seen by some as abrogating the radical women's rights agenda and marginalising key activists (Sandler, 2015).

UN Women has defined substantive equality for women as encompassing 'three interconnected dimensions along which actions need to be taken' (2015, p. 42) in which women's formal rights, guaranteed by various international and national constitutions and conventions, need to be supplemented by additional processes to develop equality as a set of lived relationships:

1   Redressing women's socio-economic disadvantage
2   Addressing stereotyping and violence
3   Strengthening agency, voice and participation

This discussion does not explicitly include education. However, although education is not identified as one of UN women's priority areas for action it has been given some attention within their work, and UN Women is a member of the Steering Committee of the UN Secretary-General's Education First Initiative. In 2013, the Deputy Executive Director of UN Women, in setting out a vision for a post-2015 agenda for gender equality focused on freedom from violence; capabilities and resources; and voice, leadership and participation, argued for the importance of paying attention to education as 'a major enabling factor in achieving all [these] areas'.[2] In this view a concern with education is not simply associated with gender parity and getting girls in schools, but is linked to the strengthening of girls and women's capabilities, and the achievement of wider gender equality outcomes.

In the period around the formulation of the SDGs UN Women became more intertwined with the UN education organisations than heretofore, but at the same time, its links with the networks of women's rights campaigning organisations, many of which carried forward the history of the Beijing Conference, was tense. Much of the energy and dynamism of women's rights organisations cohered around AWID, a global feminist membership organisation working for women's human rights, sustainable development and gender equality worldwide. In 2015 AWID's priority areas were improving the resources and funds available for women's rights organisations, challenging religious fundamentalisms, strengthening efforts towards economic justice and support for women's rights organisations, defenders of women's human rights, and young feminists' activism (AWID, 2016). While this programme was not concerned with the narrow space of a school, it did take in arrange of educational sites and addressed many networks working in terrains of a middle space.

Conclusion

This chapter, in reviewing global policy concerned with gender, education and poverty, has shown how the MDGs can be associated with a shift in the framing of global policy, from procedural to purposive, linked with a particular focus on new public management. Meanwhile, although there is some diversity in the form of global, national and local connections associated with the institutional structures that were developed around the MDGs and the EFA movement, these conformed more closely to the metaphor of a ladder connecting the global to the local from the top down than the looser forms of networking and grassroots mobilisations around gender equality and women's rights associated with the Beijing Conference and the terrains of a middle space associated with the public sphere and civil society.

The data that we collected with actors working in international organisations, discussed in this chapter, revealed how the employees of multilateral and bilateral organisations, and large global NGOs, saw the global policy agenda on gender and education as a space of opportunity. They took their direction from the policy frames set by the Dakar Framework on EFA and the MDGs, and to a greater or lesser extent engaged with the vision of the Beijing Conference. The terrains of a middle space they worked on were partly institutional, and some of their work entailed building better settings for institutional collaboration at a global level. They also engaged with a public sphere of debate and some relationships with professional organisation, although this did not lead them to alter a position shaped by institutional affiliations to governments. The large global NGOs working in the capital cities of G8 countries had national offices in developing countries, and some worked with partner organisations that were rooted in local contexts. Their frame of reference was a national and local membership in terms of assessing the accountability of multilateral and bilateral organisations, but they also saw their remit as working with these organisations to establish a global space. Thus in the area termed global there was some complementarity of the different terrains of a middle space, particularly with regard to global NGOs, multilateral and bilateral organisations, all of which worked through the institutional terrain of a middle space. Amongst global NGOs there was also an attempt to harness the public sphere and some of the mixtures of global and local we have linked with the metaphor of the weather system, so that we see the global policy space as working like ladders blowing in the wind.

The historical contexts in Kenya and South Africa had particular salience for whether the global visions articulated in Dakar and the MDGs could be discussed, how these were addressed, and what the consequences were at national level. In Chapters 4 and 5, we look at some key aspects of the history of both countries in further detail, addressing in particular some of the historical conditions of the terrains of a middle space concerned with institutions, the public sphere, professional associations and civil society.

Notes

1 UN Women [online]. Available at www.unwomen.org/.
2 www.unwomen.org/en/news/stories/2013/9/ded-speech-on-right-to-education-post-2015#sthash.5qgBTKWe.dpuf

References

Arat, Z. F. K. (2015). Feminisms, women's rights, and the UN: Would achieving gender equality empower women? *American Political Science Review*, 109(4), pp. 674–689.

AWID (2016). *Priority Areas Toronto*. Available at www.awid.org/priority-areas

Baden, S., & Goetz, A. M. Jackson, C., & Ruth Pearson, R. (1998). Who needs [sex] when you can have [gender]. In Jackson, C., and Pearson, R. eds. *Feminist Visions of Development: Gender Analysis and Policy*, 19–38. London: Routledge.

Baksh, R., & Harcourt, W. (2015). *The Oxford Handbook of Transnational Feminist Movements*. Oxford: Oxford University Press.

Beijing Declaration and Platform of Action (1995). *Beijing Declaration and Platform of Action, Adopted at the Fourth World Conference on Women*. Available at www.un.org/womenwatch/daw/beijing/pdf/BDPfA E.pdf

Benavot, A., Antoninis, M., Bella, N., Delprato, M., Harma, J., Jere, C., & Zubairi, A. (2016). Education for all 2000–2015: The influence of global interventions and aid on EFA achievements. In Mundy, K., Green, A., Lingard, B. and Verger, A. eds. *Handbook of Global Education Policy*. Oxford: Blackwell, pp. 241–258.

Charlesworth, H. (2005). Not waving but drowning: Gender mainstreaming and human rights in the United Nations. *Harvard Human Rights Journal*, 18, p. 1.

Colclough, C. (2005). Rights, goals and targets: How do those for education add up? *Journal of International Development*, 17(1), pp. 101–111.

Colclough, C., Al-Samarrai, S., Rose, P., & Tembon, M. (2003). *Achieving Schooling for All in Africa: Costs, Commitment and Gender*. Aldershot: Ashgate Press.

Gaventa, J., & Mayo, M. (2009). Spanning citizenship spaces through transnational coalitions: The case of the global campaign for education. *IDS Working Papers*, 327, pp. 1–43.

Global Partnership for Education (2016). *Gender Equality Policy and Strategy, 2016–2020*. Washington: Global Partnership for Education. Available at www.ungei.org/infobycountry/files/SRGBV_CallToAction_2016_(4).pdf

Global Working Group to end SRGBV (2016). *Call to Action*. New York: Global Working Group to end SRGBV [online]. Available at www.ungei.org/resources/6342.htm. Accessed 12 February 2017.

Gore, C. (2010). The MDG paradigm, productive capacities and the future of poverty reduction. *IDS Bulletin*, 41(1), pp. 70–79.

Jahan, R. (1996). The elusive agenda: Mainstreaming women in development. *The Pakistan Development Review*, 35(4, Part II), pp. 825–834.

Kaldor, M. (2013). *Global Civil Society: An Answer to War*. Cambridge: Polity.

Kantola, J., & Squires, J. (2012). From state feminism to market feminism? *International Political Science Review*, 33(4), pp. 382–400.

Kennett, P., & Payne, S. (2014). Gender justice and global policy paradigms. *Journal of International and Comparative Social Policy*, 30(1), pp. 1–5.

King, E., & Hill, M. (1991). *Women's Education in Developing Countries: Barriers, Benefits and Policy*. John Hopkins University Press for The World Bank.

King, E., & Winthrop, R. (2015). *Today's challenges for girls' education*. Washington DC: Brookings Global Working Paper Series.

Moser, C., & Moser, A. (2005). Gender mainstreaming since Beijing: A review of success and limitations in international institutions. *Gender & Development*, 13(2), pp. 11–22.

Mundy, K. (2012). The global campaign for education and the realization of "education for all". In *Campaigning for "Education For All": Histories, Strategies and Outcomes of Transnational Advocacy Coalitions in Education*. Boston: Sense Publishers, pp. 17–30.

Mundy, K., & Murphy, L. (2001). Transnational advocacy, global civil society? Emerging evidence from the field of education. *Comparative Education Review*, 45(1), pp. 85–126.

Naidoo, J., & Seim, O. (2013). *Report of the Global Thematic Consultation on Education in the Post 2015 Development Agenda*. New York: UNICEF & Paris: UNESCO.

Parkes, J. (2015). *Gender Violence in Poverty Contexts: The Educational Challenge*. Abingdon: Routledge.

Porter, F., & Sweetman, C. (2005). *Mainstreaming Gender in Development: A Critical Review*. Oxford: Oxfam GB.

Rose, P. (2005). Is there a "fast-track" to achieving education for all? *International Journal of Educational Development*, 25(4), pp. 381–394.

Sandler, J. 2015. 'The warrions withing': How feminism changed bureaucracies and bureaucracies changed feminism. In Baksh, R. and Harcourt, W. eds. *The Oxford Handbook of Transnational Feminist Movements*. Oxford: Oxford University Press, pp. 188–214.

Sayed, Yusuf, et al. (2013). Compare Forum: The post-2015 education and development agenda. *Compare: A Journal of Comparative and International Education*, 43(6), pp. 783–846.

Sen, G., & Mukherjee, A. (2014). No empowerment without rights, no rights without politics: Gender-equality, MDGs and the post-2015 development agenda. *Journal of Human Development and Capabilities*, 15(2–3), pp. 188–202.

Sivasubramaniam, M. (2008). Social capital, civil society and education for all: A gendered lens. In Fennell, S. and Arnot, M. eds. *Gender Education and Equality in a Global Context: Conceptual Frameworks and Policy Perspectives*. Abingdon: Routledge.

Smyth, I., & Rao, N. (Ed.). (2005). *Partnerships for Girls' Education*. Oxford: Oxfam.

Tembon, M., & Fort, L. (2008). *Girls' Education in the 21st Century: Gender Equality, Empowerment and Economic Growth*. Washington, DC: The World Bank.

Termine, P., & Percic, M. (2015). Rural women's empowerment through employment from the Beijing platform for action onwards. *IDS Bulletin*, 46(4), pp. 33–40.

Tikly, L. (2017). The future of education for all as a global regime of educational governance. *Comparative Education Review*, 61(1).

UNESCO (2003/4). *EFA Global Monitoring Report 2004: Gender and Education for All: The Leap to Equality*. Paris: UNESCO.

UNESCO (2005). *EFA Global Monitoring Report 2005: Education for All: The Quality Imperative*. Paris: UNESCO.

UNESCO (2010). *EFA Global Monitoring Report 2010: Reaching the Marginalised*. Paris: UNESCO.

UNESCO (2013). The Muscat Agreement Paris: World Education Blog. Available at https://gemreportunesco.wordpress.com/2014/06/04/the-muscat-agreement-new-proposed-post-2015-global-education-goal-and-targets-announced-today/

UNESCO (2014). *EFA Global Monitoring Report 2014: Teaching and Learning: Achieving Quality for All*. Paris: UNESCO.

UNESCO (2015). *EFA Global Monitoring Report 2015: Education for All 2000–2015: Achievements and Challenges*. Paris: UNESCO.

UNESCO (2015b). *Incheon Declaration and Education 2030 dopted at World Education Forum*. Paris: UNESCO. [online]. Available at http://en.unesco.org/world-education-forum-2015/incheon-declaration

UNGEI (2010). *UNGEI Dakar Declaration on Accelerating Girls' Education and Gender Equality*. http://www.ungei.org/index_2527.html

UNGEI (2015). *UNGEI Annual Report 2014*. New York: UNGEI [online]. Available at www.ungei.org/resources/index_old_6073.html

Unterhalter, E. (2007). *Gender, Schooling and Global Social Justice*. Abingdon: Routledge.

Unterhalter, E. (2014). Measuring education for the Millennium Development Goals: Reflections on targets, indicators, and a post-2015 framework. *Journal of Human Development and Capabilities*, 15(2–3), pp. 176–187.

Unterhalter, E. (2016a). Gender and education in the global polity. In Mundy, K., Green, A., Lingard, B. and Verger, A. eds. *The Handbook of Global Education Policy*. Oxford: Wiley Blackwell, pp. 111–127.

Unterhalter, E., & North, A. (2011). Girls' schooling, gender equity, and the global education and development agenda: Conceptual disconnections, political struggles, and the difficulties of practice. *Feminist Formations*, 23(3), pp. 1–22.

Verger, A., Novelli, M., & Altinyelken, H. K. (2012). *Global Education Policy and International Development: New Agendas, Issues and Policies.* London: Bloomsbury Academic.

Wetzel, J. W. (1993). *The World of Women: In Pursuit of Human Rights.* London: Macmillan.

4 Negotiating global gender and education policies in Kenya, 2003–2016

In the previous chapter we saw how employees of multilateral and bilateral organisations saw the global policy on gender and education as an area of opportunity to build relationships with each other, selectively engage with the currents of the women's rights movement, and establish ladders down to some governments, NGO and professional structures. In this chapter we provide some background history on the context in Kenya in which these global gender policies came to be received. We show how, despite the intentions of those who had worked to formulate and advocate for the global policies, there was a very limited engagement with global policy agendas on gender and education in the National Ministry of Education, how distant these frameworks appeared to provincial, district and school-level practitioners. For the staff of a global NGO working in Kenya, the global policy agendas framed what they were doing very clearly, but this orientation was not present for the staff of a local NGO, with limited communication with global networks.

The chapter is organised in two parts. The first part summarises some key aspects of shifts in policy on education, poverty and gender inequality in Kenya, concentrating primarily on the period from the introduction of Free Primary Education in 2003, and provides some background on the four terrains of a middle space we consider important for understanding some of the exchanges around global gender equality and education policy. We detail some shifts in institutional relationships in education linking global, national and local structures. We also provide some overview of professional organisations in Kenya, the networks of civil society, and some discussion of features of the public sphere. In the second part of the chapter we provide detail on the research we undertook in five different sites, linking some salient features of the settings with the relationships that contoured the negotiations with global policy, particularly the MDGs and EFA, described in the previous chapter.

Overview history

In the period of our analysis, Kenya was a state politically in transition from a one party autocracy. The political landscape between 1963, the end of colonial rule, up to 2000, when multi-party elections were sanctioned after a long period of authoritarian government, generated particular institutions to engage with gender, poverty and education. These began to shift their shape from 2002 with the reinstatement of multi-party elections (Murunga and Nasong'o, 2007; Ng'weno, 2009; Elischer, 2013). But the fledgling democracy was fragile as the 2007–8 post-election violence highlighted. However, a progressive programme of social development was envisaged supported by a new Constitution adopted in 2010. In 2013 with a more peaceful experience of elections and a change of political leadership, growing social development was anticipated. A Gender Commission was appointed to oversee the implementation of the gender equality components of the new Constitution.

However, against this generally optimistic outlook must be set much international and bilateral development literature. Some of this circulating at the time of data collection (e.g. UNESCO, 2010; DFID, 2009) portrayed Kenya more ambivalently. On the one hand, it was considered a progressive, emergent, reformist pro-western economy, with strong pro-poor welfare policies and programmes in education and health, which were oriented to support women and improve equity (MOE, 2009). On the other hand, its political stability and legitimacy were seen as fragile and questionable with many of the political elite tainted by a history of corruption (Odol and Kabira, 2000; Dowden, 2009; Wrong, 2010). Critiques of the inadequacy of the state to deliver on social development, were linked with a large NGO/CBO sector, and from the 1990s with an extensive networks of private schools serving poor communities that had grown up to respond to the lack of state provision (Nishimura and Yamano, 2013; Srivasta, 2013). A number of corruption scandals involving the education ministry (2009–2011) enhanced the stature of certain non-state groups to gain access to aid and funding for non-state education providers started to increase (Nasongo, 2007). A significant number of NGOs worked on poverty, gender and education projects. The launch of DFID's Girls' Education Challenge (GEC) programme from 2011, which focussed on interventions by non-state organisations, led to an expansion of funding for programmes, which gave prominence to features of girls' education and aspects of poverty.

Regional, racial and gender inequalities in education in Kenya had a long history. The British colonial government had organised schools on a racial basis with separate, and differentially resourced schools for whites, Africans and Asians (Sifuna and Otiende, 1992, p. 18). At independence in 1963, the government, in distancing itself from the colonial past, recognised education as a basic human right, linked to human and national development (Republic of Kenya, 2005 (a), p. 4). This theme was re-emphasised in subsequent policy documents, but not always fully implemented. Three periods of major education reforms since independence can be distinguished.

From the mid-1960s to the end of the 1970s, there was a focus on building a national education system and a combination of government and community efforts resulted in education expansion at primary, secondary and teacher education levels. Documents like the Ominde Commission Report envisaged education underpinning a strong national project (The Ominde Report, 1965). The

Report of the National Committee on Educational Objectives and Policies (The Gachathi Report, 1976), focused on national unity, and the economic, social and cultural aspirations of the people. It resulted in Government support for 'Harambee' schools, intended to serve the needs of the poor. A small educated African middle class began to grow, with strong affiliations to the idea of the nation articulated though government and community relationships. However, this middle class was divided ethnically and regionally. From 1986 to 2002, this nation-building project came under stain. High levels of debt, partly linked to the high costs of fuel, led to a period of structural adjustment, reductions in public spending, a retreat from an engagement with the poorest and an adjustment of the shape of the education system.

The return to multi-party democracy from 2003, led to an expansion of concern with rights and building the institutions of the state to underpin this. From 2003 programmes for Free Primary Education (FPE), and Free Day Secondary Education (FDSE) were introduced. The adoption of a new Constitution in 2010 framed education provision in terms of rights and the expansion of democracy. In the table below we link these periods of education change to accompanying policy shifts with regard to gender and poverty.

In Table 4.1 we list some key policies that addressed poverty, gender inequality and lack of education, grouping these into three phases, namely the building of a national education system c. 1963–1986, the structural adjustment period, 1986–2002, and the period of multi-party democracy, from 2003 to the present (2016).

The policy changes in these periods were reflected in the enrolment statistics, which show growing numbers of children in primary school, and girls comprising an increasing proportion of all school enrolments.

Despite these achievements there were glaring regional disparities, and very large gender gaps in education in some regions. Thus, for example: in 2008 while in Nairobi primary completion rates averaged 93% (94% for boys and 92% for girls), in the North Eastern region they averaged 42%, with only 29% of girls (compared to 56% of boys) completing primary education. Similarly figures for out-of-school children in the same year show that while in the central region less than 1% or fewer girls and boys of primary age were out of school, in the North Eastern region 54% of primary aged girls and 45% of primary aged boys were not in school.[2] The global gender equality initiatives were often framed in terms of implementation through a national approach. But these marked inequalities within a single country, and the uneven dynamics of national reform, meant that there were particular features of the national landscape in which policy was to be negotiated that needed acknowledgement in some of the terrains of a middle space in order to support appropriate kinds of implementation.

The period of Structural Adjustment in the 1980s was one in which the expansion of education was halted, and those at the lower end of education and employment were hard hit. One effect of the introduction of SAPs was that gross enrolment in primary school dropped from 115% in 1980 to 87% in 1999 (Bedi et al., 2004; Somerset, 2009, pp. 242–243). According to

Table 4.1 Key policies introduced in Kenya 1963–2015 addressing education, poverty and gender

Policies on education change	Policies on gender	Policies on poverty
Building a national education system 1963–c.1986		
1963 KANU Manifesto commitment to free primary education & government policy on UPE (1965). **1969** Ominde Commission recommends integration racially separate schools, English as medium of instruction & accelerating education of girls. Cautions that care must be taken to provide sufficient schools and teachers before legislating that free primary education is available for all. **1971** Formation of Kenyatta University to develop secondary school teachers.	**1969** Constitution forbids discrimination on the basis of gender. **1974** Participation in the UN Conference on Women. 1976 Established Women's Bureau in Ministry of Culture. **1984** Ratified CEDAW.	**1965** Sessional Paper African Socialism defined government commitment to universal freedom from want, disease and exploitation, and equal opportunities. Education as tool for poverty reduction. **1979** National school feeding programme. Free milk in schools in remote areas Boarding Programme and Mobile Teaching Units.
The structural adjustment period (1986–2002)		
1988 Presidential Working Party recommends cost sharing between government, parents and communities in schools. Fees charged and children kept out of school. Government allocation to the education sector as % GDP increases. Donor involvement in teacher development e.g. SPRED. **1990** Acceded to Convention on the Rights of the Child. **1997** Poverty eradication plan includes bursaries to poor and vulnerable groups. **2001** Children's Act recognised education as a basic right.	**1985** the UN women's conference in Nairobi. **1994** UNICEF established Girl Child Project at Kenya Institute of Education (KIE). **1995** Women's organisations mobilise widely from farming to political action and go in large numbers to Beijing. **From 1998** Women's Bureau develops implementation strategies for Beijing agreements. **2000** Gender and Development Plan published	**From 1986** Structural adjustment and reduction of support for poor. **1997** National Poverty Eradication Plan developed **2000–2003** Poverty Reduction Strategy Paper (PRSP)

Multi-party democracy, 2003 to present

2003 Introduction of FPE; estimated 1 million children return to school & National conference on Education and Training

2003–2007 Large donor involvement in Education sector strategic plan and **2005–2010** the Kenya Education Sector Support Programme (KESSP)

2005 Sessional paper Education and Training & Kenya Vision 2030 links education and economic growth, and supports children to remain in school through targeted interventions.

2006 Anti Child Labour laws, Children's Rights Acts, and the Sexual Offences Act No. 3 of 2006.

2009 Recognition of African Charter on Rights and welfare of the child '*Kazi kwa Vijana*'

From 2003 Women's organisations active in mobilization for democratization – National Commission on the Status of Women.

2003 Creation of Ministry of Gender, Sports, Culture, and Social Services incorporating National Women's Machinery.

2011 Establishment of National Gender and Equality Commission.

2005 Launch of the Poverty Eradication Commission (PEC)

2008 Launch of Vision 2030 – a national long-term development blue-print that "aims to transform Kenya into a newly industrialising, middle-income country providing a high quality of life to all its citizens by 2030 in a clean and secure environment"[1]

Table 4.2 Numbers of girls and boys enrolled in primary school in Kenya, 1963–2015

Date	Total	Girls (%)	Boys (%)
1963	892,000	305,000 (34)	587,000 (66)
1984	4,380,230	2,110,992 (48)	2,269,238 (52)
2000	5,034,858	2,486,365 (49)	2,548,495 (51)
2005	6,075,706	2,959,962 (49)	3,115,744 (51)
2009	7,150,259	3,515,413 (49)	3,634,846 (51)
2014	9,950,800	4,898,400 (49)	5,052,400 (51)

Adapted from Republic of Kenya, 1964; UNESCO, 2014, p. 252; Ministry of Education, 2007.

Somerset (2009, p. 243) the contributing factors for declining levels of enrolment include the adoption of cost-sharing in 1988, prompted by the SAP,
which reintroduced parents' contributions to school costs. Later government
studies conceded the significance of high costs of education for poor families,
early marriages, gender discrimination, and cultural rites, beliefs and practices
on who entered and progressed through schooling (Republic of Kenya, 2001,
p. 6). Research conducted in 2003 by the NGO coalition Elimu Yetu in two
rural districts in Thakara and Kajiado and informal settlements in Nairobi,
noted low value placed on girls' education so that practices such as early marriage, FGM and heavy levels of domestic work were all offered as reasons girls
were not in school (Elimu Yetu, 2005, pp. 108–110). This study also noted
that practices associated with gender inequalities, such as the late school enrolment by girls, a lack of women teachers and high levels of sexual harassment
associated with male teachers were also significant factors in girls' dropout
(Elimu Yetu, 2005, pp. 111–112).

The expansion of school enrolment after independence was accompanied by
an increase in the number of teachers and a focus on building a national education system that would seek to confront some features of poverty and exclusion,
but with little planned focus on gender equality issues associated with teacher
employment. At independence, the training of primary school teachers took
place in thirty-seven small independent colleges, mostly managed by different
religious organisations. Each college followed its own syllabus and administered
its own examinations. Many of them had inadequate qualified lecturers, facilities and equipment. Following the enactment of the Education Act of 1968 the
Government took over these colleges and reorganised them into more economic
units. At independence most of the secondary school teachers were non-Kenyans.
As late as 1989 only one-third of the teachers in maintained and aided secondary schools were Kenyans (Republic of Kenya, 1983, p. 179). At independence,
many public servants were drawn from the ranks of teachers, and this historical
background of colonial and hierarchical education was to some extent part of
the culture of the administration. King (2007, p. 360) identifies a 'local policy
discourse', at least in the first thirty to thirty-five years following independence;
which constituted 'a powerful concern that education should be oriented to the

range of work and employment in both the rural and urban economies, formal and informal; and an equally strong view that since the state could not supply sufficient funding, communities should be encouraged, through self-help, to build additional secondary schools, and later community institutes of science and technology' (2007, p. 361). However the SAP period weakened the engagement of civil servants and the central institutions of the state with supporting increased demand for education (Bradshaw and Fuller, 1996).

Policies on gender, education and poverty were affected by the oil shocks and the world recession after 1973. These meant reduced prices for Kenyan exports, just at the time that the government had to face increased fuel prices. Low levels of technology, drought and high levels of debt contributed to the government not being able to sustain initiatives for poverty reduction. In the 1980s this largely redistributive concern with free education came under considerable pressure. Structural Adjustment Programmes, initially introduced in 1980/81 as an instrument of economic management to cut government expenditure, began to be used from 1986 to abolish price controls, liberalise trade, rationalise government budgets and reform the civil service (Republic of Kenya, 1996). Thus, global and national strategies were intermixed in the policies that resulted. Programmes were introduced in collaboration with the World Bank and the IMF. Rono (2002) highlights the many harsh effects on the poor in terms of exclusions from education and health benefits, contraction of employment and the emergence of high prices. A number of other commentators also noted these effects (Ikiara, 1990; Mwega and Ndulu, 1994; World Bank and UNDP, 1993; Swammy, 1994). SAPs were associated with an increase in the gap between the rich and the poor, urban and rural communities. Data on income expenditure distribution for 1994 (Bigsten et al., 2014) showed that the bottom 20% of the rural population received only 3.5% of the income whereas the top 20% captured more than 60%. Rono (2002) noted in this period that participation rates of urban women in employment rose from 30% in the early 1980s to 56% in 1995. However, women's employment was generally characterised by low productivity, low pay and long hours of work.

Under conditions of extreme stress associated with the poverty exacerbated by the SAPs period some of the terrains of a middle space became highly visible, and organisations associated with some of these areas articulated a cogent challenge to the global policy of structural adjustment. A grassroots women's movement emerged that challenged many of the orthodoxies of state formation. The Green Belt movement led by Wangari Maathai was founded in 1977 in response to rural women's concerns at environmental degradation. Professor Maathai, highly educated, and employed in the higher education sector, used many of the techniques of education – seminars and consciousness-raising – but linked these with direct action and women's mobilisation in demands for women's rights, human rights and sustainable development (Maathai, 2004). This locally based and popularly connected movement expressed some of the connections across classes and groups that were a feature of women's movements internationally, but, although Wangari Maathai was active in mainstream politics, and became an MP and Minister in the NARC government from 2003, the women's rights mobilisation of the Green Belt Movement was primarily a mobilisation of protest exposing the failures of government to take account of the rights of the poor.

The SAP programme placed Kenya very firmly on the agenda of global aid agenda, linking national institutional sites, such as the Ministry of Education, with global bodies. The main donors up to 1995 were Unicef, UNESCO and the World Bank and the UK, which continued aid to Kenyan education throughout the period of autocratic rule, when some donor government withdrew support. Teachers were a major focus of these programmes, supporting the growth of the professional organisations as an important terrain of a middle space.

Global policy attention on Kenya was enhanced as the period of autocratic government under President Moi came to an end. Free primary education (FPE) was an election promise in 2002 generated out of the class and ethnic alliances that made up the NARC, and was effected as one of the first actions of the NARC government in 2003. The effects of the introduction of FPE were dramatic. According to data from the Ministry of Education (Republic of Kenya, 2009, pp. 2–5), primary school enrolment shot up from 6,062,763 in 2002 to 7,159,522 in 2003; an increase of 20%. The net enrolment rate rose from 77.3 to 80.4 with good levels of gender parity (Republic of Kenya, 2009, pp. 2–5). Immediately after the launching of FPE, over 1.3 million who would have remained out of school joined primary schools. Resources were stretched to breaking point and there were reports of classes with sixty children and only one teacher (Somerset, 2009; Chaca and Zani, 2015). The government sought and received financial assistance from international development agencies for a range of projects to support education expansion. These organisations policies were intended to address aspects of gender inequality and poverty, although initially these forms of social division were not singled out in Kenyan programmes (Otieno and Colclough, 2009). By 2008 enrolment had further increased, although regional and gender disparities persisted. Government goals were to ensure that by 2010 all children including 'girls, children in difficult circumstances and those from marginalised/ vulnerable groups' had access to and completion of free and compulsory primary education. Other goals included support for poor children to enter secondary school, and to improve the qualifications of teachers (Republic of Kenya, 2005(a), p. 46). However, studies of the effects of the introduction of FPE on gender gaps showed that while enrolment expanded for boys and girls, more boys than girls were successfully able to complete (Lucas and Mbiti, 2012). FPE had expanded enrolments, but there were very mixed outcome in improving quality and progression particularly for the very poor (Bold et al., 2015; Kimosop, Otiso and Ye, 2015; Omwami and Foulds, 2015; Mugo, Moyi and Kiminza, 2016). Addressing gender inequalities in access, in relationships within school and as an outcome of schooling remained a major challenge, accentuated by the many dimensions of poverty, (Elimu Yetu, 2005; Chege and Arnot, 2012; Jewitt and Ryley, 2014; Milligan, 2014).

The expansion of schooling led to increased employment of teachers, many of them women, however pay, conditions and promotion were uneven and insecure for some, although in some regions newly employed women teachers began to make their presence felt in the terrains of a middle space associated with trade unions and professional associations, although there was considerable opposition to them taking leadership roles, and the insecure terms of employment often made joining unions difficult (Onyango, 2013; Mayienga, 2013; Mungania, 2014; Buckler, 2015). In 2010, women comprised 46% of primary teachers (184,873) and 37% of secondary teachers (53,047) (Obura et al., 2011, p. 4). While the Ministry of Education (MoE) and the Teachers' Service Commission (TSC) did not hold data on female head teachers, the nationally representative school sample surveyed for the Southern and Eastern Africa Consortium for Monitoring Educational Quality (SACMEQ) assessments in 2007 reported 15% of head teachers at primary level were women – 20% in urban and just over 10% in rural schools (Hungi, 2010).

These formations of terrains of a middle space contoured some of the forms taken by development assistance and shaped some of the Kenyan participation in a global policy dialogue of education and gender. In 2006 international donors worked with Kenyan NGOs and sections of the government to develop a gender and education policy, published in 2007 (Republic of Kenya, 2007; Kibui and Mwaniki, 2014). This drew very little on the grassroots activism of the women's rights movement, such as the Green Belt Movement that had emerged in the earlier period, but the reasons for this dislocation require investigation. In the place of the grassroots participation of women's rights campaigners or women members of teacher trade unions, FAWE (Forum on African Women's Education) came to play a key role. FAWE was a leading contributor to the formulation of the Gender and Education Policy. FAWE had been established in 1992 by five African women ministers of education as a result of discussions between African ministers and donor agency representatives. It was envisaged as a network which would enable African women educationalists in leadership positions to share experiences and knowledge and build capacity for influencing and shaping policy and, in 1993 was registered in Nairobi as a pan-African NGO.[3] There was a Kenya chapter of FAWE, as well as the continental organisation based in Nairobi, and the organisation developed materials around gender sensitive pedagogies, set up some schools, and was influential in a number of international fora. But FAWE did not build substantive networks into the Kenyan women's movement, or connect well with some of the grassroots civil society activism around education, a theme which awaits detailed historical investigation, although the shifting and difficult contours of alliances around women's rights and cross-cutting inequalities in Kenya were not only an issue in the field of education (Sanya and Lutomia, 2016).

The gender and education policy formulated by groups working on terrains of a middle space in the Ministry of Education, with multilateral and bilateral donors, FAWE, and selected global NGOs expressed its key aim to promote gender equity and equality in education, training and research to contribute to the economic growth and sustainable development of Kenya (Republic of Kenya, 2007, p. 7). The policy directed the government to undertake a wide range of actions in support of girls' education, including lobbying parents and communities to support girls' education, providing in-service training of teachers in gender-responsive methodology, and deploying more female teachers in rural and urban slums areas. Government was required to

> ensure learning environments were gender responsive and enforce rules and regulations that prohibited sexual harassment in schools. A gender balance in school management committees was called for and gender equity in teacher training.
>
> (Republic of Kenya, 2007, pp. 11–15)

This policy, with its consideration of teaching, school management and learning processes went much further than previous government documents, which had mainly focussed on access, and identified girls as a group in need of specific attention. But it is also striking that the document was rather silent on issues of poverty.

A new Constitution was promulgated in 2010, guaranteeing equality to women and men in all fundamental freedoms including education. Under the Constitution a National Human Rights and Equality Commission was established, tasked with overseeing government actions to ensure promotion of the equality goals of the Constitution. The Commission was accorded significant resources and engaged in reviewing a number of aspects of the implementation of gender equalities and women's rights (Tripp, 2016).

Terrains of a middle space

The Kenyan history reveals that the process of trying to form a national identity and a democratic state, given some of the deep regional, ethnic, wealth and gender divisions was uneven. The terrains of a middle space we have distinguished, – notably the civil service, the public sphere, professional organisations and civil society, – were all areas where perspectives on gender equality and education played out as ideas and relationships, sometimes deemed global, sometimes national, and sometimes local. All these terrains had their own histories, which coloured these dynamics.

The Kenya civil service has been analysed as a site both of the mobilisation of ethnic power bases for ruling elites (Bienen, 1974; Stubbs, 2015) and as an area of public enterprise working with an institutional culture oriented to development (Ghosh, 1991; Leonard, 1991). Thus, political–economic relations within state institutions have been primarily national and local, carrying many of the fault-lines of the country within them. The bureaucracies concerned with education replicate this pattern. Osumbah (2011) analysed the numbers and level of seniority of women in the Ministry of Education in 2005. She concluded that individual, socio-cultural and organisational structures put obstacles in the way of women's career progression. In 2011, Obura et al. (2011) built on her study and found that there were fewer women in senior positions in the Education Ministry than ten years previously, that women comprised about one-sixth of the intake at the lower level of the Ministry, and 38% of middle-rank officials. A number of studies (Goetz and Hassim, 2003; Dahlerup, 2013) consider that women's absence from institutions makes a proactive policy on gender equality more difficult to maintain. The gender profile of the staff of the Ministry is a salient feature in the discussion of our data collection methods later in this chapter, and the views analysed in Part 2.

A number of studies of the education policy process in Kenya note how policies have changed as they move from sites of adoption to implementation (Otieno and Colclough, 2009), so that despite a clearly organised organisational structure within the Ministry of Education, and discussion with the donor community, the way policies are implemented is highly variable and linked with local processes. Thus, the move from global, through national to local through the terrain of the middle space concerned with the institutions of the Ministry of Education, could not be assumed to be a simple onward transition of the key ideas of EFA and the MDGs.

Similar pathways are evident in relation to gender policy, and gaps in the rungs of the ladder that linked global policy through national administrative structures to local implementation. True and Mintrom (2001)identified Kenya as having high level central structures for gender mainstreaming with a number of apex Ministries and strategies responsive to UN initiatives. In 1999, gender focal points were appointed in ten districts, under a UNDP plan to support gender disaggregation in planning. In 2011 the Ministry of Gender Report (2011) monitored gender affirmative staffing outcomes across ministries. However, Elsey et al. (2005) found that the process of district-based gender focal points had limited support at the local level, and that there were few linkages with civil society. As will be evident from the discussion in Part 2, we did not note any gender focal points working in education at province and district level, despite global policy aims of these themes.

The formation of institutions in Kenya, thus, has some connection at the top ends of the ladder with global organisations concerned with education, gender and poverty, and support through national structures, particularly in the expansion of education provision. But the extent to which ideas and processes about gender and poverty pass up and down is highly variable and linked with a local politics, where ethnicity and other ties of local affiliation were highly salient.

The second terrain of a middle space we have distinguished, drawing on Habermas, is the public sphere. Habermas (1989) develops his notion of the public sphere as network communicating information and points of view reproduced through communicative action. His analysis derived from his interpretation of European history from the 18th century, and the growth of an open discussion of all issues of general concern, where issues relevant to the public good could be subject to informed debate and examination. The public sphere presupposed freedoms of speech and assembly, a free press, and the right to freely participate in political debate and decision-making. This concept of a public sphere is sometimes invoked in discussions of the media in Kenya, and the expansion of the news and discussion linked with a deepening of democracy (Mak' Ochieng, 1996; Omwoh, 2014), but accounts also draw out pervasive sexism in the media (Macharia, 2016) and the ways in which freedom of speech and assembly are experienced in practice. Often these express local affiliations, which are strongly marked by gender politics (Kiluva-Ndunda, 2001; Isaksson, Kotsadam and Nerman, 2014). While critical assessments of gender, the public sphere and the public good, are often linked with national aspirations (Fraser, 1990; Fraser, 2014), that are somewhat distant from local realities, local contexts can have an important bearing on how the notion of public good is interpreted. Frederiksen (2000), in a study with young men and women engaging with global culture in a poor Nairobi neighbourhood, brought out how ideas about the nuclear family, considered conservative in the global north, presented an aspiration for independence from large collectivities in which the young people lived and experienced gender subordination. Linke et al. (2015) notes the importance of face-to-face negotiations amongst poor farmers in rural areas facing the harsh effects of climate change. These personally mediated negotiations were much more significant than institutional processes in preventing violence linked to scarce resources. These studies suggest appreciation of the terrain of the public sphere in Kenya is highly contextual, and linked with national and local historical relationships.

The third terrain of a middle space we have identified is that of professional organisation. Kenyan teachers have been organised nationally through the trade union KNUT, which was established in 1957, and which brought together regional teachers' organisations which had been active since the early 1950s.[4] However, the union's history is tied up with the politics of the state, and some commentators highlight limited engagement with issues of professional practice by KNUT and its membership, divisions with senior management which exacerbated disputes, and strikes (Kibe, 2014; Watila, 2016), However, concern with gender and poverty has not been much documented in the unions or in other forms of teacher professional organisation. Onyango (2013) presented data from a survey of women members of KNUT in Kisumu county, showing how few women stood for leadership in the union because of negative attitudes. The union's most recent strategic plan cites the establishment of a gender desk as a recent achievement, and contains an objective to "Advance gender parity in education and in the ranks of KNUT" (KNUT, 2014, p. 38). However, while the associated activities include "ensuring that every branch and region maintains gender desk equal in weight with other offices" and carrying out gender mainstreaming (KNUT, 2014, p. 38), the focus appears to be largely on parity of numbers, rather than addressing issues around leadership or forms of discrimination.

Outside KNUT in other areas of the third terrain of a middle space we have identified, professional associations for teachers, head teachers and education researchers have generally not given much attention to gender, but have stressed issues of professional practice. In 2002 Herriot et al. (2002) documented the development of primary school head teachers' support groups (HTSGs) in all zones and communities. Heads were encouraged to form small clusters of approximately six schools within reasonable reach of one another to provide a forum for sharing ideas, but whether or not gender was discussed was not documented. Giordano (2008) reflected on the conditions that made for teacher resource centres working as successful centres for developing insight into teaching and administration, with little stress on reflection on social division. Koech's (2006) doctoral research in Uasin Gichu district found that there was limited relationships between teachers and parents discussing educational issues, despite government policy which aimed to foster this. Women officials in the Ministry of Education interviewed by Oburo, Wamaniu et al. (2011, p. 8) described developing informal networks and support groups, because of the difficult work conditions, and gender discrimination they encountered, but they do not mention to what extent the women officers placed their personal experiences within a wider context of gender inequalities within the education system. All these examples document forms of professional organisation in which there is little attention to reflection or discussion on gender and poverty in education. Very local concerns seem to be what guide the professional work that is done collectively, and global policies and formulations around rights and poverty are not referenced in the accounts of this work.

The fourth terrain of a middle space we have noted is that of civil society. Murunga and Nasong'o (2007) reviewed a range of groups associated with civil society in Kenya and their potential to contribute to the democratisation process initiated after the introduction of multi-party democracy. In one chapter of the book Nasong'o evaluated some of the strengths and weaknesses of civil society organisations, and the ways in which they prefigured aspects of democratic engagements and Nasong'o and Ayot's chapter in the book contrasts the ways in which women were a key constituency in the independence movement, but how a number of women's groups were silenced or co-opted post-independence. Their potential for enhancing democratisation was seen as crucial. Muhula (2009) is more cautious about the potential of civil society, noting the depth of horizontal ethnic inequalities entrenched Mathi (2014), comparing civil society organisations in Kenya and South Africa, distinguishes between those that engaged uncritically with neoliberalism, those that presented a counter argument, and those concerned with service delivery. Women's groups fall into all three groups. Some of this analysis chimes with that of Mundy et al. (2010) who have looked at the evolution and role of education civil society organisations (CSOs) in Kenya. At the time of the first free parliamentary elections in 2002 civil society organisations came together as the ElimuYetu Coalition (EYC), which played an important role in lobbying for the abolition of school fees. However, according to Mundy et al. (2010), since this successful campaign, EYC 'lost much of its capacity and voice' (p. 490). Increasingly, rather than engaging actively in advocacy and monitoring work, education CSOs have instead been involved in service and contracting roles linked to the Ministry of Education. While for some CSOs this has enabled them to have some leverage in the development of policy, more generally Mundy et al. note that there is "little evidence of coordinated capacity for monitoring government and donor commitments to universalising good-quality education" (ibid p. 490). They link this lack of CSO coordination and advocacy capacity in the education sector in part to the wider political tensions within Kenya, as well as to the impact of the threat of government reprisals for critical advocacy and monitoring work.

While the education civil society organisations may have declined in importance in lobbying around democratisation and equalities from 2002, a very wide range of civil society organisations mobilised in protest at the post-election violence in 2007–8 and in support of the Constitution. Indeed Maathai (2014) argues that it was because of the issues laid bare through the violence of 2007–8 that elites conceded some of the key points civil society argued for in relation to the Constitution. The actions of CSOs in recent Kenyan politics have been highly controversial, reflecting many faultlines around the dynamics of accountability, but have also revealed energetic challenges to established centres of power and their sense of standing above the law (Hansen and Sriram, 2015; Gathi, 2016). The global–national dynamic has been part of the struggle over legitimacy for CSOs, with many who argued in favour of rights and equalities vulnerable to claims that they were the mouthpiece of donors or foreign governments (Wood, 2016). Civil society in Kenya thus cannot be neatly categorised as either a sphere for critique of government and expression of local interests. Some sections of civil society are very rooted in local contexts, and some very connected with global movements, government or the global institutions. Murunga and Nasong'o (2007) note that donors have both encouraged democratisation but also kept in place authoritarian forces. Civil society has a similar complexity and different organisations are either more global or more local in their orientation.

Our analysis suggests that the terrains a middle space in Kenya education policy making most receptive to global gender equality policy, were those associated with the national levels of the Ministry of Education and some NGOs working through EYC and linked with the global NGO community. In the next section we briefly outline our data collection strategy in Kenya to explore this in greater depth, before reporting on the on the views of a wide range of actors in organisations and institutions regarding the MDGs and EFA.

Researching global gender equality and education policy in terrains of a middle space

Our research strategy to investigate how global policy on gender equality, education and poverty was being engaged, refused or negotiated entailed using a number of approaches to collecting qualitative data in five sampled sites – three settings of government activity and two of NGO work. To investigate government work we collected data in (a) the national Ministry of Education, (b) the offices of the provincial and district administration in a region of the country with a high proportion of the population classified as poor and (c) in a government school serving a poor peri-urban community. To look at non-state work we collected data in (d) a rural NGO based in a pastoralist community, and

(e) a NGO, located in a large city, with many links to global networks. The terrains of a middle space we have distinguished cut across these five sites for data collection, and are more or less present in different sites in different ways. In the discussion below we describe the interviews and observations in each setting, give some descriptive detail of the work conditions, and report on some perspectives from people working in these sites on global gender equality policy. We draw out which of the terrains of a middle space we have distinguished appeared most salient to the respondents in each site.

The national Ministry

In 2008, when we began our data collection, the Kenyan Ministry of Education (MoE), formerly the Ministry of Education, Science and Technology, was located in Jogoo House 'B' on Harambee Avenue in the heart of the Nairobi Central Business District. At the Ministry we interviewed a wide range of officials, from some of the most senior, down to newly appointed officers with specific briefs to attend to aspects of gender or poverty. This data collection strategy enabled us to gain insight into the terrain of the middle space associated with the bureaucracy and the working of policy enactment by administrative institutions. It also allowed us some insight into how individuals within the Ministry perceived the public sphere of the press, the media, academic debate and the network of civil society organisations and NGOs in dialogue with the MoE.

We conducted eighteen interviews and two focus groups over two phases of data collection. All interviews were conducted in the Ministry. Some were interspersed between officers' meetings in a busy schedule, and some happened after the working day had concluded. At the end of the first year of data collection we presented our findings to a selection of staff at the Ministry (13/02/2009). This was an opportunity to reflect together on what we had found about how gender equality, education and poverty policy were being negotiated in different sites. We conducted some further interviews with selected officials in the second year of our study, attempting to track how they were responding to further discussions of global policy, including the findings from our feedback meeting. Some staff from the Ministry attended our dissemination meeting, which took place at the end of the project at the Catholic University of East Africa (CUEA).

In Jogoo House, there was a sense of compartmentalisation in many areas which imposed a strong sense of an institutional hierarchy. Professional staff were often separated physically from secretarial workers. Secretaries were frequently women, while a large proportion of officers were men. However, in the Reform Secretariat, which dealt with aspects of gender policy, about a dozen senior officers and policy makers, heads of investment programmes (IPs), including the head of the gender programme worked side-by-side with secretarial staff at computers, sharing a central meeting area. Here there were posters for the UN Decade of Education for Sustainable Development 2004–2014 and EFA. The calendars represented the Kenya Education Support Sector Programme (KESSP) partnership. Thus, global gender equality policy was visually present. One fieldwork day we saw thousands of gender posters piled on the floor next to the Gender IP team leader's work-desk. They were literally moving though his hands.

There was a strong sense in the MoE of working in a hierarchy where lines of responsibility were very clearly drawn. Officers were under pressure to deliver documents upwards to Ministers, parliament and donors, and downwards to provinces and schools. At the time of data collection some staff in the MoE were highly focussed on securing finance, and engaging with the financial regulations of the KESSP. However, the day to day rhythms in other parts of MOE and the Reform Secretariat, were less tightly governed by the ladder of global account-ability, and on some fieldwork days we discussed some academic debates and issues in the press, suggesting some openness of some officers to the realm of the public sphere, although, as the interview extract we cite below revealed, the major framing used to interpret of events was provided by the institution.

In the KESSP, a key project of the MoE at the time of fieldwork, gender was a cross-cutting theme, which was meant to be mainstreamed (MOE, 2005). This link explicitly referenced the MDGs. This cross-cutting approach, linked with a large funding project from international donors, implied that gender was dealt with by every department, but how this worked in practice was difficult to trace. There was only one officer with a specific brief on gender.

Many senior officials we discussed gender equality policy with were cautious and closed on the subject. Many appointments to talk with officers on this theme were broken, often without prior warning, and frequently, when trying to talk to officials, we were told that gender was not their brief. One Secretary for a senior officer refused to make an appointment to talk to us on these grounds. When the member of our research team mentioned gender was a cross-cutting issue in the KESSP, the response was:

> Yes, gender is a cross cutting issue. The officer in charge of gender and edu-cation is the one who handles all these issues across the board. That is the person who will help you.

(Fieldnotes 03/02/2009)

This was typical of the view of many officers, some of whom gave short interviews, some of whom agreed to interviews (but subsequently were not available at the agreed time), and some of whom said they could not make time. We were aware that in the past relations between the MoE and some academics had been strained and even hostile. It was clear some MoE officers regarded our presence as unhelpful, however others were open and willing to talk about their work. To some extent, whether or not we were able to have in-depth discussions depended on the area of work, whether or not we had prior contacts with an official, and their level of confidence in where they stood in the institutional hierarchy. Gender was a cross-cutting theme on paper in the KESSP, but willingness to talk about it was more a matter of personal relationships.

In discussions with staff in the MoE about the MDGs and EFA, there was a formal acknowledgement of the MDGs requiring particular organisational actions but with little room for critical reflection on the process of agreeing them:

> Let me say, those goals and MDGs, they are very good because . . . these goals keep the government and NGOs, all of us, on our toes. If we had no goals, we would go back and be in our own comfort and pretend every-thing is OK.
>
> (National Official 1, 21/05/2008)

A large number of officials identified the MDGs with requiring particular organisational relationships within the Department. The stress, for more senior officials, was on identifying the officers or systems tasked to deliver on the MDGs. One official, for example identified a problem with lack of public awareness of the MDGs, yet also emphasised that although one person alone could not deliver the necessary actions, much responsibility rested with the gender desk in the Ministry (staffed by only one official), the guidelines on implementing policy and relationships with the donor community:

> The people at the grass roots may not really be aware of the MDGs, in terms of achievement. I think sometime back, the President did give status for Kenya. We were still far [from] achieving the targets of the MDGs. You see now this depends what actions have been in place. . . . But . . . I feel in the education sector we have . . . developed a gender policy. I know we have got . . . maybe draft . . . guidelines for the implementation of the gender policy. Gender, being an IP within KESSP, we have got an officer who mans gender issues . . .
>
> (National Official 2, 08/04/2009)

Here, there is a strong sense of the MDGs entailing bureaucratic practices of policy delivery, rather than any sense of discussion, dialogue or accountability. Other terrains of a middle space, such as the public sphere, professional associations or CSOs are not mentioned.

For other officials, the MDGs were valuable because they stressed outcomes, but this too, presented difficulties for civil servants in managing delivery:

> These global declarations are good, and they are relevant to us. But I think the issue I have with them is implementation . . . I know there is a monitor-ing mechanism by NEPAD [New Partnership for Africa's Development][5] about the MDGs, but I don't think it is grass root based. I know one time when I was in Garissa, they came there to monitor how best the Kenya government is implementing. They went and compiled the report. And the feedback never came to Garissa to show that this is the progress. These are the gaps, and these are the corrective measures you are supposed to take to close the gaps so that we attain the goals. So, to me, the gaps are in imple-mentation. Especially provision of resources.
>
> (National Official 3, 07/04/2009)

For many the MDG framework was a key way to secure resources:

> So even though each time you have specific themes but there [are] also side issues which are used to address issues of resource mobilization. . . . We get all the development partners at the global level to come and make their commitment. Last time when we were in America on this invitation of the MDGs . . . many of the prime ministers, leaders in the world were there to make their commitment.
>
> (National Official 4, c. April 2009)

Nonetheless, for some officials, sometimes at a lower level of seniority, while they had the sense of the MDGs imposing a regulatory regime with regard to monitoring enrolment or attendance, they also considered they provided a platform for more engagement with questions of education content and process. For example, one official when asked for views on the MDGs, replied describing work to support learning:

> We ensure that the teachers are teaching in a more interesting manner so that the kids don't fall out. . . . You can see the type of topics we are teaching: collaborative teaching, importance of talk, ensuring that even we improve their attendance . . .
>
> (National Official 5, 09/05/2008)

Here the official interpreted his work as implementing the MDGs, but in fact he was going much further than the MDGs specified.

The sense that their work fell outside the MDG framework was discussed by a small minority of officials who saw the MDGs as too constraining:

> You see, the MDGs do not talk of early childhood, they talk of universal primary education. But how do you get universal primary education without charting up early childhood? How do you achieve school readiness without addressing issues of early childhood?
>
> (National Official 6, 20/05/2008)

Implicitly and explicitly, for these officials, their practice exceeded the MDG framework, considering how education was more than enrolment and completion of primary school. But for Kenyan officials working in the national department, who saw their work as wider than the MDG framework, or who advanced some critical views on this, their argument was generally focussed on an operational approach to particular programmes. The terrain of a middle space that appeared most frequently in their talk concerned the institutional structures and the bureaucratic form of the MoE. Global gender equality and education policy was viewed as passing down rungs of a ladder, and the Ministry portrayed itself very much as an institution organised hierarchically. There was little comment on the terrains of a middle space, either global or national that linked to the public sphere, professional reflection by teachers or critique and contestation by civil society.

Responding to global gender equality policies in a provincial and district office

There was a similar wariness in commenting on gender among staff in the provincial and district offices where we collected data. We chose a particular province as a research site because official data indicated some districts had large populations living below the poverty line. In some, this was more than a third, and in others more than half the district population. In 2008 we conducted in-depth interviews with a number of officials who dealt with aspects of gender and poverty in both provincial and district offices. On our initial visits we noted some details of the work environments of officials. A feedback meeting with provincial and district office staff was held in 2009, and follow up interviews took place in 2010 and 2011. In total we conducted seventeen interviews with provincial and district level staff over the two phases of data collection. The bureaucratic structures of administration shaped the terrains of a middle space even more sharply in the province and the district than they did at the MoE. Here, it was impossible, even informally to discuss issues circulating in the public sphere, or to comment on teachers in any other terms but as a resource. The terrains of a middle sphere appeared very constrained, and the sense of global policy making at some considerable distance away.

In 2001, one and a half million pupils had been enrolled in the province's primary schools and the teacher pupil ratio was 1:37. By 2007, there were 2 million pupils, and the teacher pupil ratio had increase to 1:45. In the district, where detailed observations of provincial officials at work were conducted, the teacher pupil ratio was 1:50. There was a pronounced gender gap in primary enrolments and completion. Thus there were thus a host of gender issues to consider with regard to enrolment, participation, progression and attainment.

The provincial administrative headquarters was in a large town, several hundred kilometres from the capital. The Provincial Director of Education (PDE) was welcoming but considered the project focus on gender and poverty not to be in his remit. He pointed out his officers dealt with quality assurance, standards, staffing, examinations, special education, secondary education and auditing. His account of how his work was organised, and indeed the prominent display on the walls of his office of education data for the province, written on manila paper, indicated how the administration of education at the provincial level was primarily concerned with audit, ensuring particular forms for monitoring. The Provincial Director managed district officers, but did not feel comfortable to talk or reflect on policy, values, gender or the distribution of resources. Detailed implementation of policy on poverty and gender, we were told, was a matter for district officers. This discussion illuminated how the institutional organisation of the education system located work on gender and poverty in particular spaces of the bureaucracy. Other terrains of a middle space, such as teacher organisation, CSOs or discussion in the public sphere were not discussed or commented on.

Definitions of poverty were highly contentious. The official surveys, which had led us to select this province, as a research site were disputed with some heat by the provincial education officials we interviewed. When officers were asked to comment on statistics on poverty (which showed the province had some of the highest levels of poverty in the country) most felt that whatever was reported did not actually reflect the situation on the ground. In the view of one officer a constituency, considered rich according to the poverty data, was one where, in the experience of local officials, most children dropped out of school when no school feeding programme was in place. Community members had lost large herds of cattle due to prolonged drought. These tense engagements around official data suggested that critical discussion about how poverty was defined and understood was not part of a public sphere where debate on these issues was engaged by officials in government and people who lived close to experiences of poverty.

The institutional hierarchy was a very clear set of delimiting processes. Provincial officials were forthright that gender equality, as a global or national concern, was not their brief, but was the remit of district officials, because gender issues were matters of local household or community relationships. One of the senior provincial officers said, "Gender issues are not found at the provincial headquarters but in the villages [. . .], where early marriages take place and . . . where they practice FGM" (Fieldnotes, 16/09/2008). From his perspective gender was a set of relationships around particular forms of sexuality. It was not a matter of policy concern from the perspective of the provincial administration. The only way the single female officer at the provincial office felt she could engage with our interest in gender was to share her frustrations as the only senior woman education officer. She said that, as the only senior woman in the education department, she did not get any respect even from junior male officers recruited after her. She was expected to perform traditional gender roles like typing and organising catering. For her gender was a matter of personal difficulty, and there was no opening to discuss this in the realm of institutional organisational relationships.

In this formally delimited space, it was difficult for officials to understand why we had come to talk to them. One officer upon looking at the interview guide said:

> What do you mean gender, education and poverty? You see I do not understand all these things you have put here. I do not know what you really want.
> (Fieldnotes, 16/09/2008)

The institutional hierarchy and some constraints on the public sphere made it difficult for this official to know how to respond to the research team and our interest in the negotiation of global gender policy. From his perspective he did not 'do' gender or poverty, and therefore had nothing to contribute on these themes.

Some officials knew about the gender and education elements of the MDGs, but there was a strong sense that goals had been set a long way away from their day-to-day experiences. Some had heard about the MDGs, but did not know what they were. Their distance from the goals was framed by the rungs of the ladder linked with the institutional order. An officer interviewed in 2008 said:

> I tell you the first time I heard about the MDGs and you will not believe, it was last year when I went for a ministry of planning had a dissemination kind of workshop organized at the province here. I went to represent my boss and that's the first time I heard about MDGs and really it's like they belong to other people.
>
> (Province Official 1, 16/09/2008)

Another officer said:

> You know sometimes those people have a point because some of these decisions are made at higher platform and we are in . . . . A person who is to implement is in . . . and does not even know Nairobi and those policies the beneficiaries are the people at the grassroots so there should be a way like let's talk about MDGs the millennium development goals how many people understand? They are few, even the teachers do not understand . . . people do not know [the MDGs] and yet they are meant for them. So one of the things we need to do is let this policy be made but is there a way that the policies can really go down to the ground. Instead of having decisions from top down it should be from down up. So that people can create a sense of ownership.
>
> (District Official 1, 24/11/2008)

For both these officials, decision taken about the MDGs were at considerable distance from their work, and they had a sense that their professional engagements with education or gender were not being built into the global policy. In contrast to the confidence about working to achieve the MDGs at the national MoE level, provincial officers appeared pessimistic. There was a sense that the very ambition of the MDGs in the face of the difficulties they encountered was a mockery. One official said:

> Another thing to this MDG. We are operating like crisis as far as the human resource is concerned. For us we have a number of schools actually [and not enough teachers]. Even sometimes we doubt the quality of the curriculum that we are offering.
>
> (District Official 1, 24/11/2008)

In these conditions of delivering the most basic resources to secure teachers in post the concern of the Beijing Platform with intersecting inequalities around gender and poverty is not known, and while the EFA and MDG programmes around enrolment and progression have a clearer resonance they are seen to come from far away.

Travelling to the district highlighted how there was considerable distance from the provincial capital, reached on a tar road from Nairobi. A drive to the district headquarters entailed taking a dilapidated tarmac road marked with potholes. Tracts of desolate land filled the landscape. The dry spell in the first phase of data collection hit so hard that no green vegetation could be seen. Along the road were carcasses of dead animals because of drought. A few herdsmen were driving emaciated herds to try to get water and pastures. After twelve months, during the second phase of data collection the rains came. The whole area began turning green. Many pastoralists were returning with healthier animals and larger flocks. But the fragility of the economy of the district was evident.

At the district education offices there was no desk or office to deal with gender issues, although we had been told at the provincial office, that this was where gender was handled. Unlike in Jogoo House, there was no visual depiction of the MDGs, international or national gender policy in the district offices. However, despite the lack of a formal structure to deal with gender we had some very engaged interviews on this theme. Officials had strong opinions on gender and poverty, but, as discussed in Chapters 6 and 7, many of the views they expressed emphasised their social distance from people who were poor, or practiced forms of gender discrimination linked to early marriage. They drew on particular local formulations, in which global frameworks concerned with rights or equality were rarely referenced. Thus, responding to global gender equality policy in the province and district offices, was strongly shaped by the relationships of administration linked to the institutional structures of the Ministry of Education, but other terrains of a middle space, such as dialogues around a public sphere, engagements with professional associations or CBOs were less evident.

The school

The school we selected as a research site, was located in a peri-urban area, close to a main road, adjacent to a settlement with many shacks. Pupils enrolled in the school came from informal settlements along the main road, and some more distant villages. There was a wide ethnic mix. Economic activities in the area included small-scale agriculture, dairy farming, small-scale trading and manufacture. At the school we conducted in depth interviews with the head teacher, thirteen teachers and representatives from the School Management Committee (SMC). We also interviewed learners and members of local organisations, observed a number of school meetings, interactions during some teaching days, and had some group discussions with teachers. We presented our findings from the first round to a meeting at the school in July 2008. In the second year of data collection we did follow-up interviews and observations at the school. In total we conducted twenty-nine interviews and two focus groups over the two phases of data collection.

The school is surrounded by quite extensive grounds, and a *shamba*, where crops grow. The school grounds are fenced, but there is no elaborate security. A church stands next to the school. Only one teacher appeared to have a car, an old model. Other teachers walked to the main road to pick up transport. Many spoke of ties of affiliation to community members, either through the Church or a shared history. The space between the school, the houses of the settlement and the main road appeared to blend into each other. We can thus read the school as a site of connection to the terrains of a middle space framed institutionally by the administration of education, framed dialogically by the terrain of the public sphere, where teachers and members of the community exchanged views as they moved between work and home, and framed organisationally by the relationships of civil society linked to various religious, social and economic relationships of the neighbourhood.

The school motto was 'Strive to do better', its mission was to develop pupils 'to work hard in life for better results'. Its vision was 'To help our pupils develop their talents and realise their potential' (Head Teacher, 22/02/2008). However, these aspirational statements were not displayed. At the entrance to the head teacher's office a handwritten sign noted the mean score of the school in the KCPE exams over the past three years. There was no visual representation of national or global goals regarding education.

There were nineteen classrooms (eighteen used for lessons and one as a store for broken furniture and building materials) one staffroom, three offices (one for the Head Teacher, one for the Deputy Head Teacher and one for the Senior Teacher), one book store, pit latrines, with nine doors for girls, seven doors for boys, and one urinal for the boys. There was also a pit latrine for the teachers (one door for the male and two doors for the female). A library was under construction in the early phases of fieldwork, and completed by the end. Here posters advertising the national gender policy, brought to the school by the research team, were prominently displayed. But, the room was kept locked and used only for staff meetings. It did not appear the posters were seen by many visitors.

Although the living conditions of children attending the school were poor, by standards of many schools in Kenya this was a reasonably well equipped school in terms of buildings and facilities. Each of the sixteen teachers, including the senior teacher, was a class teacher. All learners sat at bulky desks, which each child was required to bring to school when they first enrol. Three pupils sat on one desk in class one to six while in classes seven and eight two learners shared a desk. During the first period of field work, pupils shared text books at a ratio of 1:3 for the lower primary and 1:2 for upper primary. One year later the school was almost achieving a ratio of 1:2 for lower and 1:1 for upper primary in all subjects. Reference books such as dictionaries, kamusi (*Swahili dictionary*), atlases, bibles and story books were issued on short loan. A feeding scheme had been discontinued in 2002 amidst allegations of mismanagement by the school administration. The head teacher and members of the SMC felt there had been a drop in the academic performance because of the withdrawal of the school feeding programme.

The head teacher and a few of the other teachers had some knowledge of the MDGs, but a sense that they came from far away. One teacher said:

> I have only heard some of the millennium development goals like universal primary education. I think it was declared in Dakar.
>
> (Teacher 1, 12/06/2010)

EFA and the MDGs had blurred together for her, but she was one of only a handful who knew about the global policy framework at all. Thus although the school was close to a main road, and not that distant from a large city, well connected to global flows of information and ideas, there was very little direct engagement by the head teacher, the staff or members of the SMC with global gender equality and education policy processes.

The engagement of teachers with the terrains of a middle space we have identified were uneven. Some were members of the KNUT, which was reforming at the time of data collection. Some were considering enrolling at private universities to take degrees. Thus there was some limited engagement with professional terrains, but this was largely focussed on skill development and work conditions. A number of teachers and members of the SMC were involved with the Church and some of the organisations of civil society. Although members of our research team spent many weeks in the school, the relationships remained formal, and it was difficult to engage in open discussions on contentious themes like gender and poverty. While the school was clearly a site where many terrains of a middle space converged, conditions were fragile to facilitate an engagement with global gender equality and education policy, understood using any of the forms we have selected to describe this process. The school was not well located on the ladder of administrative exchanges, being quite a long distance from the attention even of the district education offices. Although it was not very far from a main road, its links with the global, national mix of information exchanges was not well established, and there were no meaningful connections between members of the school committee and social activists concerned with gender or poverty engaged with international movements and networks.

A global and a local NGO

The headquarters for the global NGO where we collected data was located in an affluent part of a major city in extremely well equipped offices in a modern building. The NGO oversees the disbursement of funds originating from NGOs in G8 countries to local implementing partners. We interviewed the Director, five members of staff working on policy and projects, and held some group discussions. We made fieldnotes on the work conditions and went with one staff member to visit one of the projects in a rural district. Report back meetings to the NGO on our findings took place on 25th July 2009. In 2009 and 2010 follow up meetings and interviews took place with selected staff.

In the offices of this NGO large posters with photographs of children and slogans linked to the MDGs and various international gender campaigns were on display. On the door to the front office was a poster '*Let us stop child abuse*' and '*Engaging children in prostitution is a violation of their rights*'. Other posters on the walls read, '*Gender and Education*' and '*Education, Peace and HIV/AIDS are gender issues*'. Posters in the crowded offices where staff worked stressed child rights. One was a picture of a child saying '*Let me play*', another referred to the '72 Hour' campaign to stop sexual harassment and spread of HIV/AIDS with guidelines of what one should do when raped. There were some overtly political posters with a call relating to the work of the Electoral Commission: 'Beware of division, selfish and empty promises'. Another affirmed 'everyone has a right to education. Stop the violation now' and 'your vote is precious: use it wisely to build a united Kenya'. These visual invocations mixed the global and the national in an affirmation of rights, education and gender equity. A KESSP Calendar with the message *FPE implies that all children MUST be in school* was displayed on a desk. A T-shirt with message 'Let's stop FGM and educate girls for future development' was displayed on the wall. There was a sense of being in a nerve centre for work on human rights and gender equality, and the mobilisations around the Kenyan Constitution, were very much linked with this. This was not a space of formal administrative rungs of policy exchange, but a space where the global and the national were shaking hands with each other.

The interviews with the staff of this NGO took place in these offices, and on fieldwork visits to projects in a very rural and remote district, where some work on gender was being conducted. During these interviews and visits there were more cordial, and less guarded exchanges, compared to those with government officials and teachers. At the time of the first round of interviews there was much public debate about the proposed Constitution, and some of the direct political engagements with how rights were being thought about came up repeatedly in the interviews. On our initial visit the Director made a point of coming out of her office, introducing the researcher to members of staff and giving assurances of welcome, and interest in the study. Thus, the terrain of the public sphere, the civility and critique, which are sometimes noted as features of the communicative action Habermas depicted coloured our engagements.

A number of staff members we interviewed were young highly educated women and men. One programme director talked about the distance you had to travel from your presuppositions in order to connect with the scope of a project concerned with gender. In describing her work she said:

> You will first of all leave civilization in [. . .] Now you start life, because the road even ends at some point, then you use four wheel drive cars. There is no other car, unless you are using a bus.
>
> (National NGO, staff member 1, 16/03/2009)

To inspire girls to remain at school the NGO organised educational tours so that they have an opportunity to get out of their villages and see what is happening outside. Girls' forums or clubs are held where girls can discuss reproductive health, FGM, life skills and rights. In some districts there is work to provide rescue centres for girls at risk of early marriage and in others there is work on the distribution of sanitary towels. There are also a number of projects linked to out of school youth, special needs and young offenders. Some projects work with schools to make them more oriented to children's needs. They build latrines, girls' changing rooms, construct water tanks and provide training for girls and boys on child rights.

In reflecting on this wide range of activities and the global gender equality and education policy NGO staff we interviewed, gave quite a measured assessment that the MDGs and other global declarations. They considered they were good on paper but their effects were not being felt on the ground.

> . . . if you go to a place like [very rural area] and you ask them about the millennium development goals, they are not aware of that, so there is also lack of community awareness on MDGs.
>
> (National NGO, staff member 2, 19/03/2009)

However, while there was concern that the MDGs may not be achieved, staff were quick to point out that, because of FPE, many learners would access education, who would have been shut out without the combined agendas of the MDG, EFA and FPE. Thus the MDGs, EFA and a rights agenda framed their work more visibly than in other research sites, even though they were cautious not to over-claim on what could be achieved. There was thus a sense here of the terrains of a middle space concerned with national administration, the public sphere, teacher professional association and CBOs were in some kind of connection, and that the global gender and education policy was seen from many angles, expressing our metaphors of a ladder, a letter and the gusts of weather. However, it was striking that this was a special node of interaction, with good access to funds, but politically quite apart from the MoE, and with connection only to its projects schools in particular districts, not to large national networks.

The local NGO, where we collected data, did not receive grants from large international NGOs, but from some individuals in the global north as well as locally based donors. Most of their work concerned livestock breeding and income generation. Although the NGO worked in a rural area. It was led by a highly educated coordinator, who lived in a town. It took its remit, not so much from the framework of the MDGs, but from particular local conditions of poverty it was seeking to remedy. Thus there was a sense that the organisation's priorities were not being framed by or linked to the global policy framework. The organisation was an instance of the terrains of a middle space linked to CBOs, somewhat guarded about the extent to which staff might interact with the institutional spaces of the MoE, the professional organisations of teachers, or the critical dynamics of the public sphere. The focus was particularly local and ethnically framed. One NGO worker said 'there are so many policies around here [. . .] we don't disseminate those policies' (Local NGO, staff member 1, 19/05/2010).

On the MDGs the view was one of indifference and distance to the goals. When, for example, in one exchange with an interviewer the issue of how the MDGs could be discussed at the grassroots, was raised, the view of the NGO worker was that the MDGs were too particular, and that the nature of the work which the organisation did was general, linked to the locale and integrated with its own programme of education, not the steer from the MDGs. Another explained:

> The MDGs are very far off, it is only those people who can read and hear it in the media and actually interacting a lot that can actually know what Millennium Development Goals are.
>
> (Local NGO, Staff member 5, 22/06/09)

We interviewed the Coordinator, three field workers, and spent some days observing the work of the NGO including a training course to strengthen the work of local SMCs. We held a report back meeting for the NGO on 2nd November 2009. In contrast to our interviews with the global NGO, most of these interactions were in Swahili or the mother tongue of the district. On the walls of the education office room of the NGO were posters, one with a picture of a child saying '*Let me play*', and another declaring 'everyone has a right to education'. Data charts were pinned up with the names of board members, the number of enrolments and exam results in the schools in which the NGO works. There was little visual evocation of global policy. Thus the NGO interfaced with the terrains of a middle space concerned with the public institutions of education and discussions in the public sphere concerning rights, but the explicit connection to global or national policy or debate on this issue was not evident.

On one of the fieldwork days when we were in the NGO offices a daily newspaper was discussed animatedly. Our fieldwork notes record:

> A woman worker settled at a table to look through the daily paper before beginning work. One of her colleagues asked her turn to a page that carried a story titled, '*Pupils skip school due to hunger*'. She quickly read through the news article and picked a few issues from the story that became subject for a brief discussion engaging all present in the room including the researcher. The issues she picked included the government's announcement that it would allow over 2.5 million children in famine-hit areas to remain in schools during the August holidays to be fed under the School Feeding Programme that year (2009), measures to enrol the 1.5 million minors, believed to be engaged in child labour, the issue of teacher-pupil ratio which, the report suggested, were as high as 1:100 in some areas and the government's move to recruit 12,600 temporary teachers.
>
> (Fieldnotes, 11/06/2009)

This engagement with the public sphere, involving the researchers, was very different to the more guarded approach to discussing political events in the government offices and the school. It resonated more with the informal discussions about current events in the offices of the global NGO. However, in contrast to the global NGO there was little focus on gender. The NGO reports did not highlight these issues. During the training on SMCs we observed the NGO carry out gender issues were not mentioned. Although the limited participation by women in the event was noted with the comment that 'women are shy' (Local NGO, staff member 1, 19/05/2010).

Reflections on researching terrains of a middle space in Kenya

This chapter has provided some of the political, economic and education context in Kenya at the time we collected data, drawing out some of the ways in which gender equality policy was being or not being addressed in different terrains of a middle space evident in the research sites we selected. How these terrains of the public sphere, institutional arrangement, professional association (or its absence) and community formation help shape some of the relationships of engagements or distance with the global gender policy take different forms in the contrasted research sites. They also provide some detail and texture regarding the form in which global education policy come to be seen. Our fieldnotes indicate how the terrains of a middle space in Kenya are marked by particular forms of poverty associated with climate, housing, distance, struggles over the implementation of law and the sense of connection or disconnection from central government. It can be seen that the connections between gender equality, poverty and education, was not a strong or well recognised discourse in any site apart from the global NGO. In the next chapter we give an overview of similar features concerning terrains of a middle space and the history of engagement with global gender equality policy in South Africa.

Notes

1 www.vision2030.go.ke/about/
2 World Inequality Database on Education (WIDE). [online]. Available at www.education-inequalities.org/. [Accessed 12 February 2017].
3 FAWE [online]. Available at www.fawe.org/about/index.php . [Accessed 12 February 2017].
4 See www.knut.or.ke/index.php/2015-06-08-17-07-02/history for detailed history.
5 NEPAD is the economic development programme of the African Union.

References

Bedi, A. S., Kimalu, P. K., Mandab, D. K., & Nafula, N. (2004). The decline in primary school enrolment in Kenya. *Journal of African Economies*, 13(1), pp. 1–43.
Bigsten, A., Manda, D. K., Mwabu, G., & Wambugu, A. (2014). *Incomes, inequality, and poverty in Kenya: A long-term perspective* (No. 2014/126). WIDER Working Paper, United Nations University, Helsinki.
Bold, T., Kimenyi, M., Mwabu, G., & Sandefur, J. (2015). Can free provision reduce demand for public services? evidence from Kenyan education. *The World Bank Economic Review*, 29(2), pp. 293–326.

Bradshaw, Y. W., & Fuller, B. (1996). Policy action and school demand in Kenya. *International Journal of Comparative Sociology*, 37(1), pp. 72–96.

Buckler, A. (2015). *Quality Teaching and the Capability Approach: Evaluating the Work and Governance of Women Teachers in Rural Sub-Saharan Africa*. Abingdon: Routledge.

Chaca, B., & Zani, A. (2015). The impact of free primary educaiton on puil teacher ratios in Kuria East constiutency, Kenya. *Journal of Humanities and Social Science*, 20(5), pp. 1–12.

Chege, F. N., & Arnot, M. (2012). The gender – education – poverty nexus: Kenyan youth's perspective on being young, gendered and poor. *Comparative Education*, 48(2), pp. 195–209.

Dahlerup, D. (Ed.). (2013). *Women, Quotas and Politics*. Abingdon: Routledge.

DFID (2009). *Eliminating World Poverty: Building Our Common Future*. London: DFID.

Elimu Yetu (2005). The challenge of educating girls in Kenya. In Aikman, S. and Unterhalter, E. eds. *Beyond Access: Transforming Policy and Practice for Gender Equality in Education*. Oxford: Oxfam, GB, pp. 106–125.

Elischer, S. (2013). *Political Parties in Africa: Ethnicity and Party Formation*. Cambridge: Cambridge University Press.

Elsey, H., Kilonzo, N., Tolhurst, R., & Molyneux, C. (2005). Bypassing districts? Implications of sector-wide approaches and decentralization for integrating gender equity in Uganda and Kenya. *Health Policy and Planning*, 20(3), pp. 150–157.

Fraser, N. (1990). Rethinking the public sphere: A contribution to the critique of actually existing democracy. *Social Text*, (25/26), pp. 56–80.

Fraser, N. (2014). *Transnationalizing the Public Sphere*. Cambridge: Polity.

Frederiksen, B. F. (2000). Popular culture, gender relations and the democratization of everyday life in Kenya. *Journal of Southern African Studies*, 26(2), pp. 209–222.

Gathii, J. T. (2016). Assessing the Constitution of Kenya 2010 five years later. In Ginsburg, T. and Haq, A. eds. *Assessing Constitutional Performance*. Cambridge: Cambridge University Press, pp. 337–364.

Giordano, E. (2008). *School Clusters and Teacher Resource Centres* (Fundamentals of Educational Planning No. 86). Paris: IIEP.

Goetz, A. M., & Hassim, S. (Eds.). (2003). *No Shortcuts to Power: African Women in Politics and Policy Making*. London: ZED Books.

Habermas, J. (1989). *The Structural Transformation of the Public Sphere*. Cambridge: Polity.

Hansen, T. O., & Sriram, C. L. (2015). Fighting for justice (and Survival): Kenyan civil society accountability strategies and their enemies. *International Journal of Transitional Justice*, ijv012.

Herriot, A., Crossley, M., Juma, M., Waudo, J., Mwirotsi, M., & Kamau, A. (2002). The development and operation of headteacher support groups in Kenya: A mechanism to create pockets of excellence, improve the provision of quality education and target positive changes in the community. *International Journal of Educational Development*, 22(5), pp. 509–526.

Hungi, N. (2010). *Characteristics of school heads and their schools*. SACMEQ Working Paper No. 3, September 2011. SACMEQ. [online]. Available at www.sacmeq.org/sites/default/files/sacmeq/publications/03_schheads_final_24nov2011.pdf

Ikiara, J. (1990). *Industrialization in Kenya: In Search of a Strategy*. London: Heinemann.

Isaksson, A. S., Kotsadam, A., & Nerman, M. (2014). The gender gap in African political participation: Testing theories of individual and contextual determinants. *Journal of Development Studies*, 50(2), pp. 302–318.

Jewitt, S., & Ryley, H. (2014). It's a girl thing: Menstruation, school attendance, spatial mobility and wider gender inequalities in Kenya. *Geoforum*, 56, pp. 137–147.

Kibe, J. W. (2014). *Factors Affecting Settlement of Industrial Disputes by the Kenya National Union of Teachers (KNUT)*. Unpublished Doctoral dissertation, University of Nairobi.

Kibui, A., & Mwaniki, B. (2014). Gender equity and educaiton development in Kenya and the new Constitution for Vision 2030. *International Journal of Scientific Research and Innovative Technology*, 1(2), pp. 1–14.

Kiluva-Ndunda, M. M. (2001). *Women's Agency and Educational Policy: The Experiences of the Women of Kilome, Kenya*. Albany: State University of New York Press.

Kimosop, P. K., Otiso, K. M., & Ye, X. (2015). Spatial and gender inequality in the Kenya certificate of primary education examination results. *Applied Geography*, 62, pp. 44–61.

King, K. (2007). Balancing basic and post-basic education in Kenya: National versus international policy agendas. *International Journal of Educational Development*, 27(4), pp. 358–370.

Koech, P. (2006). *Parent-Teacher Partnerships for Enhancing Pre-School Children's Education in Uasin Gishu District, Kenya*. Kenyatta University.

Linke, A. M., O'Laughlin, J., McCabe, J. T., Tir, J., & Witmer, F. D. (2015). Rainfall variability and violence in rural Kenya: Investigating the effects of drought and the role of local institutions with survey data. *Global Environmental Change*, 34, pp. 35–47.

Lloyd, C. B., Mensch, B. S., & Clark, W. H. (2000). The effects of primary school quality on school dropout among Kenyan girls and boys. *Comparative Education Review*, 44(2), pp. 113–147.

Lucas, A. M., & Mbiti, I. M. (2012). Does free primary education narrow gender differences in schooling? Evidence from Kenya. *Journal of African Economies*, 1(5), pp. 691–722.

Maathai, W. (2004). *The Green Belt Movement: Sharing the Approach and the Experience*. New York: Lantern Books.

Macharia, J. (2016). Gendered media and political communication in Africa: The Kenya experience. In Mukhongo, L. and Macharia, J. eds. *Political Influence of the Media in Developing Countries*. Hershey: Information Science Reference, pp. 216–233.

Mak' Ochieng, M. (1996). The African and Kenyan media and the public sphere. *Communication*, 22(2), pp. 23–32.

Mathi, M. (2014). Neoliberalism and the Forms of Civil Society in Kenya and South Africa. In Obidare, E. ed. *The Handbook of Civil Society in Africa*. New York: Springer, pp. 215–232.

Mati, J. M. (2013). Antinomies in the struggle for the transformation of the Kenyan constitution (1990–2010). *Journal of Contemporary African Studies*, 31(2), pp. 235–254.

Mayienga, D. M. (2013). *Success Stories: Biographical Narratives of Three Women School Principals in Kenya*. Unpublished Doctoral dissertation, Michigan State University.

Milligan, L. (2014). 'They are not serious like the boys': Gender norms and contradictions for girls in rural Kenya. *Gender and Education*, 26(5), pp. 465–476.

Ministry of Education (2005). *Kenya Education Sector Support Programme I, 2005–2010: Delivering Quality Equitable Education and Training to All Kenyans.* MOEST: Nairobi.

Ministry of Education (2007). *Education Statistical Booklet 2003–2007.* Nairobi: Ministry of Education, Planning Division, Republic of Kenya.

Ministry of Education (2009). *KESSP II 2010–2015.* Nairobi: MOE.

Mugo, J. K., Moyi, P., & Kiminza, O. (2016). Education in Kenya, 1963 to 2015. In Muene, J. ed. *Achieving Education for All: Dilemmas in System-Wide Reforms and Learning Outcomes in Africa.* London: Lexington Books, pp. 81–106.

Muhula, R. (2009). Horizontal inequalities and ethno-regional politics in Kenya. *Kenya Studies Review*, 1(1), pp. 85–105.

Mundy, K., Haggerty, M., Sivasubramaniam, M., Cherry, S., & Maclure, R. (2010). Civil society, basic education, and sector-wide aid: Insights from Sub-Saharan Africa. *Development in Practice*, 20(4–5), pp. 484–497.

Mungania, M. M. (2014). *Institutional Factors Influencing Affiliation of Secondary School Teachers to Trade Unions in Igembe North District, Kenya.* Unpublished Doctoral dissertation, University of Nairobi.

Murunga, G. R., & Nasong'o, S. W. (2007). *Kenya: The Struggle for Democracy.* London: ZED Books.

Mwega, F. W., & Ndulu, K. (1994). Economic adjustment policies. In Barkan, J. D. ed. *Beyond Capitalism versus Socialism in Kenya and Tanzania.* Nairobi: East African Educational Publishers.

Ng'weno, H. (2009). *The Making of a Nation: A Political History of Kenya.* [DVD]. Kenya.

Nishimura, M., & Yamano, T. (2013). Emerging private education in Africa: Determinants of school choice in rural Kenya. *World Development*, 43, pp. 266–275.

Obura, A. P., Wamahiu, S., Kariuki, W., Bunyi, G. W., Chege, F., Njoka, E., . . . Education, M. (2011). Gender Equality in Education Planning and Management in Kenya. In *Gender Equality in Education: Looking Beyond Parity.* Paris: IIEP. Retrieved from http://doc.iiep.unesco.org/wwwisis/repdoc/sem313/sem313_13_eng.pdf

Odol, W., & Kabira, W. M. (2000). The mother warriors and her daughters: The women's movement in Kenya. In Smith, B. G. ed. *Global Feminisms Since 1945.* London: Routledge, pp. 101–118, Rewiting Histories series.

Omwami, E. M., & Foulds, K. (2015). The persisting challenge of age-for-grade non-compliance in post-free primary education in Kenya. *Development in Practice*, 25(6), pp. 832–842.

Omwoha, J. R. (2014). *Talk Radio and The Public Sphere: Jambo Kenya's Role in Democratization.* Unpublished Doctoral dissertation, University of the Witwatersrand, Johannesburg.

Onyango, A. A. (2013). *Participation of Women in Trade Union Leadership in the Kenya National Union of Teachers, Kisumu County.* Doctoral dissertation, University of Nairobi.

Otieno, W., & Colclough, C. (2009). Financing education in Kenya: Expenditures, outcomes and the role of international aid. In *Research Consortium on Education Outcomes & Poverty.* Cambridge, UK: University of Cambridge.

Republic of Kenya (1964). Kenya Education Commission Report (The Ominde Commission). Nairobi: Republic of Kenya.

Republic of Kenya (1976). The Report of the National Committee on Educational Objectives and Policies (The Gachathi Report). Nairobi: Republic of Kenya.

Republic of Kenya (1983). *Kenya 1963–1983 Official Handbook*. Nairobi: Government Printer.
Republic of Kenya (1996). *Statistical Abstract 1996*. Nairobi: Central Bureau of Statistics.
Republic of Kenya (2001). *Poverty Reduction Strategy Paper for the Period 2001–2004*. Nairobi: Ministry of Finance and Planning.
Republic of Kenya (2005a). *Sessional Paper No. 1 of 2005: A Policy Framework for Educational Training and Research*. Nairobi: Government Printer.
Republic of Kenya (2007). *Gender Policy in Education*. Nairobi: Ministry of Education.
Republic of Kenya (2009). *Education Facts and Figures*. Nairobi: Ministry of Education.
Rono, J. K. (2002). The impact of the structural adjustment programmes on Kenyan society. *Journal of Social Development in Africa*, 17(1), pp. 81–98.
Sanya, B. N., & Lutomia, A. N. (2016). Feminism unfinished: Towards gender justice and women's rights in Kenya. In Koster, M. ed. *Kenya After 50*. New York: Palgrave Macmillan, pp. 227–252.
Somerset, A. (2009). Universalising primary education in Kenya: The elusive goal. *Comparative Education*, 45(2), pp. 233–250.
Srivastava, P. (Ed.). (2013). *Low-Fee Private Schooling: Aggravating Equity or Mitigating Disadvantage?* Oxford: Symposium Books.
Swammy, G. (1994). *Adjustment in Africa: Lessons from Country Case Studies*. Washington, DC: The World Bank.
Tripp, A. M. (2016). Women's movements and constitution making after civil unrest and conflict in Africa: The cases of Kenya and Somalia. *Politics & Gender*, 12(1), pp. 78–106.
True, J., & Mintrom, M. (2001). Transnational networks and policy diffusion: The case of gender mainstreaming. *International Studies Quarterly*, 45(1), pp. 27–57.
UNESCO (2010). *EFA Global Monitoring Report 2010: Reaching the Marginalised*. Paris: UNESCO.
Watila, M. W. (2016). *Surviving State Corporatism in Kenya: The Case Study of the Kenya National Union of Teachers (KNUT) 1982–2013*. Unpublished Doctoral dissertation, University of Nairobi.
Wood, J. (2016). Unintended consequences: DAC governments and shrinking civil society space in Kenya. *Development in Practice*, 26(5), pp. 532–543.
World Bank, & UNDP. (1993). *Kenya: Challenge of Promoting Exports*. Washington, DC: World Bank.
Wrong, M. (2010). *It's Our Turn to Eat*. London: Fourth Estate.
Yates, C., Foster, D., & Barasa, L. (2009). *Education Reform in Kenya: Institutionalising the Provision of Instructional Materials and In-Service Teacher Education for Quality Primary Education*. Nairobi: DFID.

5   Exchanges around global gender equality and education policies in South Africa, 1991–2016

In this chapter we provide some background history on the context in South Africa in which global gender policies came to be received. We show how there was a somewhat different engagement with the global policy agendas on gender and education in the research sites compared with those in Kenya, and that a national project concerned with overcoming inequalities associated with poverty and gender discrimination were very central to the political goals of the ANC in government, but hard to realise. Difficulties of delivery on equality, coupled with many processes that reproduced attitudes of discrimination against women, particularly around aspects of sex and reproductive rights, were evident in the sphere of education shaping and shaped by the terrains of a middle space we sketch. These concerns meant that global gender equality policy was generally refracted through national and local perspectives, and the metaphors of weather and a message appear to characterise the context more appropriately than the notion of a ladder connecting global, national and local.

The chapter is organised in two parts. The first part summarises some key aspects of shifts in policy on education, poverty and gender inequality in South Africa, concentrating primarily on the period after the end of apartheid in 1990, and provide some background on characteristics of the four terrains of a middle space we consider important for understanding some of the exchanges around global gender policy – the institutional relationships around the civil service, the public sphere, professional association and civil society. In the second part of the chapter we outline the research we undertook in the five research sites, describing how some of these settings and the relationships we examined reflected negotiations with the global policies concerning gender, poverty and education outlined in Chapter 3, particularly EFA, the MDGs and the Beijing Platform of Action.

Global gender, education and poverty reduction initiatives

As we described in the previous chapter, some features of engagements with the global gender equality policy in Kenya had links with old histories of colonial relationships and contemporary links around aid, geopolitics and economic exchange. The global women's movement, although networked to some individuals in Kenya, did not have deep roots of connection to the many locally based forms of women's association in the country. South Africa, therefore, provides a number of salient contrasts while sharing a history of white settlement, black land dispossession and a racially divided education system.

The nature of colonialism in South Africa is much debated. The early history of white settlement was not different in form from that in some other African countries. However, the large migration of settlers (primarily from Europe over four centuries) with their own diversities, and the particularities of an economy built on gold, grain and sugar with imported slave labour and indentured workers, largely from India, meant that South African colonial relationships had particular formations. Although whites had the franchise in South Africa from the 19th century, and South Africa was self-governing from 1910, the forms of political domination by the white minority only ended in 1994 with the first democratic elections.

This particular history filtered global relationships in diverse ways. The national liberation movement, which had begun to form at the beginning of the 20th century, had been a crucible for many ideas and strategies to address gender, poverty and education. These drew explicitly on ideas about rights, equality and participation garnered from gusts of global discussion. Key spokespeople from this movement positioned these values in opposition to the racial segregation and authoritarianism of the apartheid education system (Lodge, 1983; Nkomo, 1990; Unterhalter and Wolpe, 1991). International anti-apartheid support mobilised diverse constituencies, from the UN, through governments of different political complexions, religious organisations, civil society, the media and family networks. Thus, before 1994, we can see the three metaphors we have used to discuss global, national, local relationships all in play in relation to the ideas circulating on changing gender, education and relations of poverty in South Africa.

South Africa's exemplary Constitution, adopted in 1996, was seen as a beacon with regard to human rights, setting out a framework for a redistributive, egalitarian state, challenging poverty and inequality, and linking education with other programmes for social change (Motala and Pampallis, 2002; Steiner, Alston and Goodman, 2008). The Truth and Reconciliation Commission offered a blend of legal process and religiously inspired catharsis to help chart a new path for social relations in the country (Tutu, 1999; Posel and Simpson, 2002). Both were formulated through processes of democratic iteration in a public sphere that shattered older regimes of censorship and repression. South Africa's international relationships were often moral exemplars with President Mandela taking a role in work on international peacebuilding. Thus while South Africa also received aid, in the immediate post-apartheid period these relationships were not shaped primarily within the prism of the politics of decolonisation and the Cold War – a major theme in Kenya.

Commentators on the post-apartheid South African however often point out there was a considerable gap between what was envisaged in the ferment of the early 1990s, after the release of Mandela, the unbanning of the ANC and all political parties, and what was achieved (Habib, 2013; Hart, 2014; Clark and Worger,

2016). In periodising this process, a conventional division separates the period of the Redistribution and Development Programme (RDP) from 1991–1996, from that of the Growth, Employment and Redistribution programme (GEAR) from 1996 to approximately 2008. The RDP period was associated with initiatives around equity, redress and building democratic institutions. It was also the period of South Africa's return to an international stage and open engagement with human rights agendas (Wilson, 2001; Alden and Le Pere, 2004). Under GEAR the emphasis shifted towards growth, trade liberalisation, increased privatisation, relaxing some labour legislation and putting in place minimal safety nets against poverty, rather than working towards equalities and redistribution (Hart, 2002; Habib, 2009). The prominence of a South African, Phumzile Mlambo-Ngcuka, appointed in 2013 as Executive Director of the United Nations Entity for Gender Equality and Empowerment of Women, UN Women, signalled the importance of the international stage for the South African government. But this appointment also highlighted some disjunctures between international position and some of the developments around gender in South Africa (Andrews, 2016; O'Manique and Fourie, 2016).

From around 2009, when Jacob Zuma became President, some of the contradictions in the unification achieved in 1994 became evident, with enormous inequalities between those securely in work (which include those working in government departments or NGOs) and those subsisting on casual contracts or grants. The effects of electricity shortages and a downturn in the demand for minerals has weakened the economy. Long-running strikes in some sectors have pushed the political alliance (the ANC, the Communist Party and the trade union allice COSATU), which shaped the RDP, almost to breaking point. Government response to some of these issues has been concern to address aspects of poverty but generally there has been limited or inadequate action and widening inequalities most notably in education (Ashman et al. 2010; Habib, 2013; Hart, 2014; Suttner, 2015). More affluent urban African voters in 2016 local elections voted against the ANC and for the more centre Democratic Alliance, while a segment of poorer voters turned to the left and supported a new political party the Economic Freedom Fighters (EFF).

Table 5.1 summarises three phases of policy change linked to the RDP, GEAR and the period after 2009, when Jacob Zuma became President. It can be seen from this periodisation that the RDP period was associated with broad brush-stroke assurances of rights to education. A range of gender equalities were features under the Constitution. Poverty was to be addressed through redistributive policies of the state, with only one clear targeted practice for this in education, namely school feeding. In the GEAR period, there were a host of initiatives in education, to make delivery more efficient and ensure even the poorest children could enter school. In addition, there was work to support curriculum development, and to address particular problems around HIV and school-related gender-based violence (SRGBV). In the Zuma period, there has been an emphasis on monitoring learning outcomes, directing teachers and clear evidence of very stark inequalities, articulated most powerfully in university student protests in 2015

Table 5.1 Key policies introduced in South Africa 1991–2015 addressing education, poverty and gender

Policies on education change	Policies on gender	Policies on poverty
The Reconstruction and Development Programme (RDP) period (1991–1996)		
ANC Education Policy Framework stresses equalities. 1996 Constitution guarantees compulsory 12 years schooling for all. Curriculum overhauled to foster learning of human rights, multilingualism, multi-culturalism and values of reconciliation and nation building.	Laws on abortion & sexual and reproductive rights. 1996 ANC education policy IPET committee has gender cross-coordination group. RDP stress need to open up opportunities for women in income-generating employment; girls and women to pursue non-traditional subjects such as maths and science; 1996 GETT established in Ed Dept.	Provision for one meal per child per day at primary schools located among poor communities. Provision of housing, health, social security and social services
Growth, Employment and Reconstruction (GEAR) (1996–2008)		
1996 Fee free schools. Struggles over Curriculum content and pedagogic approach. *National Policy on HIV/Aids for Learners and Educators (1999)* Tirisano programmes (2000): HIV/Aids; school effectiveness & teacher professionalism; illiteracy; FET & higher education; system organisation effectiveness (national & provincial). Acknowledged gaps in gender equity, ECD and special needs. 2000 Moral Regeneration Movement launched. 'Values, Education and Democracy' policy prescribes equity, tolerance, multilingualism, openness, accountability and social honour. 2000 Employment Educators Act provides for immediate dismissal of a teacher guilty of sex with pupil. 2001, the Curriculum Review Committee affirms need to promote awareness of social justice, human rights, a healthy environment and inclusivity 2003. Establishment of GEM clubs 2007 *Measures on the prevention and management of learner pregnancies.* Pandor establishes Ministerial committee on gender equality. 2008	The *Employment Equity Act* (1998) gender equality in new appointments in all government departments. Customary Marriages Act (1998) abolished minority status of women married under customary law and legalised these marriages. 2000 Nation Policy Framework for Gender Equality and empowerment of women	GEAR aimed to achieve a 6% annual growth rate and reduce the budget deficit. Claimed this would lead to savings that could be directed to social services and infrastructural expenditure. Introduction of child support grant
The Zuma era		
Testing regimes. Concession of no fee increases for university students in 2015. Fee increases for students above a means tested limit adopted in 2016.	2008 Formations Ministry of Women, Children and People with Disabilities	2010 The child support grant was extended to children up to 18 years of age

and 2016, led by those who had succeeded in education despite many problems of distribution and inequalities.

The approach to addressing poverty therefore has shifted. In the transition from apartheid, there had been a general social democratic approach. Under GEAR there was a means tested focus on child support grants and various ameliorative concessions regarding pregnant school girls and establishing girls' and boys' clubs. In the Zuma period there was an attempt to support the poorest students in higher education, and an attempt to review the lack of provision in post-school education for those who did not enter university. Table 5.1 offers a chronology of these policy shifts, and notes the changes between a generally redistributive policy set up in the RDP period, to a programme of selective means tested interventions and government directed initiatives on gender equality in the subsequent decades.

At the time of data collection enormous challenges existed in delivering social development, orienting the economy to meet the needs of the majority and engaging politically with the aftermath of the divisions and exclusions associated with apartheid. While ambitious programmes in poverty reduction, housing provision, building infrastructure and improving access to health and education were being put in place, realising these in practice was an enormous challenge. There were many initiatives associated with popular participation through a vibrant civil society, which had grown out of the mass democratic movement (MDM), active in overthrowing the apartheid regime. But many demands of this movement remained unfulfilled, and government was frequently criticised for being out of touch with the needs of the poorest (Ashman et al., 2010; Hart, 2014; Suttner, 2015). The relationship between a state, which considered itself closely tied to the mass of the people, and oriented to an equalities agenda, and civil society organisations, which aimed to hold the state to account became particularly strained with struggles over lack of service delivery, wage levels and conditions in higher education (Ballard et al., 2006; Robins, 2008; Habib, 2013; Seekings and Nattrass, 2015; Allais, 2016).

In 1991 changes in policy and practice associated with gender, poverty and education were linked by processes of nation building where ideas of democratic institutions, the public sphere and an open civil society intermixed. The interests of the middle classes, the working classes and the dispossessed were fused in a process of bringing together under a rubric of equal rights guaranteed through the Constitution. Later, as the RDP period shifted to GEAR, the form of the nation invoked was one engaged in processes of economic growth, trade liberalisation supporting the more affluent sectors of the middle class, with minimal support for the most disadvantaged in practice, although a great deal of policy discussion on these issues continued and institutional structures, like those of the education system were much concerned to engage with this.

In the RDP period, while race was noted as a feature of inequality which the Constitution and the new education system sought to transform, discussion of race and class as aspects of lived relationships put much store in the transformation of institutions. From 2008, as inequalities persisted, discussion of race became a major component of reflections on education change, poverty and divergent politics of gender. The student protests of 2015–2016 highlighted these issues starkly (Deegan, 2011; Badat and Sayed, 2014; Mbembe, 2016).

Under apartheid, racial segregation and unequal distribution of schooling were associated with both political and economic strategies of the regime but were often deeply contradictory aiming at some periods to limit the provision of education and in others to expand it for certain groups. However, class and race were key characteristics of the provision of schooling, and the success of the regime partly rested on the benefits of this education for some. However, this was also one of its Achilles heels as it was often through the reflections within and through educational relationships that opposition movements grew (Kallaway, 1984; Alexander, 1990; Nkomo, 1990; Unterhalter and Wolpe, 1991). Gender inequalities were a feature of the classed and racialised division of the education system (Unterhalter, 1991a; Truscott, 1993). Thus, for example, while white middle-class women had excellent access to secondary and tertiary education from the 1960s, and some black women shared this access, the nature of their education experience and its outcomes were marked by racialised and gendered exclusions (Martineau, 1997; Unterhalter, 1999; Mwabu and Schultz, 2000; Morrell and Moletsane, 2002).

With the end of apartheid there was extensive interest in working within and through the education system to undo the unjust structures, attitudes and practices linked with the racism of the past, and there were enormous assumptions made regarding what education could achieve in relation to developing equalities (Jansen and Christie, 1999; Chisholm, 2004). Extensive policy borrowing from around the world took place, looking to develop high levels of skill, participatory pedagogies and a curriculum, focussed on outcomes that could undo the inadequacies and inequalities of the past (Jansen and Sayed, 2001; Motala and Pampallis, 2002; Chisholm, 2004; Spreen, 2004). Poverty was noted as a severe risk factor for children dropping out of school and not achieving well (Fiske and Ladd, 2004; Bhana, 2007; Hargreaves et al., 2008; Morrell et al., 2009; Feisch, Shindler and Perry, 2012) as was the HIV epidemic (Coombe, 2001; Aikman et al., 2008; Archer and Boler, 2008). Statistics showed the high level of risk associated with being a poor girl (Poku and Whiteside, 2004; Hargreaves and Boler, 2009). In the projects developed to respond to these risks terrains of a middle space were reconfigured as teachers, administrators and NGO workers built relationships to keep children in school; partly to support the realisation of rights to education, partly to deliver the new curriculum, and partly to support health promotion addressing HIV.

In South Africa the challenges around girls' participation and gender equality in school were somewhat different from Kenya. In 1991, there were already high enrolment ratios for girls in primary schools in South Africa (Unterhalter, 1991b). Analysis in 2007 showed that by the age of eighteen far more boys than girls were failing to complete twelve years of school (Fleisch and Shindler, 2009). Girls overall fared well at the school-leaving examinations compared to their male counterparts, but there were differences linked to class and location

(Perry and Fleisch, 2006, p. 108). Generally it was both girls and boys from the black middle classes who did well, often at what had been historically white state or private schools, gained access to top tier universities and entered the professions (Southall, 2016, p. 108–123). For those with good education qualifications and access to political and social networks there were widening opportunities in new employment sectors (Bhorat et al., 2014). But for large proportions of the population there was only insecure, casual work, and jobs in some areas of manufacturing and mining disappeared. Poverty and inequality were extensive and intensive. In 2008, approximately 12.4 million people received social grants, of whom 8.1 million were poor women who received the child support grant (in that period given to children up to the age of fourteen years) (Presidency: Republic of South Africa, 2008. p. 28). In 2016, 11.97 million children were receiving the Child Support Grant, generally paid to a mother or female guardian. The grant was means tested, and while the threshold for claimants had risen from when it was initially introduced, so too had the value of the grant (Hall and Sambu, 2016). However despite the social transfers associated with a system of pensions, disability grants and child support, poverty is widespread and clearly associated with children repeating classes, dropping out and failing to complete school (Spaull, 2013; Branson, Hofmeyr and Lam, 2014).

Poverty and gender inequalities thus connected in how children experienced schooling, but issues concerning sex, sexuality and reproductive rights came prominently to the fore as the HIV epidemic which became a national emergency because of the high numbers of infections in the late 1990s, and the lack of treatment. The numbers of deaths associated with infection only started to dip after about ten years as anti-retrovirals came to be widely available and well supported. Through the trauma of the high levels of mortality associated with the HIV epidemic sexuality came to dominate debate concerning gender equity issues, and the public sphere became a terrain both of rational discussion, confronting issues like the lack of treatment for those with HIV, and of abusive prejudice articulating sexist and homophobic attitudes (Posel, 1994; Bhana et al., 2007; Mbali, 2013). Several youth education campaigns and televised drama series highlighted the risks of contracting HIV, teen pregnancy and gender-based violence. Policy initiatives aimed to prevent discrimination against HIV-positive learners, students and educators, protect confidentiality and create safe school environments (Republic of South Africa, Department of Education, 1999). But a number of studies showed how these were not always interpreted in this way, and, when not well understood or implemented sometimes exacerbated fear and discrimination; however those programmes with a clear framework dealing in depth with gender equality issues, appeared to offer promise of some change in behaviours (Campbell and Macphail, 2002; Bhana, 2007; Harrison et al., 2016).

Some research, conducted during the period of rising anxiety about the HIV epidemic, flagged connections between violence, sexuality, gender inequalities and schools. Human Rights Watch (2001) reported that girls in South African school regularly encountered violence in school, including rape, sexual abuse, sexual harassment and assault by male classmates and teachers. A South African

Medical Research Council report on data from the same period revealed that 10% of learners in their study had experienced being forced to have sex, 15% had been threatened or injured on school property and 32% felt unsafe at school (Reddy et al. 2003, pp. 33–35). In 2008, the Department of Education released guidelines on how to prevent and manage sexual violence and harassment at schools, and how learners could report abuse without fear of reprisals (Republic of South Africa, Department of Education, 2008). The prominence given to traditional values (such as *ubuntu*) in curriculum discussion and to a moral approach to citizenship in the work of the Department of Education after 2000 may in part have been a reaction to a new visibility of sexuality, partly linked to the HIV epidemic. Posel argues that 'one of the most striking features of the post-apartheid era has been the politicization of sexuality' (2005, p. 125). That sexuality came out into the open was a result of a number of factors: a rolling back of censorship laws, the formal recognition of sexual preference, legislated protection against sexual violence and the escalation of the HIV/Aids pandemic. This newfound openness around rights-based sexuality awakened public recognition of masculinities and sexual violence (Posel, 2005). On the one hand, this opened up avenues for women to assert their rights, but on the other hand, as Posel points out, this also led to 'reactions [rimmed with anger, pain and uncertainty] from a range of men to the constitutional provisions for gender and sexual equality, who feel their masculinity under threat' (Posel, 2005, p. 137).

If gender-based violence was often the silent statistic of adolescent sexual relationships, then teenage pregnancy became its visible marker. While the Council of Education Ministers confirmed in July 2000 that pregnant learners could not be expelled from schools, anecdotal reports through the media indicated that expectant girls were pressured to leave (Panday et al., 2009) and research studies showed this empirically (Grant and Hallman, 2008; Bhana et al., 2010; Branson, Hofmeyr and Lam, 2014). The forms of sexual and reproductive health education offered in school were often silent on the issues relevant to young women, or biological and moralistic in tone, offering little guidance about how to deal with pregnancy at a young age (Moletsane, 2014). Girls' feelings of trauma and shame were, some studies showed, compounded by the negative attitudes of health care professionals (Shefer, Bhana and Morrell, 2013; Moletsane, Mitchell and Lewin, 2015). Gender was thus a feature of poverty and school dropout, but in complex relationships, which policy, professional practice and civil society was not always refined enough to address.

Terrains of a middle space

Against this background, the four terrains of a middle space we have identified shaped particular relationships and perspectives on the dynamic of global, national and local engagements with gender equality policies.

Unlike Kenya, in South Africa women were a significant political presence, with a large number of Members of Parliament, and many women working in government Ministries at all levels. The institutional space of the bureaucracy was thus not closed to women, and many gained access to senior positions because of their level of education, and political experience. However, Hassim (2006) has argued that although women were formally included into government institutions and have given voice to organised constituencies through legislative processes, this has made little practical difference to 'the redistribution of resources and power in ways that change the structural forces on which women's oppression rests' (Hassim, 2006, p. 184). She identified a form of elite politics, associated with women representatives or members of elites consolidating their positions within existing power arrangements without necessarily upturning socio-economic structural relations. She noted women in government used "tactics, demands and rhetoric [which were] moderated to fit the discourses of the state in order to make incremental gains and retain hard-won openings into the state" (Hassim, 2006, p. 185). As a result, she considered most gains were made on women-specific policy (such as maternal health) while policy that addressed power relations between men and women (such as customary law) lagged behind. The argument she makes is that the institutional terrain of a middle space was necessary for women to enter, but not sufficient to allow them to effect radical transformations of power, partly because of the ways in this space became cut off from other centres of mobilisation around gender equality, women's rights, and against poverty and multiple inequalities. Waylen's (2007) comparative study of gender in historical transitions to democracy is concerned with the complexities of institutional arrangements, the relationships with women's movements, political parties and the forms of gendered institutional relationship that require change. She draws illuminatingly on examples from South Africa. Her concern with descriptive and substantive representation of women, that is the presence of women in the institutions of government, and their capacity to advance women's rights provides detail on the nuance of the terrains of a middle space we have distinguished as institutional and civil society. However, she does not comment on professional associations or formations of the public sphere. The analysis of Hassim and Waylen illuminates how the institutional terrain was one where interest and concern with issues of poverty and gender inequality could develop, but where access to power was constrained to bring about change in deeply entrenched relationships associated with race, class, gender and regional inequalities.

The dynamics of global gender equality policy, as formulated at the Beijing Conference were incorporated institutionally in South Africa much earlier than in Kenya. A Gender Policy Framework was adopted in 2000, drawing explicitly on ideas about gender mainstreaming at all levels of government from national, provincial to local outlined in the Beijing Conference Platform of Action (Republic of South Africa, The Office on the Status of Women, 2000). The Office on the Status of Women was located in the executive, the Joint Monitoring Committee on the Improvement of the Quality of Life and Status of Women in the legislature and the Commission on Gender Equality set up to monitor, educate and inform the public, research, investigate and ensure that South Africa complied with international commitments to gender equity (Hassim, 2006). All government departments were to appoint gender focal points, and had processes for them to report and review their work. Developing this rational plan around gender mainstreaming evokes aspects of the image we have deployed concerning global policy as a ladder. The location of these structures in the offices of the executive and legislature indicate how close to important centres of power the ladder of concern with global gender equality policy was placed, and how central the state as a site of change was to this vision.

However realising these plans for gender mainstreaming within the institutional terrain of a middle space was much more complex than the plan envisaged. Analysts noted there was often inadequate resourcing of the gender machinery in government departments; in some work settings staff responsibility for gender matters was merely added onto their existing job descriptions (Hassim, 2006; Waylen, 2007). In 1996, the Minister of Education had established a Gender Equity Task Team (GETT) to advise the Minister on setting up gender structures (Wolpe et al., 1997). The report reflects on some of the processes of the Beijing Conference concerned with gender mainstreaming, but also takes account of wider debates around feminism and the women's movement, attempting to summarise some salient features of gender and education in South Africa. It thus evinces all three facets of the relationship with global gender equality policies we have distinguished in that it suggests forms of bureaucratic structure that evoke the metaphor of the ladder, comments on a global national regarding debates around feminism and gender that recalls our metaphor of the weather, and is written reflecting on some of the personal values of the authors, with echoes to the notion of a letter of some considerable personal significance, as emphasised by Wolpe eight years later in her reflections on the process (Wolpe, 2005).

One of GETT's recommendations was a Gender Equity Unit in the national office of the Department of Education, so as to influence departmental policies and 'ensure that gender equity is a systematic consideration' (Wolpe, Quinlan and Martinez, 1997, p. 237). But support for this unit sometimes appeared fragile. For example, at a GETT National Consultative Conference, 7–9 July 1997, a national department official is reported to have cast doubt on the need to consider gender in the context of budget constraints (Motala, 2003, p. 403). Chisholm and Napo (1999) argued that while the state took steps to increase the access of women into decision-making positions concerning education, these were largely symbolic. Reflections articulated at a conference on what government had and had not been able to do regarding gender mainstreaming and connection with civil society were published by Chisholm and September (2005). These highlighted many of the complexities of working in the institutional terrain of a middle space, and the difficulties of making connections to the terrain of civil society and professional organisation, both nationally and globally.

The difficulties of the National Department of Education to deliver on an equalities agenda were not limited to gender. A number of criticisms were made with regard to its capacity to deliver on gender and other equalities and adequately address the education effects of poverty (Jansen and Sayed, 2001; Chisholm and September, 2005; Van der Berg, 2008; Spaull, 2013). McLennan (2000) analysing the governance structures within the education system and the forms of training available argued that the institutional capacity of the Department of Education was constrained by relationships characterised by inherited inequalities and strongly established hierarchies, which prevented fulfilling goals and the development of democratic governance structures. Thus initially the institutional space accorded by the nation building project to develop in the direction of equalities and right based approaches to poverty was somewhat constrained. Whether the gender machinery put in place in response to GETT was able to change this is one of the issues we set out to investigate.

Waylen (2007) and Hassim (2006) argue that the South African feminist movement, which they depict as a formation of civil society and the public sphere, became detached from women trying to effect institutional change within the bureaucracy. The feminist movement drew on some of the ideas circulating in a 'weather system' where global and local ideas about gender and women's issues intermixed. But they also articulated very personal connections between feminist activists in South Africa and many other countries (Steyn, 1998; Bennett, 2010 Fester, 2014; Bennettet al., 2016). For some leading figures who went into government or guided the establishment of gender machineries, their first involvement in women's politics had been as part of the ANC in exile and their activism had always had an international orientation. Over the period from the mid-1990s the relationships between gender activists inside government and feminist voices in civil society were to become fraught, although the areas of tension were primarily around national politics or the practices in particular education institutions, rather than global policies. In this there was some telling difference with Kenya, where it was the very links with international civil society that were the point of contention between some state bodies and civil society.

In South Africa the civic and political organisations that had collaborated to raise women's issues and political participation through the Women's National Coalition in the early 1990s changed as their leaders moved into government. But feminists moving into positions associated with the institutional order of the bureaucracy did not easily translate into realisation of women's rights demands. Hassim and Gouws (1998) showed that 'as the demand for inclusion [of gender advocates] is nominally met . . . the demands for transformation [associated with gender are] sidelined' (1998, p. 70). The institutionalisation of gender in the post-1994 period shifted the focus of demands initially to 'state-centric policy-related issues' (Hassim and Gouws, 1998, p. 69), but the uneven achievements of these with regards to women's rights issues was a long-standing area of struggle (Hassim, 2003; Waylen, 2007; Gouws and Hassim, 2014; Gouws, 2014). The terrain of the public sphere including the media, public lectures, academic debate, literature, theatre, film and music were all areas where ideas about women's rights, the persistence of gender and multiple other inequalities and how to change these were discussed, reviewed and critiqued (Gunne, 2014; Bennett et al., 2016; Ngcobo, 2015; Byrne, 2016). While sometimes these discussions were highly polarised and charged with unresolvable tensions around race, gender and what the limits of the public sphere might be (Hassim, 2014), they nonetheless gave testimony to the importance of this terrain of a middle space. The public sphere was a space where the issue of what an African feminism might look like in South Africa or how a southern theory of gender might be formulated came to be explored and debated, although the student struggles of 2015–2016 placed this process under enormous strain for the higher education sector. If there were limits on what could be achieved on the institutional terrain there was enormous creativity and dynamism in the terrain of the public sphere. While many global feminist currents of ideas fed into this process it was very strongly rooted in the complexities of South Africa.

The terrain of professional organisation amongst teachers, researchers, social workers was one where gender equality and women's rights issues appeared and disappeared from national and local levels of practice. Mannah (2005) describes how women's rights and gender equality issues were raised by activists in the South African Democratic Teachers Union (SADTU) in the 1990s, and then came under pressure as splits around union support for different factions in the ANC emerged. Fleisch (2010) in an analysis of accounts of teachers strikes in Soweto in 2010 draws out how different threads concerned with wider equalities agendas, pay and conditions, and critical engagements with government were wound together in teacher union activity. SADTU was a key player in the fraught politics of COSATU and tensions within the ANC, and the implications of the teachers' strikes it led were controversial regarding the effects on children's education and teacher's professional status (Balfour, 2015; Beresford, 2016). In this process the union focus on gender and women's rights issues was not much commented on. However, the case studies of South African work organisations, including trade unions, presented by Rao et al. (2015), draw out a range of ways in which ideas about taking forward gender equality ideas were supported, and the ways that global and local processes mixed together to help support change.

As in Kenya, South African civil society had many different formations, some which were oriented to supporting gender equality and addressing poverty, and some extremely conservative focussed on maintaining patriarchal hierarchies. The potential of the terrain of civil society for activism around equalities and women's rights, meeting basic needs and engaging pragmatically with the democratising state was noted in some early studies (Britton, Fish and Meintjes, 2009) together with the potential of men's organisations to work to change gender inequalities (Morrell, Jewkes and Lindegger, 2012). But in the Zuma era the uneven processes and outcomes of civil society's engagement with the state regarding issues of gender equality, service provision and confronting gender-based violence were evident; this terrain was no longer seen as a simple site of possibility (Gouws, 2016; Hick and Myeni, 2016).

Because of the diversity of civil society it is not possible to map a single form of the relationship between global, national and local. Beall (1998) argued that because of the absence of the dependencies associated with aid in South Africa, the robustness of the local women's rights organisations that negotiated the new Constitution, and the depth of supportive connection with international women's rights organisations there was a good possibility for a dispensation to emerge receptive to global gender equality and women's rights agendas in policy making and practice, although the lack of critical engagements of South Africa at that time with a neoliberal growth agenda gave her cause for concern. A number of commentators on South Africa's international and global relationships distinguish between different threads in an agenda, partly engaging with advanced global capitalism, and forms of neoliberalism, and partly trying to build social solidarities around human rights, social democracy and equalities, and civil society organisations mirrored all these formations (Hart, 2002; Alden and Schoeman, 2015; Black and Hornsby, 2016). In the process all three of the different forms of relationship with the global gender equality policy community were evident in different terrains of a middle space.

This brief review indicates that the dynamics of global, national and local engagements with gender equality, poverty and education were extremely diverse. However, generally perspectives on global frameworks were very strongly framed by the vivid experiences of the local. There was a sense of individuals and organisations making a selection from global frameworks, and considering if they were of use nationally and locally. This cautious consideration seems to better characterise the formation of the association, rather than an eager reaching out for some different policy that might help solve local troubles, evident in some organisations in Kenya. This privileging of a national framing of the discussion is exemplified by contributors to a collection on feminist debates in South Africa ten years after the transition from apartheid. The authors reflected on the limits and achievements of working with the state, the forms of participation and agency that had and had not been possible for women's rights activists (Gouws, 2005). In this study it is striking how in the only essay that touches on the relationship with global policy discourses this connection is primarily depicted as problematic placing tensions on and compromising the richness of national relationships (Manicom, 2005, pp. 41–43). Some later studies began to bring out this global–national relationship in terms of a greater area of potential. Kuumba (2009), looking at transnational women's social justice activism and two cases of African/African diaspora action involving South Africans, concluded that the potential for transformation associated with this form of activism has been under-explored. However, other studies of transnational feminism and the spaces open for the experiences of South African activists were more cautious about what potential existed (Wilson, 2013). These different perspectives suggest that in South Africa the tension between trans-national/global forms of policy and practice and those that are locally grounded has not been a simple matter of opposing or embracing policy transfers. The engagement with the international appears to have many facets, depending on who engages in the partnership and what drives it. Thus, while there is less depiction in South Africa, compared to Kenya of global gender equality policy working as a ladder with directives passed up and down the different rungs, there are many examples of the form of global–national mix we have tried to delineate with the metaphor of the weather, and the commitments to build towards women's rights and gender equality, despite, difficulties, violence and decades of struggle a testament to how much these relationships mean to the activists involved. The empirical data will help to show these relationships in greater depth.

Researching engagements with global gender equality and education policy

Our research strategy in South Africa entailed collecting qualitative data in five sites, selected to be somewhat similar to those in Kenya, so that we could investigate comparatively how global policy on gender, education and poverty was engaged, refused or negotiated. The South African sites also comprised three settings of government activity and two of NGO work. We investigated government work at the national Department of Education, administrative offices of a province with a high proportion of the population classified as poor, and a government school serving a poor peri-urban community. The settings for investigating non-state work were a NGO based in a rural community, and a NGO located in a large city, with many links to global networks. In the discussion below we describe the interviews and observations in each setting.

At the Department of Education we conducted interviews and a focus group with a range of officials at all levels, from some of the most senior, to those who had been newly appointed. We made notes on the work environment, and the activities in hand, tracking how policies on gender, education and poverty were being put into practice. We had a report back meeting to staff mid-way through our study, and again at the end. The report back meeting at the end of phase one of data collection entailed a lively exchange of views, in which different opinions were aired between researchers and different groups in the Department. There was a strong sense that discussion and critique was useful and informative. This was in marked contrast to the more guarded and formal interviews we conducted in Kenya. In the second phase of data collection we had single and group interviews reflecting on how much policy was engaging with gender and poverty. In total we conducted thirty-nine interviews and one focus group in the Department of Education.

The Department of Education, later the Department of Basic Education, is located in Pretoria, the administrative capital. Although the international airport and the financial and commercial hub of the country, Johannesburg, are only an hour's drive away, the dynamic of the city revolves around the government ministries that are located there and there is an atmosphere of being both linked, but at some distance away from the pressures of global agendas. For the first phase of this study the Department of Education was located at 123 Schoeman Street, which had been the office of the apartheid era Department of Education and Training. Although renamed, after 1996, for an early 20th-century ANC activist, writer and linguist, Sol Plaatje, the name change could not undo the work environment of long corridors and closed off offices, inherited from an earlier period. By the second round of data collection in 2010 the Department had divided into two halves. One dealing with further and higher education remained at Schoeman Street, and a new Department of Basic Education moved to new offices in

Struben Street built around a central turret of sandstone reminiscent of the conical ruins of Great Zimbabwe, and set within indigenous gardens and a spectacular water fountain. Here, although directors still sat apart, glass partitions ensured they were part of new communal working areas.

At Sol Plaatje House there was a sense of hierarchy but this was not quite so pronounced as in Jogoo House in Kenya. The move to the new building provided staff with a restaurant/canteen downstairs, a meeting place and a state-of-the-art conference centre, which offered facilities to bring people to the Department and connect with their concerns. In Sol Plaatje House the Gender Equity Unit (GEU) had a number of offices. Posters on the wall were exhortations not to overlook violence against girls. Resources on gender were much more in evidence than in Kenya. Books aimed at learners and teachers, and pamphlets outlining guidelines on sexual harassment and the prevention and management of teenage pregnancy were stacked in the offices. However, the move to the new offices, meant some reduction in the visibility of these issues. No posters could be stuck to the walls and the only 'pictures' were large standardised placards of school children. One interviewee lamented that the posters learners had produced at a GEM (Girls' Education Movement) camp were almost thrown into the rubbish when the move took place. To save them she took them home. She said: 'this is what makes me wake up in the morning' (National Official 7, 07/11/2008).

From the vantage point of the Department relationships with schools, teachers and the provincial Ministries which oversaw education were paramount, and keeping lines of communication open to them was a key issue. There was a sense that NGOs were not particularly helpful in developing policy and positions on gender and poverty. One senior Department of Education official said:

> There are some limited relationships being built [with NGOs]. But to be honest, in the gender sector, I don't know who to really work with. For example, for the GEM camp, who can I get from outside – just somebody to do that kind of facilitating work. . . . When we did the Guidelines, the Minister had said we must check with the activists. [. . . .] The other problem of working with NGO's is that the concept of partnership has not really been developed in the relationships that government has [. . .] with NGOs. A partnership is not just about the government giving funds and someone else implementing. It's actually about developing relationships and bringing joint ideas to the table and finding the funds jointly which may well be from within government.
>
> (National Official 6, 20/10/2008).

In 1997 the Gender Equity Task Team (GETT) had reported on how gender work in the Department should be conducted. GETT had wanted the GEU structure to be mirrored in provinces. While Gender Focal Persons were appointed in each of the provinces, (sometimes as an additional function to their job descriptions), they rarely had additional support staff or a budget specifically allocated to gender work. None of the provincial departments had Gender Officers located in each branch. GETT also recommended the establishment of a Provincial Gender Advisory Committee, made up of departmental representatives and external constituencies, to advise the Minister of the direction and impact of strategies to achieve gender equity (Wolpe, Quinlan and Martinez, 1997, p. 249). Such Committees had not been set up at the time we collected data, but in some provinces intra-departmental meetings with the Office on the Status of Women located in the President's office occurred regularly.

There was awareness in the Department of how controversial gender was, and how complex dealing with the issue could be. Ramagoshi had been the director of the GEU in the DoE while Naledi Pandor was the Minister. She argued (Ramagoshi, 2004) that 'levels in government are spaces of power and . . . the position you occupy determines whether you will be listened to or not. The GFPs [Gender Focal Persons appointed in provinces] occupy spaces that have no influence with regards to programmes or policy' (p. 134). 'Instead of mainstreaming gender in the system, many of the GFPs have been reduced to events co-ordinators' (p. 134). In her view equity targets (30% of women at management level by 1999) were not met partly as a result of cultural or traditional reasons – such as school governing bodies (SGBs) preferring male appointments as principals. The National Gender Co-ordinating Committee (NGCC) she said 'is not functioning as expected', its recommendations were not taken seriously because GFPs do not have budgets and 'the unions in the committee are not empowered by their organizations to be pressure groups within government' (p. 136).

It can be seen that the politics of working on gender in government and non-government spaces was a very live issue in South Africa. Thus, perspectives on global gender equality policy we noted, were developed against a background of intense national and local engagements with the issues they raised.

Perspectives on global frameworks

In contrast to the formal recognition accorded to the MDGs in the Kenya MoE, in South Africa data from the Department of Education indicated a more reflexive form of distanced engagement with the global frameworks. This sometimes entailed a critical consideration of questions of equality, inclusion, global discussion and obligation. Among many officials, there was a sense that the MDGs were an important framework, but their implications were not of major national significance in deciding policy. A senior official in the Department said:

> . . . within senior management . . . the issues are not usually . . . discussed, but they get mentioned and the expectation, the assumption is that as a senior manager you should be aware of those issues. We do, I mean I do from time to time, bring up the discussion of the location of our work in the MDG framework. So ja, but I would say you know there should be a stronger focus than there is at the moment.
>
> (National Official 1, 07/11/2008)

Another official, when asked about the MDGs, may not have known what they were, responding 'the what?' (National Official 2, 06/11/2008). In recovering, he frankly said they had little effect on his work which was involved in monitoring teachers. For these officials distanced engagement was about distance rather than engagement.

Similarly to Kenya were data which indicated the MDGs and EFA were sometimes understood in terms of reporting. Several officials in South Africa described filling out forms linked to the MDG indicators as a mechanism for exchanging information up and down the hierarchies of government. Thus, a senior official (National Official 3, 10/11/2008) in South Africa, asked about his understanding of the MDGs, responded with a description of a report on this for consultation with the Director General (DG). Another senior central government official described attainment of the MDGs as 'obligations in terms of our membership of international bodies' and fulfilling their reporting requirements (National Official 4, 19/08/2008).

As we explore further in Chapter 6, against this engagement with the MDGs, where all that was required was documenting whether or not gender parity in NER or youth literacy had been achieved, some officials pointed to a value in the MDG targets in forcing them to disaggregate by gender. There was a sense among some that the MDGs could be used strategically to leverage action on gender equality. For many officials however, critical reflection on gender or rights was generated by frameworks other than the MDGs, even though they sometimes indicated the MDGs were the origin of their ideas. Often when officials were asked about how their work related to the MDGs, they responded describing their work, but picking up on few points of relationship with actual MDG targets or indicators. Thus, for example, an official working on assessment in the National Department was asked:

I: How do the programmes that you engage in, how do they relate to . . . the MDGs that address gender equity?
R: we particularly worked on the one of inclusion, that's our big one and that just includes everybody. And what we do find is particularly disabled children and albino children are actually shunned when they come into the schools. So that's really with Education for All – our big thing is to bring everybody into the school – whether it's a special school of a Public Ordinary School, it doesn't matter.

(National Official 5, 12/11/2008)

Here although the official was asked about the MDGs, he respond with an interpretation of EFA, that actually went considerably beyond the MDG framework with regard to inclusion. The MDGs have targets concerned with completing a cycle of primary schooling, but say very little on transforming relationships where some children may be shunned. Thus it seems the MDGs were not guiding practice, which was in fact deeper and more nuanced than the framework required.

A number of officials articulated a position of distanced engagement that was critical, but alert to possibility. They did not take the MDGs or EFA as prescriptive, but considered that international discussion was a useful resource. One senior official in the national Department, acknowledged, as other colleagues had done, how the MDGs and EFA were often associated with reporting, but went on:

> . . . people often look at that kind of data and say 'we've achieved gender parity – in a sense that those don't apply to us.' But in a way that has been the problem, because they are very generalized and they have help[ed], but now they don't help enough. Because actually what needs to be done is actually quite complex, its multi-faceted. We have to deal with really difficult issues that are not about saying we have just achieved this particular international benchmark . . .
>
> (National Official 6, 20/10/2008)

The sense here is that a clearer international steer on gender equality might be helpful to help reflect on the complexity of local problems.

In the South African Department of Education a distanced engagement with the global frameworks appears to generate a number of positions. For a majority of officials interviewed the right to education is expressed in South African policy documents on access and participation. The MDGs, in their view, do no more than give some international imprimatur to this. This is confirmed through reporting conventions upwards and sometimes reviewed in strategic planning. In this form, global relationships are considered as a form of ladder. For others, the MDG *approach*, if not the actual existing targets and indicators, suggest that broader interpretations of rights might be measured and that this could secure action globally or nationally to address this. Another version of this approach suggests that it is international collaboration which helps to better expand understanding of gender and the enactment of education rights. This is seen as the most useful possibility presented by something like the MDG or EFA project. National perspectives on their own cannot go far enough, but international thinking contributes a valuable dimension which helps to understand the problem and by implication suggest ways forward.

Province, district and school

Under the South African Constitution, provinces oversee the provision of twelve years of basic education, and early childhood care. In one South African province, we interviewed the gender focal point and senior managers in education and related programmes. Over two rounds of data collection we conducted a total of eight interviews and one focus group.

In this province in 2009 there were nearly 6,000 public schools (primary and secondary) and close to 90,000 teachers employed, mostly in rural areas. The Provincial Education Department (PED) had organised its education system into twelve geographic districts, co-ordinated by an office located at the provincial administrative headquarters in a large town. In contrast to Kenya, where at provincial level there was no particular focus on gender, here a senior manager was responsible for overseeing gender work within the schools of the province. However, although gender was her brief, neither this manager nor the deputy manager who acted as the Provincial Department Gender Focal Person (GFP) gave any overt visual representation to these roles in their offices. However, at one end of a main corridor, there was some general mention of gender-based violence. Posters about HIV were displayed with one which read 'Act against abuse: 16 days of activism, 25 November – 10 December.' Thus some selected gender issues were profiled, but there was no invocation of the MDGs or EFA.

Unlike Kenya, at district level a GFP had a post and an office. However, as we discuss in Chapter 8, her capacity to engage from this position with aspects of global gender policy was somewhat limited. Her work environment appeared to frame this symbolically. At the district offices, each staff member used their office door to represent themselves and their work to their colleagues and visitors. The GFP in the district office had stuck an A4 printed sheet of paper on the door with a heart symbol, her name, job title and the name of the section under which she fell on the district organogram. There was no mention of gender or the position she held as the GFP for the district.

In the provincial headquarters the gender manager's daily work entailed writing and reading reports, taking calls from school principals, other senior managers in the department, representatives of funding agencies, NGOs and foreign governments' development offices. One NGO visitor attended a meeting to invite the PED to collaborate on a writing project. One fieldwork day the gender manager multi-tasked, referring to reports and press clippings from the newspaper on her desk about issues such as a pregnant teenager being suspended incorrectly from a school: Unlike the provincial official in Kenya, who were dealing only with Nairobi and the districts, there was a more dynamic sense in this office of engagement with global, national and local levels of policy.

However, the interviews we conducted with provincial officers suggested that, in contrast to the distanced but critical engagement in the national department, engagement with the global frameworks (and the MDG agenda in particular) at the level of the province was largely one of managerial control rather than reflective discussion. One interviewee, for example, gave an account of the top-down process between tiers of government as they negotiated action on the global goals:

. . . they are very important in the sense that we [are] not a province in isolation to the national mandates or international mandates because it becomes the programme for implementation for all government departments. At the beginning of the year or when financial period starts, these frameworks, these new developments or areas of focus are always tabled to all government departments. Even in our own, when we have branch meetings, in which there are extended branch meetings, they are tabled. . . . Kind of like when after the state of the nation address and the report, the Premier's address, then they fall down to government departments. At the beginning of the year strategic plans are being developed [at] the level of the top management and wherever they are being developed . . .

(Province Official 1, 06/02/2009)

However, some officials suggested that, although the global goals were formally embedded in their plans, inadequate resourcing meant that the goals did not materialise in action:

we do talk about the obligations and we do know that we have a responsibility towards meeting those obligations and they do provide a framework for the policies that are implemented from National and even Provincial but the unfortunate part is that unless you have the resources to do that, they just remain on paper and for me that is the challenge. [. . .] I don't think as a department we have taken those [global processes] to implementation stage.

(Province Official 2, 04/02/2009)

For this interviewee, because strategic plans were not implementable, the global goals were merely paper goals. Another official questioned the relevance of the global frameworks, articulating the distance between aspirations of the global goals and the reality of the day to day experiences of the people in the province. She said:

We have been to those places, we took old clothes, our clothes, to give those. How do you feel when you drive your car passing? You see those people selling mangoes. How do you feel? You are busy telling people that 'no, we are addressing the millennium goals'. In what way? How do you do it?

(Province Official 3, 23/02/2009)

The school, where data were collected, was located in a peri-urban area, about 20 kilometres from a major city centre, in a neighbourhood with high levels of poverty. At the school we conducted interviews with the principal, deputy principals, teachers and parents, as well as boy and girl learners and a member of a local women's organisation. Over the two rounds of data collection we conducted a total of ten individual interviews, one group interview and one focus group.

The road from the main city to the peri-urban area passes through busy residential areas, blocks of shops, and crowded bus and taxi stops. The school was built and established in 1985 by the Department of Education and Training, the apartheid era bureaucracy that governed black education in urban areas. The school was slightly set apart from its neighbourhood. It was clustered with three other schools along a busy thoroughfare and bus route that led down to a heavily populated neighbourhood and a community hall, police station and primary health care clinic. Unlike the school in Kenya, which was quite open to the local community, this one was fenced off from the road, with a security guard at the gate. The school's external wall, facing the busy road, had a large display of the school crest and motto which is translated as 'education is the foundation'.

In the foyer of the administration block, facing the clerk's reception window, there was a photomontage of all the classes in the school, with the learners and their teacher sitting in formal rows, and some special events such as tree planting on Arbour Day. High above the reception window were glass cabinets filled with numerous trophies and awards, and a sample of the full school uniform for girls and boys. Above the entrance doorway were framed photographs of the current and past principals of the school. On the wall directly opposite the entrance was the foundation stone and a banner about the school's commitment in relation to HIV and AIDS. This display of images was a contrast to the school in Kenya, where there were no photos. These visual reference points were focussed entirely on highly local concerns. This stress on the status and history of the school continued in the principal's office. This was more spacious than that in Kenya, dominated by the principal's desk. Along the window wall, was a large school flag on a stand, a banner that depicted the school crest, vision and mission statements. In other places in the school images were more random and less formal. In the staff room the notice boards stood empty except for an occasional notice or poster from a trade union or the government's education department. On the retaining wall of the terrace above a garden area in the school grounds was a fading mural depicting a girl and boy wearing graduation outfits.

Classrooms were adequately furnished for the class size of 30–45 learners per class in the lower grades and 45–55 learners in the upper grades. Most learners had their own seat and desk area. In each classroom there was a teacher's desk, metal stationery cupboard, metal chalkboards, pin-boards for posters, a dustbin and some brooms for sweeping out the classroom at the end of every day. The classrooms were better equipped than the school in Kenya, and pupils did not have to provide their own desks. There was no library in the school and a room of computer terminals had been ransacked by thieves. A room outside the administration block was used daily as a kitchen where two female cooks, employed by the school governing body, prepared a free hot mid-morning meal. When the first break bell was rung the lower grades stopped their lessons for the learners to eat and play. Those learners wanting the free meal came with bowls, plastic plates or empty lunch boxes and lined up at the door to the kitchen to get food.

For staff and parents associated with the school, the global frameworks such as the MDGs seemed even more distant and removed from their daily lives than in the provincial department. When asked about the global goals as expressed in the MDGs, all participants talked about these as something which they knew very little about and which was mostly hearsay. The principal for example, said

> I do heard about it but I've never given my time to get an explanation about it because it's never touched [me]. I've never get the real explanation about it.
>
> (School Principal, 25/03/2008)

Mystery shrouded the MDGs which were seen as remote and lofty ideals that were spoken about in the public media, with little bearing on the things that people experience:

> . . . there is the Millennium Development Goals but where? And what the Millennium Development Goals say to whom too? You know that . . . they must come down. Don't just say when we have TV and say that there is something, that there's change what – but we don't have that change!
>
> (Teacher 1, 26/07/2010)

Here the view is that the MDGs are distant and have negligible bearing on people's lives and public institutions like schools.

The NGO research sites

We conducted research with two NGOs, one located in a large city, and net-worked with a head office in the global north. The second was in a rural area, and focused on work with women and children around literacy. In the first NGO we interviewed the country director, senior advisors as well as programme and administrative staff working at national and local levels. We also conducted interviews with staff working in a school participating in one of the NGO's education programmes. In total we conducted fourteen interviews over the two phases of data collection. In the second NGO we conducted interviews with the NGO founder, local facilitators and adult learners and children participating in the local NGO's programmes. In total we conducted seven individual interviews, one group interview and two focus groups over the two phases of data collection.

The offices for the NGO with links to a large NGO in the global north where we collected data changed over our three years of data collection. Initially this NGO was located in an upmarket business precinct close to a very affluent shopping mall. The office space was comfortable and spacious. A large poster at the reception declared a commitment to girls' education and human rights. Similar posters were displayed along the corridors. This location was very similar to that of the global NGO in Kenya, and the confident display of posters expressing commitments to gender issues and human rights was also similar to that we noted in Kenya.

With the global financial crash in 2008, reliant on donations from the North, the global NGO we were working with in South Africa, felt the ramifications of worldwide recession. Some events planned around the 16 Days of Activism Against Gender Violence and a particular computer training programme for girls were scaled down or cancelled. The office moved to cheaper accommodation in the inner-city. Here the NGO rented office space in a building owned by a large life insurance company. The staff no longer had individual work spaces and shared a single open-plan office. Framed photographs of children who received assistance replaced the large posters about gender and rights. However, this move was seen to give the NGO a closer connection to the communities it was working with. A staff member who had previously worked in the international office said:

> So where I was sitting [in the international office], you tended to be quite distant from a lot of the more on the ground work. Because the regions do quite a lot of work with the countries – who do a lot of work in communities, so you end up doing stuff for UN and MDGs but you end up not being as connected as one would like to be. I think for me it's quite nice [working in South Africa] because you do have a closer connection to the context. It's more direct because it's linking the international, regional and national. Part of my work is to make sure that we can link local to national and international.
>
> (National NGO, staff member 1, 09/12/2010)

The NGO worked with groups – mainly women – to identify needs and set up development projects. In a peri-urban area women volunteers were trained to provide home based care to HIV/AIDS patients. The NGO facilitated a group of girls between the ages of nine and fifteen to taxi into a large city for monthly ICT training, which involved discussions and reflections in a circle about their lives and school, before sitting behind computer screens, writing blogs and playing educational games. The idea was to use ICT for empowerment. This ICT project for girls was replicated in a rural setting, at some distance from the city, where the NGO has ran several projects with women's groups – producing leather shoes, art work and building a safe house for abused women. The NGO also has a number of projects working directly with a school in this community. On women's day, a national holiday in South Africa on 8 August, the NGO used the school to provide a meeting place for women from different villages to gather together in a classroom to discuss gender-based violence in their communities. Many walked a very long distance to be part of this celebration.

This NGO was very clearly connected into global networks, and many staff were familiar with and comfortable discussing the MDG framework. However, there was a sense in which the global campaigns where tailing behind the NGO:

> I think our work is already targeting aspects of the MDG's and the MDG's came along and happened. There were goals that were set, and I think the MDG's whether they were implemented or not is not necessarily going to change the way [the NGO] is focused, although, I know that there are people working on MDG's sort of policy stuff and that kind of thing. I tend to see the MDG's as a bit more of, it is a way to create more awareness, it's a potential way to get more government commitment and things like that, but I feel again it's another surface level thing . . . I think it plays out a very critical role, but if they would have to come and go they wouldn't so much affect my work.
>
> (National NGO, staff member 2, 23/07/2009)

The MDGs were thus seen as a useful mechanism in leveraging government action, but were not viewed as playing a significant role in shaping the organization's own work or priorities.

The second NGO focused on supporting local literacy initiatives and providing reading materials in rural areas. It was directed by a white South African woman, whose office was in her home in an affluent suburb, some considerable distance from the work of the project. The NGO had an office in a small town about 40 kilometres from the villages where the literacy work took place. Here the village-based facilitators sometime met the NGO staff. During the time of data collection the NGO was going through an evaluation in order to respond to some of the concerns of funders who comprised both local donors, and, as in the Kenya rural NGO, some located overseas. The NGO had worked, since its inception in 2000, in two villages that were some distance from the town. These were a slow 45-minute drive off the main road along a gravel road, through commercial farms, past a mission station and a government hospital. Goats grazed near the roadside and cattle wandered in the many fallow fields. There were also donkeys, chickens and sheep. People walked along the road, stopping to exchange greetings with neighbours or shielding themselves from the dust of passing vehicles.

On either side of the mountain road homesteads were crowded in by spreading thickets of trees. Although the woods were a ready source of fuel, the trees were depleting the underground water. In the past villagers had been able to feed themselves from their own plots. However now few homestead yards had fields of crops. Most homesteads were fenced off. They comprised several thatched huts, perhaps an animal enclosure, pit latrine, and granary, and sometimes a vegetable patch. A few homesteads also had square buildings in addition to the traditional round huts. The economy of the village centred on the state grants -child support, pension and disability grants – and the trickle of earnings from family members who had found jobs in towns and cities. Most adult villagers were unemployed. On grant pay-day grantees took minibus taxis to the nearest payout point about 10 kilometres away. There was a primary school offering grades 1 to 7 to children. From mid-afternoon adult basic education classes were run from the primary school. Not far away was a crèche which worked in partnership with the school to offer a Grade R (pre-school) class. A mobile clinic visited the village every one or two weeks.

The villages were more connected than those in the research site in Kenya. The cellular phone network operators' signals reached the mountains so that many adult villagers had their own mobile phones even though they had no electricity at home. There was also television reception and families with TVs powered their sets off bulky car batteries. Some boys worked in afternoons carrying batteries to a workshop where a man ran a business connecting o the national grid to recharge batteries.

The NGO employed a facilitator, who had been born and lived her whole life in the village among the women attending the literacy class. But she stood out from them in several ways. Although she was a young unmarried single parent, she held status as the educated daughter of the village headman, busy with postgraduate studies through a distance-learning university. Her work within the NGO had enabled her to travel and attend conferences in Africa, Europe and North America, opportunities the Kenya NGO workers had not had.

The NGO had a reading centre with shelves filled with books sorted by language and reading level. Above some of the shelves there were posters advocating literacy and giving information about HIV and AIDS. Photographs of events organised by the NGO were displayed. We observed sessions the NGO ran. One was for women to borrow books. A story session was held with children aged five to eight after school. A discussion group with fourteen girls mostly from grades 5 and 7 also took place after school. This session was about virginity and the dangers of becoming sexually active in the context of the HIV and AIDS epidemic. The girls were given a large seed and plant bag and told to plant the seed when they were home as a symbol of their aspirations, which would flourish as would their health if they retained their virginity. After a quick quiz about how HIV was spread, the girls knelt on the floor, using their chair seats as a desk. They all wrote sentences about their future actions on sheets of paper.

Although one of the facilitators had represented the NGO at a number of international meetings the global policy frameworks of the MDGs or EFA were either something they had heard of very generally or not at all. Most of the six village-based facilitators who participated in a focus group discussion (05/06/2009) had only heard of the global goals by name and did not know what they meant. Village-based NGO officials reluctantly recognised that gender equality was a legal right in the national Constitution (I, 05/06/2009), and that there were policies governing these rights in schools. A village facilitator said: 'the NGO never talks about the global goals' (Local NGO, staff member 1, 03/06/2009).

Reflections on researching terrains of a middle space in South Africa

This chapter has provided some of the political, economic and education context in South Africa at the time we collected data, drawing out some of the ways in which national and global gender equality policy was being or not being addressed in the research sites. It can be seen that, in contrast to Kenya, there was a designated office and work stream associated with gender in the formal institutional space of the Department of Education at national, provincial and district level. But only in the national Department was this seen as a space of critical engagement with global gender equality agendas. In the other locations the global policy frameworks were viewed as directives passed down a line of command. The space of the public sphere was documented in the national Department of Education and as a central feature of the work of the globally linked NGO, but was less evidently part of the texture of work at the provincial, district and school level, or in the rural NGO. Professional organisations of teachers were key partners to the work of the national, provincial and district level bureaucracy, and were evident in the daily life of teachers at the school, but did not seem to be connected to the work of the NGOs. NGOs and CBOs were connected with the work of the national and provincial department, but more in terms of service delivery than critical engagement. This was also their relationship with the rural and poor urban communities they worked with. However, the global NGO did organise discussions around women's rights and violence, in contrast to the rural NGO, with its stress on girls protecting their virginity.

These relationships in the terrains of a middle space help explain some of the engagements and distance from the global gender equality policy agenda of EFA and the MDGs. Our data indicate how the terrains of a middle space in South Africa are very different, depending on whether they were located in urban areas close to centres of power, or in rural or peri-urban areas marked by particular forms of poverty associated with climate, lack of food, housing, employment, distance and dependence on social grants. Grants were an important feature of a link with central government. It can be seen that, with the exception of some individuals in the national, provincial and district offices of the Department of Education and in the international NGO, for others we interviewed connections between gender equality, poverty and education, was not a strong or well recognised discourse. In Part 2 of the book we draw further on this data to explore how particular facets of global policy on gender, education and poverty was negotiated, interpreted and enacted in all the research sites. Some of the ways in which the terrains of a middle space textured these relationships will be considered.

References

Aikman, S., Unterhalter, U., & Boler, T. (2008). *Gender Equality, HIV, and AIDS: A Challenge for the Education Sector*, Oxford: Oxfam, GB.

Alden, C., & Le Pere, G. (2004). South Africa's post-apartheid foreign policy: From reconciliation to ambiguity? *Review of African Political Economy*, 31(100), pp. 283–297.

Alden, C., & Schoeman, M. (2015). Reconstructing South African identity through global summitry. *Global Summitry*, 1(2), pp. 187–204.

Alexander, N. (1990). *Education and the struggle for national liberation in South Africa*. Sea Point: Skotaville Publishers.

Allais, S. (2016). Towards measuring the economic value of higher education: Lessons from South Africa. *Comparative Education*, 1–17.

Andrews, P. (2016). *From Cape Town to Kabul: Rethinking Strategies for Pursuing Women's Human Rights*. Abingdon: Routledge.

Archer, D., & Boler, T. (2008). *The Politics of Prevention: A Global Crisis in AIDS and Education*. London: Pluto Press.

Ashman, S., Fine, B., & Newman, S. (2010). The developmental state and post-liberation South Africa. In Misra-Dexter, N. and February, J. eds. *Testing Democracy: Which Way Is South Africa Going?* Cape Town: ABC Press for Institute for a Democratic South Africa, pp. 23–45.

Badat, S., & Sayed, Y. (2014). Post-1994 South African education: The challenge of social justice. *The Annals of the American Academy of Political and Social Science*, 652(1), pp. 127–148.

Balfour, R. (2015). *Education in a New South Africa*. Cambridge: Cambridge University Press.

Ballard, R., Habib, A., & Valodia, I. (2006). *Voices of Protest: Social Movements in Post-Aparthied South Africa*. Pietermaritzburg: University of KwaZulu-Natal Press.

Beall, J. (1998). Trickle-down or rising tide? Lessons on mainstreaming gender policy from Colombia and South Africa. *Social Policy and Administration: An International Journal of Policy and Research*, 32(5), pp. 513–534.

Bennett, J. (2010). Connections to research: The Southern African network of higher education institutions challenging sexual harassment/sexual violence. In Armfred, S. and Adamako, A. eds. *African Feminist Politics of Knowledge: Tensions, Challenges, Possibilities*. Uppsala: Nordiska Afrikainstitutet.

Bennett, J., Boswell, B., Hinds, T., Metcalfe, J., & Nganga, I. K. (2016). Activist leadership and questions of sexuality with young women: A South African story. *Feminist Formations*, 28(2), pp. 27–50.

Beresford, A. (2016). *South Africa's Political Crisis: Unfinished Liberation and Fractured Class Struggles*. London: Palgrave.

Bhana, D. (2007). The price of innocence: Teachers, gender, childhood sexuality, HIV and AIDS in early schooling. *International Journal of Inclusive Education*, 11(4), pp. 431–444.

Bhana, D., Morrell, R., Hearn, J., & Moletsane, R. (2007). Power and identity: An introduction to sexualities in Southern Africa. *Sexualities*, 10(2), pp. 131–139.

Bhana, D., Morrell, R., Shefer, T., & Ngabaza, S. (2010). South African teachers' responses to teenage pregnancy and teenage mothers in schools. *Culture, Health & Sexuality*, 12(8), pp. 871–883.

Bhorat, H., Hirsch, A., Kanbur, R., & Ncube, M. (Eds.). (2014). *The Oxford Companion to the Economics of South Africa*. Oxford: Oxford University Press.

Black, D. R., & Hornsby, D. J. (2016). South Africa's bilateral relationships in the evolving foreign policy of an emerging middle power. *Commonwealth & Comparative Politics*, 54(2), pp. 151–160.

Branson, N., Hofmeyr, C., & Lam, D. (2014). Progress through school and the determinants of school dropout in South Africa. *Development Southern Africa*, 31(1), pp. 106–126.

Britton, H. E., Fish, J. N., & Meintjes, S. (2009). *Women's Activism in South Africa: Working across Divides*. Durban: University of KwaZulu-Natal Press.

Byrne, D. (2016). "Stealing the fire": Language as theme and strategy in South African women's poetry. *Scrutiny2*, 21(2), pp. 27–43.

Campbell, C., & MacPhail, C. (2002). Peer education, gender and the development of critical consciousness: Participatory HIV prevention by South African youth. *Social Science & Medicine*, 55(2), pp. 331–345.

Chisholm, L. (2004). *Changing Class: Education and Social Change in Post-Apartheid South Africa*. Pretoria: Human Science Research Council.

Chisholm, L., & Napo, V. (1999). State and bureaucracy: Symbolic access? *Agenda: Empowering Women for Gender Equity*, 15(41), pp. 32–37.

Chisholm, L., & September, J. (2005). *Gender Equity in South African Education 1994–2004: Perspectives from Research, Government and Unions: Conference Proceedings*. Pretoria: HSRC Press.

Clark, N. L., & Worger, W. H. (2016). *South Africa: The Rise and Fall of Apartheid*. Abingdon: Routledge.

Coombe, C. (2001). HIV/AIDS and Trauma among Learners: Sexual Violence and Deprivation in South Africa. In Maree, J. G. and Ebersöhn, L. eds. *Lifeskills within the Caring Professions*. Cape Town: Heinemann, pp. 1–18.

Deegan, H. (2011). *Politics South Africa*. Abingdon: Routledge.

Feisch, B., Shindler, J., & Perry, H. (2012). Who is out of school? Evidence from the statistic: South Africa community survey. *International Journal of Educational Development*, 32(4), pp. 529–536.

Fester, G. (2014). South Africa: Revolution protracted or postponed? In *Voicing Demands: Feminists' Reflections on Strategies, Negotiations and Influence*. London: ZED Books.

Fiske, E. B., & Ladd, H. F. (2004). *Elusive Equity: Education Reform in Post-Apartheid South Africa*. Washington: Brookings Institution Press.

Fleisch, B. (2010). The politics of the governed: South African Democratic Teachers' Union Soweto Strike, June 2009. *Southern African Review of Education with Education with Production*, 16(2), pp. 117–131.

Fleisch, B., & Shindler, J. (2009). 'School participation from birth-to-twenty: Pattern of schooling in an urban child cohort study in South Africa.' Paper prepared for UKFIET Conference, Oxford University, September 2007.

Gouws, A. (2005). *(Un)thinking Citizenship: Feminist Debates in Contemporary South Africa*. Aldershot, UK: Ashgate Publishing.

Gouws, A. (2014). Recognition and redistribution: State of the women's movement in South Africa 20 years after democratic transition. *Agenda*, 28(2), pp. 19–32.

Gouws, A. (2016). Women's activism around gender-based violence in South Africa: Recognition, redistribution and representation. *Review of African Political Economy*, 43(149), pp. 400–415.

Gouws, A., & Hassim, S. (2014). Who's afraid of feminism? *South African Democracy at 20: An Introduction*, 28(2), pp. 4–6.

Grant, M. J., & Hallman, K. K. (2008). Pregnancy-related school dropout and prior school performance in KwaZulu-Natal, South Africa. *Studies in Family Planning*, 369–382.

Gunne, S. (2014). *Space, Place, and Gendered Violence in South African Writing*. London: Palgrave.

Habib, A. (2009). South Africa's foreign policy: Hegemonic aspirations, neoliberal orientations and global transformation. *South African Journal of International Affairs*, 16(2), pp. 143–159.

Habib, A. (2013). *South Africa's Suspended Revolution: Hopes and Prospects*. Johannesburg: Witwatersrand University Press.

Hall, K., & Sambu, W. (2016). Income poverty, unemployment and social grants. In *ChildGauge*. University of Cape Town, pp. 111–116. http://www.ci.org.za/depts/ci/pubs/pdf/general/gauge2013/Gauge2013ChildrenCountIncomePoverty.pdf

Hargreaves, J., & Boler, T. (2009). Girls' education and vulnerability to HIV infection in Africa. In Aikman, S., Unterhalter, E. and Boler, T. eds. *Gender Equality, HIV, and AIDS: A Challenge for the Education Sector*. Oxford: Oxfam, pp. 33–44.

Hargreaves, J., Morison, J., Kim, C., Bonell, J., Porter, C., Watts, J., Busza, G., Phetla, & Pronyk, P. M. (2008). The association between school attendance, HIV infection and sexual behaviour among young people in rural South Africa. *Journal of Epidemiology and Community Health*, 62(2), pp. 113–119.

Harrison, A., Hoffman, S., Mantell, J. E., Smit, J. A., Leu, C. S., Exner, T. M., & Stein, Z. A. (2016). Gender-focused HIV and pregnancy prevention for school-going adolescents: The Mpondombili pilot intervention in KwaZulu-Natal, South Africa. *Journal of HIV/AIDS & Social Services*, 15(1), pp. 29–47.

Hart, G. P. (2002). *Disabling Globalization: Places of Power in Post-Apartheid South Africa*. Berkeley: University of California Press.

Hart, G. P. (2014). *Rethinking the South African Crisis: Nationalism, Populism, Hegemony*. Atlanta: University of Georgia Press.

Hassim, S. (2003). Representation participation and democratic effectiveness: Feminist challenges to representative democracy in South Africa. In Goetz, A. and Hassim, S. eds. *No Shortcuts to Power: African Women in Politics and Policy Making*. London: Zed, pp. 81–109.

Hassim, S. (2006). *Women's Organizations and Democracy in South Africa: Contesting Authority*. Madison: University of Wisconsin Press.

Hassim, S. (2014). Violent modernity: Gender, race and bodies in contemporary South African politics. *Politikon*, 41(2), pp. 167–182.

Hassim, S., & Gouws, A. (1998). Redefining the public space: Women's organisations, gender consciousness and civil society in South Africa. *Politikon: South African Journal of Political Studies*, 25(2), pp. 53–76.

Hick, J., & Myeni, S. (2016). The impact of gender, race and class on women's political participation in South Africa. In Shaw, M. and Mayo, M. eds. *Class Inequality and Community Development*. Bristol: Policy Press, pp. 107–120.

Human Rights Watch (2001). *Scared at School – Sexual Violence against Girls in South African Schools*. [online]. Available at www.hrw.org/reports/2001/safrica/

Jansen, J. D., & Christie, P. (1999). *Changing Curriculum: Studies on Outcomes-Based Education in South Africa*. Johannesburg: Juta.

Jansen, J. D., & Sayed, Y. (2001). *Implementing Education Policies: The South African Experience*. Johannesburg: Juta.

Kallaway, P. (1984). *Apartheid and Education: The Education of Black South Africans*. Johannesburg: Ravan Press.

Kuumba, M. B. (2009). You've Struck a Rock comparing gender, social movements, and transformation in the United States and South Africa. *Gender & Society*, 16(4), pp. 504–523.

Lodge, T. (1983). *Black Politics in South Africa since 1945*. London: Longman.

Manicom, L. (2005). Constituting "women" as citizens: Ambiguities in the making of gendered political subjects in post-apartheid South Africa. In *(Un)thinking Citizenship: Feminist Debates in Contemporary South Africa*. Aldershot, UK: Ashgate Publishing, pp. 21–54.

Mannah, S. (2005). The state of mobilisation of women teachers in the South African Democratic Teachers' Union. In Chisholm, L. and September, eds. *Gender Equity in South African Education 1994–2004: Perspectives from Research, Government and Unions: Conference Proceedings*. Pretoria: HSRC Press, pp. 146–155.

Martineau, R. (1997). Women and education in South Africa: Factors influencing women's educational progress and their entry into traditionally male-dominated fields. *The Journal of Negro Education*, 66(4), pp. 383–395.

Mbali, M. (2013). *South African AIDS Activism and Global Health Politics*. London: Palgrave.

Mbembe, A. (2016). Decolonizing the university. *Arts and Humanities in Higher Education*, 15(1), pp. 29–45.

McLennan, A. (2000). *Education Governance and Management in South Africa*. University of Liverpool.

Moletsane, R. (2014). *The Need for Quality Sexual and Reproductive Health Education to Address Barriers to Girls' Educational Outcome in South Africa*. Washington: Center for Universal Education at Brookings.

Moletsane, R., Mitchell, C., & Lewin, T. (2015). Gender violence, teenage pregnancy and gender equity policy in South Africa. In Parkes, J. ed. *Gender Violence in Poverty Contexts: The Educational Challenge*. Abingdon: Routledge, pp. 183–196.

Morrell, R., Epstein, D., Unterhalter, E., Bhana, D., & Moletsane, R. (2009). *Towards Gender Equality? South African Schools During the HIV/AIDS Epidemic*. Pietermaritzburg: University of KwaZulu-Natal Press.

Morrell, R., Jewkes, R., & Lindegger, G. (2012). Hegemonic masculinity/masculinities in South Africa: Culture, power, and gender politics. *Men and Masculinities*, 15(1), pp. 11–30.

Morrell, R., & Moletsane, R. (2002). Inequality and fear: Learning and working inside Bantu Education schools. In Kallaway, P. ed. *The History of Education under Apartheid, 1948–1994*. Cape Town: Pearson Education, pp. 224–242.

Motala, E., & Pampallis, J. (Eds.). (2002). *The State, Education and Equity in Post-Apartheid South Africa: The Impact of State Policies*. Aldershot: Ashgate.

Motala, S. (2003). 'Literature review on equity.' Written for EPC Research Project, Investigating Governance and Equity in the South African Schools Act at School Level within the Context of Democracy, Social Justice, and Human Rights.

Mwabu, G., & Schultz, T. P. (2000). Wage premiums for education and location of South African workers, by gender and race. *Economic Development and Cultural Change*, 48(2), pp. 307–334.

Nkomo, M. (1990). *Pedagogy of Domination: Toward a Democratic Education in South Africa*. Trenton, NJ: Africa World Press.

Ngcobo, N. (2015). The use of film as an intervention in addressing gender violence: Experiences in a South African secondary school. *Agenda*, 29(3), pp. 32–41.

O'Manique, C., & Fourie, P. (2016). Gender justice and the Millennium Development Goals: Canada and South Africa considered. *Politikon*, 43(1), pp. 97–116.

Panday, S., Makiwane, M., Ranchod, C., & Letsoalo, T. (2009). *Teenage Pregnancy in South Africa: With a Specific Focus on School-Going Learners*. Pretoria: Department of Basic Education.

Perry, H., & Fleisch, B. (2006). Gender and educational achievement in South Africa. In Reddy, V. ed. *Marking Matric: Colloquium Proceedings*. Cape Town: HSRC Press, pp. 107–126.

Poku, N. K., & Whiteside, A. (2004). *The political economy of AIDS in Africa*. Aldershot: Ashgate Publishing.

Posel, D. (2004). 'Getting the nation talking about sex': Reflections on the discursive constitution of sexuality in South Africa since 1994. *Agenda*, 18(62), pp. 53–63.

Posel, D. (2005). Sex, death and the fate of the nation: Reflections on the politicization of sexuality in post-Apartheid South. *Africa*, 75(2), pp. 125–153.

Posel, D., & Simpson, G. (Eds.). (2002). *Commissioning the Past: Understanding South Africa's Truth and Reconciliation Commission*. Johannesburg: Witwatersrand University Press.

Presidency: Republic of South Africa (2008). *Development Indicators 2008, Policy Coordination and Advisory Services (PCAS) in The Presidency* [online]. Available at www.info.gov.za/view/DownloadFileAction?id=84952

Ramagoshi, M. (2004). National department of education initiatives. In Chisholm, L. and September, J. (eds.) (2005). *Gender Equity in South African Education*

1994–2004: Perspectives from Research, Government and Unions: Conference Proceedings. Pretoria: HSRC Press.

Rao, A., Sandler, J., Kelleher, D., & Miller, C. (2015). *Gender at Work: Theory and Practice for 21st Century Organizations*. London: Routledge.

Reddy, S. P., Panday, S., Swart, D., Jinabhai, C. C., Amosun, S. L., James, S., Monyeki, K. D., Stevens, G., Morejele, N., Kambaran, N. S., Omardien, R. G., & Van den Borne, H. W. (2003). *Umthente Uhlaba Usamila – The South African Youth Risk Behaviour Survey 2002*. Cape Town: Department of Health.

Republic of South Africa, Department of Education (1999). *The National Policy on HIV/AIDS for Learners and Educators*. Pretoria: Department of Education, Republic of South Africa.

Republic of South Africa, Department of Education (2008). *Guidelines for the Prevention and Management of Sexual Violence and Harassment in Public Schools*. Pretoria: Department of Education, Republic of South Africa.

Republic of South Africa, The Office on the Status of Women (2000). *South Africa's National Policy Framework for Women's Empowerment and Gender Equality*. Pretoria: The Office on the Status of Women, The Office of the Presidency, Republic of South Africa.

Robins, S. (2008). *From Revolution to Rights in South Africa: Social Movements, NGOs and Popular Politics after Apartheid*. Pietermaritzburg: University of KwaZulu-Natal Press.

Seekings, J., & Nattrass, N. (2015). *Policy, Politics and Poverty in South Africa*. Dordrecht: Springer.

Shefer, T., Bhana, D., & Morrell, R. (2013). Teenage pregnancy and parenting at school in contemporary South African contexts: Deconstructing school narratives and understanding policy implementation. *Perspectives in Education*, 31(1), pp. 1–10.

Southall, R. (2016). *The New Black Middle Class in South Africa*. Auckland Park: Jacana.

Spaull, N. (2013). Poverty & privilege: Primary school inequality in South Africa. *International Journal of Educational Development*, 33(5), pp. 436–447.

Spreen, C. A. (2004). Appropriating borrowed policies: Outcomes-based education in South Africa. In Steiner-Khamsi, G. ed. *The Global Politics of Educational Borrowing and Lending*. New York: Columbia University Press, pp. 101–113.

Steiner, H. J., Alston, P., & Goodman, R. (2008). *International Human Rights in Context: Law, Politics, Morals: Text and Materials*. New York: Oxford University Press.

Steyn, M. (1998). A new agenda: Restructuring feminism in South Africa. *Women's Studies International Forum*, 21(1), pp. 41–52.

Suttner, R. (2015). *Recovering Democracy in South Africa*. Johannesburg: Jacana Media.

Truscott, K. (1993). *Gender in Education*. Johannesburg: EPU WITS/NECC.

Tutu, D. (1999). *No Future without Forgiveness: A Personal Overview of South Africa's Truth and Reconciliation Commission*. New York: Random House.

Unterhalter, E. (1991a). Can Education Overcome Women's Subordinate Position in the Occupation Structure? In Unterhalter, E., Wolpe, H. and Botha, T. eds. *Education in a Future South Africa: Policy Issues for Transformation*. London: Macmillan, pp. 65–84.

Unterhalter, E. (1991b). Changing aspects of reformism in Bantu Education, 1953–1989. In Unterhalter, E., et al. eds. *Apartheid Education and Popular Struggles*. Johannesburg; Ravan, pp. 35–72.

Unterhalter, E. (1999). The schooling of South African girls: Statistics, stories, and strategies. In Bunwaree, S. and Heward, C. eds. *Gender, Education and Development*. London: Zed, pp. 49–64.

Unterhalter, E., & Wolpe, H. (1991). Introduction: Reproduction, reform and transformation: Approaches to the analysis of education in South Africa. In *Apartheid Education and Popular Struggles*. Johannesburg: Ravan Press, pp. 1–18.

Van der Berg, S. (2008). How effective are poor schools? Poverty and educational outcomes in South Africa. *Studies in Educational Evaluation*, 34(3), pp. 145–154.

Waylen, G. (2007). *Engendering Transitions: Women's Mobilization, Institutions and Gender Outcomes*. Oxford: Oxford University Press.

Wilson, A. (2013). Feminism in the space of the world social forum. *Journal of International Women's Studies*, 8(3), pp. 10–27.

Wilson, R. (2001). *The Politics of Truth and Reconciliation in South Africa: Legitimizing the Post-Apartheid State*. Cambridge: Cambridge University Press.

Wolpe, A. (2005). Reflections on the gender equity task team. In Chisholm, L. and September, J. eds. *Gender Equity in South African Education 1994–2004: Perspectives from Research, Government and Unions: Conference Proceedings*. Pretoria: HSRC Press, pp. 119–132.

Wolpe, A., Quinlan, O., & Martinez, L. (1997). *Gender Equity in Education: A Report by the Gender Equity Task Team*. Pretoria: Department of Education.

Part 2

In the first Part of the book we provided background on our three research settings in global organisations, Kenya and South Africa, and gave some detail of our approach to data collection and the range of perspectives participants developed on the MDGs. In Part 2 we look across all the differently located research sites examining how global policy was negotiated, refused and some of the practices that resulted. Chapter 6 looks at how the meanings of gender equality and education changed shape in different locales, and how the terrains of a middle space had a bearing on which interpretations were selected and acted on. Chapter 7 considers ideas about poverty and how blame and disconnection from the lives of the poor featured in some ideas and actions about implementing global policy, reflecting on the implications of different settings for these iterations. Chapter 8 investigates gender mainstreaming and considers how some of the approaches outlined at the Beijing Conference came to be seen or resisted.

6 People and policies
Negotiating meanings of gender in education

Gender is not a simple concept. Interpreting gender as a feature of work on global policy, education and poverty takes many forms. These interpretations are partly shaped by, and, in their turn, condition, the terrains of a middle space we have distinguished. These overlap in international organisations and in the two national settings of Kenya and South Africa where we collected data. Thus many meanings of gender, poverty and education are in play. However, as we show in more detail in this chapter, the most widespread ideas are those that do least to call into question the power relations associated with inequalities. Sometimes this process is linked with pragmatism, sometimes with a sense of procedural fairness and doing the same by every girl and boy. Sometimes procedural fairness is supplemented with a particular notion of affirmative action for a homogenised group of girls, conceived largely in terms of deficits. The relational notion of gender, or the concept of what gender does or dreams is much less used than the descriptive term. Often gender is used to mean girls. For some of the groups we held discussions with their portrayal of girls is linked with hostilities. These can be expressed in a sense of girls competing against boys or a demonisation of young women's sexuality. What emerges from this analysis of how gender as a concept is used in different terrains of a middle space is how difficult it is, for the groups of practitioners positioned on these terrains, to hold together a coherent and reflexive set of ideas that connect gender, the right to education and addressing intersecting inequalities. An emphasis on what gender is, does not seem to sit easily with ideas of what the concept of gender does, or where aspirations around gender might lead.

These different meanings of gender and the relationships they illuminate are located in institutional, professional, civil society and public sphere terrains of a middle space where speaking, listening, reflecting, connecting and acting are sometimes possible, but sometimes thwarted or difficult. Examining these nuances allows us to consider some of the debates around defining rights, obligations, intersection and connecting between global, national and local. We try to map how and why discussion around gender resolves in particular directions, and what additional resources of time, education and experience, and amplifications of the terrain of a middle space might be needed to deepen these reflections.

Global goals and national reflections

The MDG policy text with its focus on targets stressed gender parity – equal numbers of girls and boys in school – as a key objective. While the Dakar Framework had a looser notion of gender equality in education, it was the tight focus of the MDGs on parity that took centre stage in much of the work on monitoring conducted through education institutions or in NGOs. Some discussion of policy transfer has suggested that policy makers or officials in national bureaucracies adopted gender parity as a policy directive because of the authority of these frameworks (Keddie and Mills, 2009; Fukuda-Parr, 2014; Khalema, Andrews and N'Dri, 2015). The data we collected suggests a more engaged and critical discussion of the concept in some sites, often linked with a pragmatism or a local strategic engagement.

For a number of practitioners located in multilateral and national institutions, with some taking a leadership role in international civil society organisations concerned with education (as discussed in Chapter 3), gender parity was seen as useful but limited. Policy officers working in international agencies based in the global North, many of whom had direct access to high level global policy meetings, voiced critiques of the narrow focus on parity, often linked simply to access for education, which

> . . . has skewed the way we look at education . . . and the whole box of teaching and learning and what actually happens in school has somehow got lost in this ten years of push for access.
> (Bilateral agency 1, staff member, 28/01/2009)

Gender parity was seen to be part of this 'skewing'. Despite this recognition of the limits of gender parity as a concept, it could not be separated from the MDG framework as a whole, and this was viewed as strategically important. Thus, for a number of employees of global organisations negotiation around the concept of gender parity is simultaneously critical and pragmatic.

But the strategic pragmatism these policy officers in global organisations expressed about the concept of gender parity and the access it gave to action took a different form in other terrains of a middle space in Kenya and South Africa where officials in education institutions or NGO workers engaged with global policy. We distinguish three threads in how the idea of gender parity, linked with the MDG and EFA agenda, was engaged with. In addition, we outline two ways in which ideas about gender parity were refused.

Firstly, in complying with the policy text regarding gender parity, we have instances of a neutral interpretation, where monitoring of gender parity in education associated with the MDGs was a form of practice passed up and down a ladder of global, national and local reporting. Secondly, we document an extending form of engagement, where the reporting required by the MDGs was seen by some officials located in education bureaucracies as opening the door to understanding national dimensions of what gender inequality or poverty may entail.

While this practice did not question the notion of gender parity, it did reposition how the form of the ladder connecting global, national and local was viewed. In this form, global frameworks, as exemplified by the MDGs, always had to be understood in relation to national policies, which were pre-eminent. In some cases this was associated with a tactical engagement with the notion of gender parity similar to the stance taken by some of the employees of international organisations described in Chapter 3, whereby the reporting required by the MDGs was seen by some officials and some NGO workers, (particularly those linked to global networks), as opening windows to the weather systems of wider global debates and mobilisation around violence against women, sexual and reproductive rights, or challenging existing hierarchies. In a third kind of response, seen in all our research sites, there was a sense that gender parity required a form of practice, which entailed an equal presence of numbers of girls and boys. We have termed this interpretation of gender parity a form of procedural fairness. For some this was seen as useful, in making a broader gender equality agenda possible, but for others this approach was viewed as failing to grasp the nature of inequalities. A fourth approach we distinguish is one where a salience for gender is ignored, either by insisting gender is linked with other forms of social division, or by arguing that gender difference is more appropriate than gender equalities. A fifth strand in the discussion suggests that gender concerns privileged girls and ignored the needs of boys. In this strand of discussion, particular homogenised identities are attributed to both groups.

Monitoring gender parity in education: a neutral stance

The first type of engagement with gender parity as framed in the texts of the MDGs and EFA is a generally neutral response which complies with the surface meanings of monitoring numbers of girls and boys accessing and progressing through school. In South Africa and Kenya, for many education officials employed by the government, gender parity was a useful way to manage data and reporting upwards from the provincial level to national and global level structures. The simplicity of the notion provided a clear specification of what was needed. For these officials, gender parity was a transparent comparative technique for monitoring work. Some South African officials described filling out forms linked to the MDG indicators as a mechanism for exchanging information across tiers of government reaching up to international forums. Thus, a senior official (South Africa National Official 3, 10/11/2008), described looking at a report on gender parity for consultation with the DG, while a provincial official described being required to make a ten-year report using MDG gender parity indicators. Another provincial official described work on the strategic plan of the department requiring review of the MDG indicators of access, particularly with regard to gender and enrolment. A senior central government official described attainment of the MDGs as 'obligations in terms of our membership of international bodies' and fulfilling their reporting requirements (South Africa National

Official 4, 19/08/2008). For all these officials, their responses were bureaucratic rather than political. Gender parity was a neutral mechanism of exchanging information which helped monitor who was where in the education system, and this was what global policy required. This view was echoed in the Kenyan national Ministry of Education, although here the sense of reporting was not neutral about passing information between tiers of government, but of enacting some kind of accountability up and down the rungs of the ladder from global down to local.

> Let me say, those goals and MDGs, they are very good because . . . these goals keep the government and NGOs, all of us, on our toes. If we had no goals, we would go back and be in our own comfort and pretend everything is OK.
>
> (Kenya National Official 1, 21/05/2008)

This official expresses the view that the monitoring brings Kenya into a sphere of global shared enterprise to improve education provision. Implicitly monitoring is thus beneficial.

Extending engagements through gender parity: reviewing gender and women's rights issues in national contexts

A second way in which the gender parity requirements of the MDGs were interpreted was not a simple neutral activity of monitoring. For a group of actors the gender parity stipulations in the MDGs and EFA frameworks prompted national reflections on a number of issues concerning the nature of gender inequalities and how to address these. This view was voiced particularly by officials working on the terrain of institutional space in South Africa and Kenya. For them the presence of gender parity in the MDG framework could help open further interrogation of questions of gender or distribution of resources to attend with inequalities in national settings.

> It forces us to think about it. . . . From the meetings I have attended, gender is always a big thing. Gender in South Africa – in the education sphere – we may not have foregrounded it as much as international organisations have done . . .
>
> (South Africa, National Official 8, 19/08/2009)

What [I] like about the EFA, the MDG and other international commitments is that they give us something to work towards. For example, when you talk of this near gender parity at the national level. . . . We talk about the regional disparities, and then the government is able to address those regional disparities. I talked about the distribution of sanitary towels towards the needy girls. That is already a case showing that there are girls who are disadvantaged in term of performance or participating in the school activities because of biological functions. So they give us something to benchmark, they give us something to work towards, and they give us a hope. And they tell us where we are. Because without them we would just be process oriented. We [instruct officials that we] expect to have this result by this time, by this year. And they give us reports on a yearly basis.

(Kenya, National Official 7, 02/04/2009)

For both these officials, the gender parity targets in the MDGs framework were a means through which other issues they considered connected with gender could be exposed and leveraged. While they are working within the ambit of global and national policy organised as a ladder, the global policy concerns were reviewed from a national set of steps on the ladder and, for some, this opened some new discussion, while for others it merely confirms some existing policies. A senior official in the Kenyan Ministry spelled this out:

. . . the Ministry is doing much more than that – the gender policy – because they are many things that the Ministry is doing to coordinate the MDGs. But you may not say he is addressing the MDGs. Because when we are addressing poverty and we are providing Free Primary Education that is MDG. When we are moving towards parity and we want to have parity in enrolment the Ministry from the top is addressing the MDGs. But the children may not know that the Ministry is addressing the MDG, parents may not also know. When we are fighting HIV/AIDS and we are reducing malaria improving sanitation from the Ministry point of view we are addressing it, And we are even providing the facilities to the school like toilets, piped water and advising them to wash their hands that is actually MDG . . .

(Kenya, National Official 8, 17/10/2008)

Here, gender is associated with parity in enrolments and poverty reduction with FPE. The government is responding to a global agenda, but on its own terms, and the global rungs of the ladder are not considered appropriate for the government to discuss with parents or communities.

The ways in which gender equality could be linked with the right to education gave officials, who were interested in these connections, some purchase on the nexus of gender inequality, poverty and education. Although the frame of reference for work on this tended to be national, rather than global, sometimes the MDGs and other currents from the global women's movement were referred to. This extended, more strategic, engagement with the global policy frame was much more evident amongst South African education officials than those in Kenya, and more articulated by the international civil society organisations in both countries than in the local civil society.

For a majority of officials in the South African Department of Education the right to education is expressed in South African policy documents on access and participation and the MDGs do no more than give some international imprimatur to this, confirmed through reporting conventions, and sometimes reviewed in strategic planning. However, for some, the MDG *approach*, if not the actual existing targets and indicators, suggest that it is possible that a broader interpretations of rights, taking in gendered experiences at school, violence or discrimination, might be measured. This approach to measurement is seen to be a useful strategy to help deepen an engagement with equality, raising issues concerning women's rights. Another version of this, expressed by some South African officials, suggests that it is international collaboration, and exposure to the gusts of debate around gender, which helps to better expand understanding of gender equality and the enactment of education rights. This is seen as the most useful possibility presented by the MDG or EFA project. National perspectives on their own cannot go far enough, but international thinking contributes a valuable dimension which helps to understand the problem and by implication suggest ways forward.

A handful of officials working on the institutional terrain of the South African Department of Education, many of whom had a concern with gender issues as part of their work or background experience, believed they could use the gender parity clauses of the MDGs to help effect action. For them, this was not a distanced engagement, but a very active appropriation of the framework. The MDGs, they said, helped them to justify gender policies to colleagues within and beyond the Education Department. One official, with long experience of working on gender who worked in the national Department, said in the focus group discussion that things that can be measured ensure action is taken. The MDGs, by focussing on measurement and targets, had secured action on the right to education:

> . . . we don't have an indicator on how many girls are raped in schools. We're not tracking that. So what is not measured does not get done. What is measured gets done. It's about the indicators. What we have found is that indicators drive what becomes important. At an international UNESCO level, the MDGs, EFA, influence must be at the level of indicators. And that's where the money goes to . . .
>
> (South Africa, Focus Group Discussion, 19/08/2008)

This reflection suggests going considerably beyond the framing of gender parity in the MDGs, drawing not just pragmatically, but also strategically on this kind of managerialism, to force a discussion on a different meaning of gender linked with what gender inequality does in relation to violence against women.

In the international civil society organisations, the views of some staff in the head office, engaging in dialogue with counterparts in G8 capitals drawing on the Beijing Framework of Action, EFA or the MDGs, also expressed the potential of the MDGs. In the global NGO in South Africa there was a view that, although their own work on gender proceeded and went beyond the MDGs, the global goals were, nonetheless, useful in terms of advocacy and ensuring government commitment:

> I think our work is already targeting aspects of the MDGs and the MDGs came along and happened. There were goals that were set, and I think the

MDGs whether they were implemented or not is not necessarily going to change the way [our work] is focused, although, I know that there are people working on MDGs sort of policy stuff and that kind of thing. I tend to see the MDGs as a bit more of, it is a way to create more awareness, it's a potential way to get more government commitment and things like that, but I feel again it's another surface level thing, . . . , so the MDGs I think they do provide an avenue but it's very important to interact on a global level and to discuss these things and try to push all our thinking and shift our thinking.

(South Africa, National NGO, Staff member 2, 23/07/09)

In Kenya, there was some sense that the MDGs could be used to ensure attention to gender in areas that did not yet receive adequate attention. One staff member, for example spoke about the need to pay attention to gender within early childhood education, and referenced the MDG on gender parity as something that could support this:

And one of the MDGs is to reduce the gender gap so if the ECD teachers can try to show these young ones that they have equal abilities and those teachers who are supposed to do this are the ones the government has not availed.

(Kenya, National NGO, staff member 3, 19/03/2009)

However, generally staff in the national NGOs were more pessimistic than in South Africa about the potential of the MDGs to leverage action, explaining that there was not sufficient widespread awareness of the global goals to ensure that they were taken seriously at national or local levels:

Maybe one thing that I have said is barrier to realization of MDGs is lack of political will, lack of implementation of policies that have been put in place. There is lack of community awareness on existence of some of these policies like if you go to a place like Kajiado and you ask them about the Millennium Development Goals, they are not aware of that, so there is also lack of community awareness on MDG.

(Kenya, National NGO, staff member 2, 19/03/09)

These examples from some officials working within the institutional space, and some engaging with the global dynamics of civil society, show the MDGs being drawn on partly to support or amplify national policies on rights or equality, and sometimes to connect with the currents of the debates in the global women's movement. We did not document this resignification of the MDG agenda much amongst teachers, and there was little explicit reference to the media or the terrain of the public sphere in these reflections. While these examples show the global policy space as an area of debate and reflection for some, this was not a widespread view. Much more common across all sites was the interpretation of the idea of gender parity, expressed in EFA and the MDGs, as a notion of procedural fairness, but not political engagement with inequality.

Procedural fairness

In the third approach evident from the data we analysed, gender was spoken about in terms of ensuring equal access, attainment or achievement for girls and boys, or ensuring balance in terms of the composition of the teaching community in a particular school. Equality is thus a measure of sameness, a formal equality of numbers as envisaged in the MDGs or EFA, although not everyone knew about these documents. The procedural fairness associated with this stance often had the consequence of compartmentalising work on poverty, which was seen to be suffered by girls and boys together, and work on gender, where an equal balance needed to be attended to.

Amongst Kenyan officials at the national level this meaning of gender equality linked to sameness was often expressed, and seen as an outcome of national, not global, policy:

> . . . in our gender policy we have been keen to incorporate both boys and girls in school we make it plain. Our agenda is to have both boys and girls in school.
>
> (Kenya, National Official 1, 21/05/2008)

> We are also looking at the girls and the boys, continuing assessing them and we are looking at the scores for the girls and the boys.
>
> (Kenya, National Official 9, 17/10/2008)

> At the TSC [Teachers' Service Commission] we have policies to ensure that we bring gender on board, for example in a mixed school, if the head teacher is male, if the female is head then the male is deputy.
>
> (Kenya, National Official 7, 02/04/2009)

> So as we implement activities we always ensure there is gender equality, like you can see, this report I am making now, we always have male and female.
>
> (Kenya, National Official 2, 08/04/2009)

At the provincial level the difficulties of attaining this kind of equal access required by national government policy was stressed. One senior Kenyan educational officer said:

> . . . the challenges we are facing here are related to enrolment because, even if we talk of enrolment, we go to the community. What they will do is that they will give us the boys leaving the girls at home. Even if we went, got the girls and brought them to school, after a while they move out. The parents participate in this. They look at the physical appearance of the girl and then they start now withdrawing them from school. . . . In early childhood education they [government] emphasise increasing girl child enrolment . . . because they are looking for ways of encouraging these people to enrol more

girls in schools . . . so there is a lot of gaps on gender policy . . . implementation is difficult.

(Kenya, District Official 2, 25/11/2008)

The head teacher we interviewed also saw gender in terms of numbers enrolled, and making improvements responding to national aspirations:

It has changed in that it has improved. Last time the number of boys was bigger than the number of girls. But now, more girls are coming than boys. So the turnout has changed and it is not like the way we started.

(Kenya, Head Teacher, 28/01/2010)

There was some consciousness among national officials that learning support materials should be gender sensitive, but the term seemed to lack precision. An official explained how INSET learning resources had been developed for teachers each with its own section on gender and with careful scrutiny of gender balance in the examples:

Even when we came to develop our materials we ensured that we took care of gender both in terms of the materials we are developing, and even language used, and even the kind of examples we are giving. . . . And in addition we ensured that there was a gender unit in each and every material that we developed.

(Kenya, National Official 5, 09/05/2008)

Compared to South Africa, there were fewer officials interviewed in institutional spaces in Kenya who had histories with a women's rights activism. This might explain why here we documented fewer instances of an attempt by officials to expand the concept of gender beyond this notion of balance in the work of the Ministry.

In South Africa, the school principal we interviewed (25/03/2008) described procedural fairness in relation to gender equality as being 'like a quota' and maintaining a 'balance'. A teacher said 'We are doing things equally because now we are in the equal' (Teacher 1, 26/07/2010). Procedural fairness in South Africa sometimes led to a strange inversion of initiatives that aimed to advance girls being joined up or complemented by programmes that focused on boys. Thus, for example, girl-friendly schools became child-friendly schools. The Gender Based Violence guidelines being discussed by the Department considered both boys and girls as being at equal risk of being victims of sexual violence. The 'take a girl-child to work' was followed by a similar project for boys. The Girls' Education Movement (GEM) was a specialist extra-curricular club where girls can consider aspects of gender, sexuality and schooling, set up in response to work with UNICEF (UNICEF, 2006). Officials in the Department decided this initiative should include the organisation of a Boys' Education Movement and the slogan was changed from 'I am my sister's keeper' to 'I am my brother and my sister's keeper'.

> The boys' programme came after we have introduced the Girls' Education Movement. Within the UN strategy of the GEM, what we were saying let us rope in the boys to come and become partners, to make sure that girls receive effective teaching and learning but later in the process we realized that the boys don't want to come in under the banner of the girls. Then we decided that we need to come up with their own movement, where they will talk about their frustrations, where they will talk about gender power relations, where they will talk about their role in terms of ensuring that girls' rights are not violated, whether due to sexual violence or whether due to violence itself.
>
> (South Africa, Gender Focal Point 1, 22/10/2008)

This may have been a strategy of avoiding conflict or upsetting a fragile system, where procedural fairness was a necessary move. One participant explained:

> I was recently talking to someone in the Northern Cape. He was working with school kids from 15–19 years and talking about the girl child. There was booing from the boys.
>
> (South Africa, National Official 9, 25/07/2008)

Such comments appear to indicate the emergence of the form of backlash against girls and women and a resistance to girl-focused projects that threatened their sustainability. This led to a conundrum: on the one hand, officials in the Girls Education Unit in the national Department wanted to strengthen projects that empowered girls beyond 'once-off' interventions, and on the other hand, they were well aware that they needed to extend projects beyond girls:

> If you are going to work with boys what are you going to work with them on? Indeed they also need self-esteem, they also need life skills but actually what we need to be doing is working in the areas in between; teaching young people about what the gender equitable society looks like, and what role they can play.
>
> (South Africa, National Official 10, 04/02/2010)

These negotiations suggest gender parity and procedural fairness are only partially a response to top-down initiatives from the MDG framework. It is evident how officials in the institutional space of a Department of Education responded to particular demands of a national and local context, and some attempted to negotiate for particular concerns with a more expansive concept of gender without strong relationships with a constituency to support this.

Meanwhile, a cruel application of 'equal' or 'sameness' understandings of gender equality became evident during an interview with learners in South Africa.

Notwithstanding that corporal punishment is illegal, girls and boys said some of their teachers subjected both groups to beatings with a red polypropylene pipe to 'two to five lashes, depending on the offence', 'beneath the foot and on our buttocks' if they had not done their work (Interview with grade 5 learners, 28/07/2010). The example indicates a consequence if there is no deliberation at staff meetings about what gender equality and child rights means for the day-to-day practice in the school.

Ignoring gender: a gender blind approach

The fourth approach to interpreting gender parity was to ignore the salience of gender. This took two forms. In one there was a stress that gender could not be understood outside other social relations, and should not be monitored or reviewed as the MDG frameworks suggested. In a second form there was the notion that gender was primarily about girls, and giving attention to policies on girls would undermine boys. These notions were somewhat linked with the idea of procedural fairness, but different to it.

The salience of looking at gender as a category on its own is a commonplace view in theoretical debates about gender and development (discussed in Chapter 2), but the form this took in policy documents sometimes meant that gender was not discussed at all. A number of South African policy documents being used by the national Department relied on a notion of developing equalities, in which gender and other markers of social division needed to disappear. In our earlier work analysing this process we called this a gender blind approach (Dieltiens et al., 2009). This discourse does not deny that gender is important but it seeks to restrict or minimise the salience of analysing gender. For example, in South Africa there was very little monitoring for gender equity in education beyond an assessment of enrolment numbers or matric passes. Gender did not appear in the National Policy and Guidelines on Whole-School Evaluation and there were few opportunities for gathering information in the system on the claims that girls or boys might make for special attention, or differential needs in particular settings. Monitoring thus focused on the attainment of parity and this was seen to be procedurally fair. Without nuanced data available on the needs of girls and boys in particular settings, there were no real principled differences between girls and boys that policy needed to address. For the gender blind approach, emphasising differences ran into the danger of essentialising a gendered identity and blocking procedural fairness. If girls were to be considered a universal category, this would overlook the way in which other social identities, such as class and race, intersect with gender. As one official explained:

> You know the one risk you run with too much emphasis on gender issues is, generally speaking, issues like this would be taken more in more well-resourced areas and what then happens is you get a lot of attention on women who are in well-to-do sectors of society and if that happens at the

expense of the poor, then your anomalies, your asymmetries still remain. So you know it has to be both.

(South Africa, National Official 1, 07/11/2008)

This respondent suggested that policy could give girls preferential treatment as a homogenous group, as though all girls experienced subjugation in the same way. Middle-class girls are able to use their existing cultural capital to leverage policies that aim to give their gender a heads-up in ways that poor learners cannot. An assumption is that 'this happens at the expense of the poor' – in other words, if the same opportunities are not afforded to poor learners, then you produce a gap for entrenching inequality that might not otherwise have existed. Poverty, therefore, was seen as a more urgent issue requiring attention. For some South African departmental officials what was most salient was ensuring the poor were regarded as equal moral subjects. Thus, the interests of girls and boys must be taken together for common purpose. Poverty and poor school quality were regarded as overwhelming problems which did not discriminate on gender terms:

Like I say, it [gender] is much more secondary to us because we deal much more with poverty and poverty is poverty whether you are male or female.

(South Africa, National Official 11, 14/11/2008)

So that's why I say it's more and more poverty alleviation. I think that's what would make life easier for many children to attend school irrespective of their gender.

(South Africa, National Official 12, 04/11/2008)

We deal with hunger and hunger does not discriminate. For us gender doesn't come out as an issue.

(South Africa, National Official 11, 14/11/2008)

Participants' responses thus suggest that when developing and implementing policy you either 'do gender' or you 'do poverty' without considering the ways in which poverty and gender inequality interact. Procedural fairness on poverty required that gender, understood primarily in terms of what gender 'is', could not be foregrounded.

Ideas around connected inequalities were not mentioned as often in Kenya. In the Kenyan Ministry of Education it was also difficult to find forms of actions that linked together poverty eradication, educational expansion, the complexities associated with different formations of the concept of gender and addressing forms of discrimination. There was a sense that action to support gender equality might mean over-privileging girls and neglecting boys, with the implication being that it would undo procedural fairness. In the focus group discussion in the National Ministry one female official said:

We are not only targeting girls. We do target boys as well, that is why we give them the Free Primary Education for access so that everybody gets to go to school. For example in central Kenya we have majority of boys leaving school, dropping out to go and work in the plantations – you know we call it child labour – we find we have come up with our districts and our Provincial Directors of Education (PDEs) are really sensitising the public so that they should not drop out but be in school because of what we are calling Vision 2030.

(Kenya, National Official, Focus Group Discussion, 26/11/2009)

The slightly defensive implication is that to have a concern with girls' education or gender inequalities might entail one was less concerned with boys out of school.

Although some officials chose to emphasise the procedural fairness of legal interpretations of equality, there was recognition by some working in the institutional terrain in South Africa that additional efforts would be necessary to achieve equality of opportunity. Girls were in some instances seen to be disadvantaged – and interventions were thus required to ensure that they could compete equally with boys but this should not come at the expense of procedural fairness that alerted them to the needs of boys.

Because our job is to ensure that every child is in school, that every child is accessing quality teaching and learning. Our job is not to make sure that girls get it – we do it for everybody – but pushing the girls because they need that harder push than the others. [. . .] What some of the research is showing is that the top achievers, some of the provinces tend to be dominated by girls. Which says that if a girl is good and given the support and encouragement – in fact she flies much higher than the boys anyway. So we have to make sure that as the girls reach puberty, they don't drop back and leave the guys to take the lead.

(South Africa, National Official 5, 12/11/2008)

Gender difference could therefore be recognised where it was justified – where there was evidence that parity had not been achieved. Affirmative action was here a technical approach to ensure commensurability and procedural fairness. Girls could be encouraged, for example, to study subjects where they had previously been under-represented, such as maths, science and technology, but they should not exceed their share of the distribution of rewards or question the framework of distribution.

In Kenya, participants used the interviews to express equal concern with girls and boys in school. However, this was not always linked to the same ideas about procedural fairness or intersecting inequalities discussed by officials in South Africa. Indeed, a number of participants registered that the problems and issues of girls and boys might be different, and that focusing too much on gender might mean these differences were underplayed. For example, a Kenyan official in the Ministry of Education raised the influence of the violent Mungiki sect on boys, particularly in the context of high levels of poverty:

I think even we are going towards there and actually even that equality we have a problem with the boy especially in central province . . . we are losing

boys . . . boys are not going to school because one of the things is Mungiki and you know the connection between Mungiki and the economic factor.
(Kenya, National Official 5, 09/05/2008)

In Kenya, the notion of procedural fairness was much more controversial for parents and community members than in South Africa. It was seen to come from outside, and thus to be illegitimate. The school governing board focus group felt that promoting girls disrupted the traditions and cultural values of the society:

a society where the girl child was stressed was spoiling the cultural set up of the area and that even in the church the women had taken all the seats for officials . . .
(Kenya, SGB Focus Group Discussion, 29/05/2008)

We are always talking about the girl child and not the boy. The impact it is creating on the nation is great. . . . Even if you go to the roads banks and all the good jobs you get girls. Now where are our boys? We have left the boys with drugs. What society is this of girls only? Look at the church leadership, it is for women and even for the youth, men are not here. Now the boy child is forgotten. . . . This is a great challenge to us . . . we need to look at this otherwise the equality we are fighting for will lead to inequality.
(Kenya, Head Teacher, Focus Group Discussion, May 2008)

But the head teacher's view was not held by all. In the focus group discussion women teachers said there was a struggle going on against cultural practices that were anti-equality. They argued that women do a lot in life, associated with pregnancy, birth and rearing a child, which was frequently not acknowledged. In contrast, male teachers said gender equality was against the cultural set-up in Africa. Their view was that women must respect men and not feel they should be equal. However, teachers all agreed that women were disadvantaged in the provision of education '[. . .] in our culture, education was denied to women and given to men'. The inclusion of girls through procedural fairness into activities that may previously have been considered to be "masculine" does not necessarily counter the cultural and institutionalised sidelining of traditionally 'feminised' activities. Neither does it deal with the status of girls and the relational and power dynamics associated with the notion of gender inequality, as some officials in the South African Department acknowledged.

In both schools, while participants emphasised their understanding of gender in terms of parity and 'balance', it was clear that a parity approach was not consistently practiced. Only girls cleaned the school's foyer and administration offices in the South African school (Principal, 25/03/2008). The explanation for this was given in terms of culture and tradition:

You know in our culture . . . the female person used to collect the wood in order to make a fire at home. Same applies here . . . it happens naturally.
(South Africa, Principal, 25/03/2008)

In Kenya, this too was girls' work although boys helped: 'The girls mop the floors while the boys fetch water from the water point in the school for them' (Fieldnote, 18/02/2008). One of the teachers explained that this was because,

> the girls prefer to clean and they say 'Mwalimu, let us clean so that we can go home early because when the boys clean they are not as fast as we are'.
>
> (Kenya, Teacher 2, 20/02/2008)

A number of officials working in the institutional space, commenting on their concerns to address procedural fairness, tended to cast girls as deficient, or in some ways embodying forms of deficit. For example, in South Africa, a government programme to encourage girls to take part in school sports drew on homogenising ideas about girls, sexuality and attendant inadequacies:

> Well because the girl learner is of concern and especially if you have a look at obesity, diabetes and other health related diseases that can be controlled through exercising and the lifestyle patterns. And you know keeping girls busy after schools so that they are not doing or engaging in other activities that will lead to unwanted pregnancies etc. So definitely it's in the interest of the girls; that's number one. And because we know that especially in our previously disadvantaged schools, it's the boys will pick up the ball and play soccer and it's very difficult to get girls to participate.
>
> (South Africa, National Official 10, 11/11/2008)

Procedural fairness was both a political position, a way of analysing problems largely using national policy frameworks, but it was also, for some working in the institutional terrain of a middle space, a clear response to a backlash posed to efforts to advance women's or girls' rights. However, for officials who had these concerns, the pragmatism associated with the use of gender parity provided for in the MDG framework, with its resonances with global authority, did not seem to be much help in addressing some of the deep hostilities and power struggles associated with advancing women's rights in conditions of poverty and intersecting inequalities.

In the local NGOs in both countries there were rather ambiguous ideas about gender equality, and this did not appear a language with which people felt comfortable or familiar. In the rural NGO in Kenya there was a strong affirmation of the link between education and realising rights '. . . education will directly liberate these people to demand for their rights' (Local NGO 2, staff member, 22/06/2009), but this was not connected with a perspective on gender equality. The NGO did work on the 'construction of classrooms, and training of SMCs' which was not seen as 'gender related'. One worker in the education section commented on how the organisation worked equally with boys and girls, but did not have a broader understanding of equality:

> Sure they involve issues of gender, poverty in that we sensitize and mobilize on the community the importance of education for both boys and girls [. . .] we also sensitize the community on the participation of education.
>
> (Kenya, Local NGO, staff member 2, 22/06/2009)

For a number of NGO workers, gender was emphatically not their brief:

INTERVIEWER: Now the project you are doing, you get special grants that are really geared towards gender related initiatives?

EDUCATION OFFICER: Gender! No! Education related! For construction of classrooms, training of SMCs, things like that.

INTERVIEWER: [. . .] Reduce poverty by 2015, reduce child mortality by 2015, what do you think we should focus on?

EDUCATION OFFICER: I think we should be focusing on two goals education and reduction of poverty [. . .] because if people are educated and poverty is reduced, I think that will be a very big achievement.

(Kenya, Local NGO, staff member 2, 19/05/2010)

In South Africa, one rural NGO worker acknowledged the positive changes that had come about in terms of women's representation in local assemblies and the provision of the child support grant to single mothers. Thus the effects of gender equality were evident, even though the origins of these policies, either nationally or internationally were obscure to her.

. . . even to the cabinet of chief, they now put the women . . . if the headman is asking for the meeting in the community, they even ask the women. Like at first we used to have a challenge that if you are a girl and you got a child before married, you are like the group of those women on the outside. But now they are including us in all things that happening. . . . So the issues around gender are coming down.

(South Africa, Local NGO, staff member 1, 03/06/2009)

Despite these important local shifts, the NGO facilitators and director insisted on being gender neutral, and thus the organisation did not see gender equality issues as a focus of the work on literacy and reading. Girls and boys were often seen as the same and collapsed into the category of 'children'. As one local staff member said:

. . . our focus is on the very young child. We don't focus on the very young girl-child or boy-child. We really focus on the very young child . . . we haven't gotten into gender because we're so focused on providing what we can for that very young child.

(South Africa, Local NGO report back meeting, 04/02/2010)

Another NGO worker explained that 'the gender issue has not been our banner' (Local NGO report back meeting, 04/02/2010). In 2007 the phrase '. . . making the community a better place for children' was the central theme for the year. Gender equality had no presence in the material that facilitators used for their group work (Local NGO 1, staff member, 03/06/2009). The drawback of this approach meant that facilitators could avoid advising girls and boys about gender relations even though the girls and boys in their groups were experiencing relationship dilemmas, as these extracts from focus group discussions with girls (11/03/2010) reveal:

> [Boys] propose love by force, they feel we are old enough now (GIRL 3)
>
> Boys force us to have relationships with them. They lie saying we love them. (GIRL 1)
>
> People will start talking about [relationships] and eventually it will reach the office [at school]. In the office they will ask why you are dating him. If you say you don't, then they will punish you so that you never do it. (GIRL 2)
>
> The boy always gives the girl money [when they're dating] (BOY 1)
>
> The boys use the money to bribe us into dating them but we don't take the money (GIRL 2)
>
> If you don't agree to date him, he and his friends will tease you and laugh at you but if you do they leave you alone (GIRL 3)

It is clear that a lack of space for discussion and reflection on gender issues and a narrow focus on gender as being about girls has not provided NGO workers with the tools necessary to deal with the complex gender issues they encountered in schools and local communities. This was exacerbated by the distance that these participants felt from international policy frameworks and national policy, which they did not feel empowered to engage with, and by the active distancing that many participants seemed to employ when talking about poor girls themselves. As a result, the work they undertook at the provincial level, in schools and in local communities, was either deliberately gender blind or focused narrowly on girls, drawing on essentialised notions of gender difference or moralistic ideas about girls' sexuality. In doing so, it did little to address the unequal power relations associated with gender and other inequalities.

Essentialising girls and blaming women

The fifth strand in the discussions of gender equality and education policy underplayed the dynamics of gender relations and structures providing unequal resources. The approach focussed on particular identities that were attributed both to groups of women and girls, and men and boys.

In both countries where gender was addressed directly it was often through actions targeting girls or commenting negatively on women taking positions of leadership. In South Africa, a number of actions associated with gender focused on the issue of teenage pregnancy. The provincial education department had held a stakeholder summit in 2006 to discuss national measures on the Prevention and Management of Learner Pregnancies (Department of Education, 2007) and raise awareness among officials and civil society about teen pregnancy. But in interviews three years later there was little critical comment from officials on how it was girls who dropped out of school to take care of young children or other family (South Africa, Province Official 1, 06/02/2009).

In Kenya, concerns with gender were linked by provincial officials to children not being enrolled in school because of the actions of particular local communities who practised early marriage or kept boys out of school to herd cattle. Gender inequities associated with education were thus located somewhere outside the responsibility of the education department. As one officer put it:

> Gender concerns are many, depending on the locality. For example in those districts where they do not believe in sending girls to schools it is a problem . . . . They see education for girls as a waste of time. The girls are married off at an early age. . . . Others worship bravery and warriors. Therefore, boys do not value education because education is viewed as something for the cowards. The brave ones go to conduct raids and they are respected by the community based on how many cattle they bring home after the raids. . . . Those raids affect education so much in these districts. For example when one community is planning a raid all the boys are withdrawn from school to go for the raid.
>
> (Kenya, Province Official 2, 16/09/2008)

The view essentialised girls, boys and the local community making assumptions about particular identities.

In South Africa we did not document this sharp ethnic sense of distance, but we did note some hostilities to women as a group. Because the greater number of teachers at the school where we collected data were women, one school official said that women were 'dominating' and hence gender equality required no further action. The adult learners in the rural NGO project in South Africa (FGD, 02/06/2009) had experienced incomplete schooling due to teen pregnancy and understood how this had affected their lives negatively. They were in favour of teenage mothers returning to school after delivery of their babies and expressed more empathy for such girls than the NGO facilitators. Although the NGO facilitator had more formal education than the women learners attending the project in the focus group discussion, many NGO workers were unsympathetic about school girls who became pregnant. They dismissed their wishes to return to school and said that rather than trying to get education: 'They should give birth to babies. That's what they do best' (Facilitator 2, Focus Group Discussion, 05/06/2009). Girls were blamed for falling pregnant, an act that they said deserved severe punishment:

> 'They wanted to have babies so they should stay at home and not go back to school' (FACILITATOR 2)
>
> 'you have to punish her by not taking her back to school' (FACILITATOR 1)
>
> 'It's very important that parents talk and tell everything to their children. Then when that thing happens, chase her away from your house' (FACILITATOR 4)
>
> (South Africa, Facilitators' Focus Group Discussion, 05/06/2009)

The wisdom of the policy allowing girls to return to school after delivery was ridiculed on the basis that it encouraged teen pregnancy. Similarly, the support from grandmothers who looked after the babies while the young mothers returned to their lessons was criticised as an endorsement of teen pregnancy that should be avoided at all costs: 'you will die working for her and her child' (Facilitator 2, 05/06/2009).

Girls and mothers were blamed whenever gender-based violence and teen pregnancy cropped up. For example, the Principal in South Africa said the response to pregnant schoolgirls of the school governing body, which has a majority of parent members, was: 'we don't want these kids in our school' (South Africa, Principal, 25/03/2008). He felt that the school's image might become tarnished. And was 'lucky . . . fortunate [. . .] helped by these parents whose learners got pregnant because they didn't bring back the kids to our school [to be a] laughing stock' (Principal, 25/03/2008).

In Kenya too there were instances of mothers being blamed for children's lack of performance at school or risk of pregnancy. For example, one teacher, when asked whether girls' getting pregnant could be associated with parents' low incomes replied:

> Yes and also that is why the parents, should I say they don't care, they don't care so much . . . about their children maybe even you can find that the child never went home even like yesterday he went somewhere else . . . but you find that some of the parents they don't even follow.
>
> (Kenya, Teacher 2, May 2008)

At the school level work on 'gender' was targeted at girls. Sometimes this had moralistic overtones, associated with control of girls' sexuality. Despite formal teaching on sex education being in the curriculum in both countries, teachers lacked confidence in how to support learners around equalities, rights and understanding gender and sex. In the South African school initially there was denial that there were any difficulties in relation to work on gender because it was a primary school, learners were younger than in high school and questions of sexuality did not arise. However, this was contradicted by statements from teachers that learners were reluctant to speak to them, take their Life Orientation lessons seriously, and confide in teachers when they were experiencing gender-based problems:

> They didn't take it [LO] as serious as a reality. They take it as a subject even though I tell them that this is what and what. And then they laugh and then they're expected to write about that thing, but not as real life. [. . .] but we found that in grade six they start that now they've seen something. They change. And they're vulnerable.
>
> (South Africa, Teacher 1, 26/07/2010)

Staff were at a loss of how to engage with older learners on gender matters:

> I don't know exactly what we gonna do but we need – I've seen this year that we need to have maybe a class like in our olden days . . . where the girls were alone and the teacher or somebody comes from somewhere and teach

these ladies about how to become a lady and how do you expect from the world now. Even the boys.

(South Africa, Teacher 1, 26/07/2010)

In Kenya, a teacher identified three main actions the school took:

We have guidance and counselling and she [volunteering parent] is given all girls and goes to church there to talk to them . . . in terms of gender there is one [volunteering parent] who is supporting girls.

(Kenya, Teacher 1, 12/06/2010)

This account indicated very little capacity from within the existing staff to deal with any gender issues, hence the reliance on a volunteer parent.

All these instances suggest that at a local level there were few frameworks for people to talk about gender, equality or women's rights. The official language of the MDGs and government policy associated with parity and procedural fairness provided few windows to think about complex issues of teenage pregnancy, sexuality, intergenerational differences or the intersections of disadvantage. The global currents associated with the gender and women's rights movements had not touched these local communities who either did not consider gender in relation to their work, or who drew on a lexicon of blame and distance to describe features of gender relations or sexuality that were troubling.

Addressing gender power relations

Despite this diversity of response, and the work that some put in to promote gender equality, we documented very few instances where people working in terrains of a middle space were able to identify gendered power relations and take action linked to global or national frameworks. The examples of this gathered were linked with the global NGO in South Africa and the statements of a few officials working in the education department, all of whom had a background in work on women's rights and gender activism.

In South Africa, one NGO worker explained to us that gender power in local communities was painfully real. She worked on a girls' computer literacy and empowerment project in a peri-urban area with high levels of poverty. Over the day she spent with a member of the research team, she felt comfortable enough to take her into her confidence about her previous experiences of women's activism and how it was currently very difficult to realise the project objectives:

At a meeting some months back before I worked for global [organisation] I stood up and I was giving a statement on gender equality. I was just talking. I think I mentioned just one statement and all the men in the room walked out. They said we cannot come here and be humiliated and be forced to give women more rights. The president has given them more rights. Now you come here and ask them. They did not just stood up and walk you know. There was a 'Whooo' in the room and there was a lot of noise. They talked and left. And we continued. And then I asked what's going on in this community? But when I slept I was like 'Hei what is happening in this community? Will I be attacked or what?' So there is a lot of opposition. And now in relation to [organisation] work, cyber training the group. We normally have parents' meetings – parents of the children that attend cyber training and things that parents say you can hear. That it's not well taken by both parents. They say we are taking their kids somewhere . . .: taking their girls particularly so these girls are going to grow up to be lesbians. . . . You know so we ended up agreeing with F . . . to make sure parents don't think we teaching their children to be lesbian. We are not teaching girls to have too much power. Women will understand, but men will have issues.

(South Africa, National NGO, staff member 3, 07/10/2010)

This project worker has had ten years of experience of women's activism, understands the complexity of local discussion and the sharp hostilities associated with raising issues of gender equality. She can see how education work with girls for the global NGO links with broader gender equality agendas. But in this work she feels has been given a prepared script and there is no space for her broader political experience of gender activism. Limiting the purpose of the project to computer training for girls does not eliminate the need to engage with and provide support in tackling deep hostilities to gender equality.

This level of reflexive insight was very rare. A few officials working in the institutional space of the Department also expressed similar perceptions. All had activist backgrounds on these issues. One official said gender was raised in internal directorate discussions or when evaluating policies and interventions, but it was expressed as "the soft issues . . . the moral issues" (South Africa, National Official 5, 12/11/2008). One senior official described how difficult it was to define and confront issues of gendered social power in a context where there are Constitutional protections and women in politically powerful positions:

We are not in a situation like . . . where you probably see no woman of any kind of public. . . . We have a situation where a lot of women are in parliament for example, a lot of women politically in power just as much as we have equal numbers of boys and girls in schools but we have an incredible discrimination against women that happens at the same time – through violence, through power relations and it's the same in schools. So we have this fantastic Constitution, but the reality is because of the social problems girls experience. So in some ways it's more difficult to deal with them – they are more invisible . . . so all the more reason why we have to keep doing things but we have to do things in a way that incorporates these kinds of debates because otherwise we reduce ourselves to just campaigning about the simplistic issues – then nobody ever really gets to understand what is it that we need to change. And what we need to change is so complicated that it's almost inexpressible in a programme.

(South Africa, National Official 6, 04/02/2010)

"Invisible" and informal processes of power took on a complexity that was difficult for the Department to action in a programmatic way. Even where training [of educators] was offered, it tended to skim over issues of power relations in favour of an interpretation of gender as acts that could be contained, managed or even policed – as if they were 'criminal activities'. 'Complex' gender issues were thus condensed into discrete, observable nouns: gender was reduced to one gender, i.e. girls, and the outcome (pregnancy, violence) was the target (managing it) rather than its causes. An additional predicament with trying to moderate the complexity of gender was that the root causes of gender oppression were overlooked in favour of keeping its obvious consequences in check. This can [partly] be explained by the idea that while the source of gender oppression was recognised to lie in patriarchal value systems, this was often seen to be outside the scope of education. Another official explained:

> I think that very often in the schools, as you go down and the further you go from the centre, you know what I mean by the centre, your town, suburb as you go out even to the sort of township areas and particularly to the rural areas, I think girls there are still very much disadvantaged . . . you find there women are expected to do a huge number of tasks and it's a man's world. You find sexual violence against girls and it's real. You find that girls will pass if they sleep with the teacher and that's unfortunately real.
>
> (South Africa, National Official 5, 12/11/2008)

An implicit assumption was that schools are not locations of equitable gender reproduction and that the problem stems from the private sphere. The challenge of fixing gender relations, therefore, is a much broader social project that cannot primarily be solved by schooling. What education could do was help girls adapt and cope with oppression, even if it couldn't change patriarchy in any real sense.

> And then, things like the Life Orientation also takes you into wellness and into sexuality and looking at the girls' role and looking at giving girls personal skills to be able to cope with – whether is violence or whether is just always battling for your place, on an equitable footing.
>
> (South Africa, National Official 5, 12/11/2008)

This frame of reference echoes Beijing, much more than EFA or the MDGs.

Across the dataset we saw how the relationships of the terrains of a middle space make it difficult to confront and change these gendered hierarchies and sites of unequal power. The South African rural NGO was started and run by strong women, with decades of political experience. Its work in rural villages wracked by poverty and disease was aimed primarily at women and girls. However, gender inequality and hierarchies of power were not made explicit in any discussion by the organisation, or referred to in decision-making and action. The pervasiveness of patriarchy was overlooked, not examined in the content and representations of the books used, or in the experiences of the child and adult learners and the village facilitators.

In Kenya, none of our interviews with officials working in the institutional space raised the issue of gendered power of institutions, and it was only raised by some women teachers in the focus group, to be pushed aside by the head teacher. Concerns with gender equality came out in the work of the global NGO with regard to abstract statements, such as those about rights evident on the posters on the office walls. But on the ground in particular projects staff appeared to have done little work to reflect on this. One fieldwork incident exemplifies this. A member of our research team travelled with the NGO to a rural community where it was doing work in a school. After discussing the project with the head teacher at a school, where the NGO was working, the member of our research team asked to talk with some girls. The NGO worker called out the name of two girls who had come into the office and said to one, 'this man [referring to the researcher from our project] has come to pick you for a wife and your friend [calling out the name of the first girl] will escort you'. The NGO worker went on to joke that our research officer was a man who had already paid bride price. The girl who had been told that she was being married off begged, "No, please teacher, no . . ." It was a joke, but an unkind one. It suggests some workers with this NGO, despite the posters on the office walls, had much work to do to understand gender, power and the vulnerability of girls.

These examples show how difficult it was in all the terrains of a middle space we investigated to work on the notion of gender power and inequality. The weather systems of global ideas about rights or equality gave little defense for NGO workers on the ground in South Africa who confronted strong opposition to women's rights activism, and the global NGO in Kenya had a long way to go to build support amongst some of its staff for values around girls' dignity and rights. These global gusts of concern, our data show, were not yet sufficient to sustain change in the direction of substantive equality and challenging gender hierarchies.

Conclusion

This chapter has identified how the lexicon of gender parity linked with global policy had currency in the institutional terrains of a middle space, partly as a means of reporting, and for some as an opening to raise more national issues of what gender inequalities meant. However, the reach of the global ladder linked to the MDGs was not very extensive. What was better known and more used were national policies associated with procedural fairness for girls and boys. However, many of these views were contested, and held together with very hostile perceptions of girls' sexuality or distanced concerns with teenage pregnancy. For only a handful of those we interviewed, all with a history of links to work on women's rights, were the gusts of global policy which referenced Beijing a resource they could draw on. For many this gave them a frame to critique their current institutional or civil society location, but few resources of time, money or political or professional support to be able to change it. The difficulties of confronting the gender inequalities of institutions or in common sense views suggest silences in the terrain of the public sphere, and very limited opportunities for professional organisations to put arguments for gender equality or the salience of global policy. In the next chapter we look at some of the barriers that were erected between different sites for the realisation of global and national policy that undermined the open kinds of exchanges suggested by the notion of a public sphere.

References

Department of Education (2007). *Measures for the Prevention and Management of Learner Pregnancies*. Pretoria: Department of Education.

Dieltiens, V., Letsatsi, S., Unterhalter, E., & North, A. (2009). Gender blind, gender neutral: Bureaucratic screens on gender equity. *Perspectives in Education*, 27(Special issue on Diversity in Education), pp. 365–374.

Fukuda-Parr, S. (2014). Global goals as a policy tool: Intended and unintended consequences. *Journal of Human Development and Capabilities*, 15(2–3), pp. 118–131.

Keddie, A., & Mills, M. (2009). Global politics, gender justice, and education. In Ayers, W., Quinn, T. M. and Stovall, D. eds. *Handbook of Social Justice in Education*. New York: Routledge, pp. 107–119.

Khalema, N. E., Andrews, N., & N'Dri, T. (2015). I Millennium Development Goals (MDGs) in retrospect in Africa. In Andrews, N., Khalema, N. and NDri, T. eds. *Millennium Development Goals (MDGs) in Retrospect*. Dordrecht: Springer, pp. 1–15.

UNICEF (2006). *Girls' Education Movement – South Africa*. UNICEF: South Africa. [online] Available at www.unicef.org/southafrica/SAF_resources_gembrief.pdf

7 Poverty and practice
Boundaries of blame and disconnection in education

Many of the actions and institutional processes discussed in the previous chapter distilled the complex notion of gender to simpler forms of parity, procedural fairness and the deficits of girls. Sometimes this drew on the global policy linked with the MDGs, and sometimes it did not. In this chapter we look at engagement with the notion of poverty and document how work on the issue had the effect of building walls or boundaries between the poor and professionals, who were tasked to deliver the gender and education policies and practices linked to the MDG and EFA frameworks. We consider some of the difficulties of establishing the bridges and connections of political membership to support democratic iteration and the establishment of a political sphere where discussions concerning addressing gender and connected inequalities could be animated by generosity and inclusion, rather than blame.

In Kenya and South Africa, blame and practices of boundary setting were evident from our data between those delivering and receiving education in contexts of poverty. We saw this in both the schools where we collected data, in certain features of the work done by the rural based NGOs, and, in Kenya, in some of the perspectives of officials in the national and provincial offices of the Ministry. In all these sites, we documented assumptions being made about poor people without providing opportunities to hear from these communities. Barriers of silencing, distancing and exclusion were put in place, which amplified the marginality of the poor. One consequence was that poor people were blamed for lack of achievement of gender equality in education and non-delivery on global goals, rather than multilateral or national institutions, the history of international, national and local relationships, and how this might affect limitations on resources and the processes of achieving specific outcomes. Poor girls and women, in particular, were stigmatised, essentialised and discursively and literally placed at some distance from the terrains of a middle space, so that their voices were not heard and their needs not acknowledged. Although some groups working on these terrains had professional responsibilities for attending to the rights of the poor, we documented a number of instances where these institutional obligations were not fully met.

The first part of the chapter draws out some of the meanings attributed to poverty in the discussions we conducted in the different research sites, and provides examples on how poverty was linked with blame, stigmatisation and marginalisation. We then look at the kinds of gender and other interventions that were then deemed appropriate connected with those meanings, reflecting on how global gender equality policy was being interpreted. In the third section, we consider how some of the practices that were evident across a number of the terrains of a middle space had the potential either to reproduce of transform these relationships of blame and marginalisation.

Groups working on terrains of a middle space as officials in the education bureaucracy, teachers or NGO workers often spoke about the poor and poor girls in ways that made it sound or look like they were to blame for being poor. This legitimated forms of exclusion and disadvantage. We loosely call this way of depicting a person or group for circumstances over which they have little control as 'blaming' (Unterhalter et al., 2012) although literature on inequalities uses terms such as constrained capabilities, marginalisation, exclusion, deficit, Othering, displaced embodiment and symbolic violence (Sen, 1999; Bourdieu, Accardo and Balazs, 1999; Farmer, 2004; IM Young, 2011; Mbembe and Blomley, 2015). Models of development, and global statements such as the MDGs, imply that a particular group are lacking in some way and they deserve attention that will bring them into better circumstances as defined by the model or statement (Colclough, 2008; Unterhalter, 2012; Clark, 2014). What the group are lacking has marginalised them, left them out and put them at a disadvantage or unequal to others in particular ways. These frameworks often fail to reflect on whether this marginalisation or exclusion is due to luck and the misfortunes of birth, or whether it is the outcome of the social relations of discrimination in the present, comprising specific actions, which fail to engage in redress for the past. These may indeed exacerbate past inequalities.

In many accounts that use data on income to assess poverty the argument is that the poor are marginalised, left behind or left out because they have failed to cross a particular line. These lines are associated with a level of income ($2 a day in the MDG framework) or level of education, or consumption of a certain quantity of calories or amount of food (Fukuda-Parr and Orr, 2014). The line is not simply a metaphor for achieving a basic education or minimum daily income or expenditure. It also works a symbol of exclusion and failure. These attributes tend to attach to the poor, rather than to the economic and political relationships or the institutions that have created the conditions in which people who are poor find themselves.

A variation on this way of understanding poverty as a line, which demarcates adequacy from inadequacy, is found in Lewin's (2009) work on zones of exclusion in education. He sees being in or out of school, attending regularly, or dropping out, and returning irregularly as signifying inclusion, marginality or vulnerability. A frequently used approach in education policy has been to incentivise the poor to cross the line demarcating zones of exclusion. Bursaries, free meals or conditional cash transfers have been some of the interventions used. An alternative approach encourages governments or local school boards not to charge school fees or gives a premium to schools who have large numbers of children deemed poor (Snilstveit et al., 2016). This way of interpreting marginalisation and how to address or reduce poverty is characteristic of the World Bank's Poverty Reduction Strategy Papers (Caillods and Hallak, 2004; Davidson-Harden, 2006). In this approach the poor are defined empirically by a science of measurement and a boundary is set in binary terms, so that learners or families are either above or below a line demarcated by income. Most surveys of poverty and schooling count numbers of girls and boys at school in families deemed poor by these measures.[1] An alternate means to distribute resources is evident in South Africa's *Norms and standards for school funding* (Department of Education, 1998), which organised schools into a quintile hierarchy setting lines to group schools to distribute resources.

By contrast, a political or sociological perspective on poverty stresses the political economic and socio-cultural relationships which structure and reproduce the many forms of structure and agency associated with the subordination, exclusion and marginalisation of poor people. As we showed in Chapters 4 and 5 inequalities in education in Kenya and South Africa were shaped around historically instituted divisions of race, ethnicity and region, which linked with poverty and were maintained or only selectively and unevenly dismantled in the decades we have been focussing on. Understanding poverty not only in terms of falling above or below a particular line, but as entailing being forced politically or socially into certain relationships which sustain inequality, injustice and exploitation, entails that the forms of remedy need to go considerably beyond incentivising the poor to engage with education. They require very systematic examinations of education systems, institutions and interactions to establish relationships of equity that are sustained and lead toward undoing unjust structures and reshaping actions in education (Raffo, 2013; Hadjar and Gross, 2016). These initiatives require groups who work on terrains of a middle space (such as government bureaucrats, teachers, nurses, social workers or journalists) to establish institutional and employment relationships, which critically examine and work to dismantle social divisions. These processes require discourses which challenge the reproduction of discrimination and subordination of the poor, building work for equalities and inclusion (Slee, 1997; Slee, 2001). Very sustained education work is needed to effect a building of understanding and professional insight and some capacity to engage difference in ways that are inclusive (Walker and McLean, 2013; de Andreotti, 2014).

Relationships with global gender equality and poverty policy frameworks can re-inscribe the exclusions and injustices of a particular society or can help to change them. The data we collected in a range of research sites showed both processes at work. In the discussion in this chapter we show how boundaries were maintained in opposition to the poor, who were characterised in terms of deficit and subject to blame. We also show how these practices were in tension with attempts to work towards inclusion. Thus global policy frameworks on gender equality and education sometimes worked to reproduce harsh exclusions associated with poverty, and sometimes, but less often, worked towards supporting a different perspective on social solidarities.

Poverty as deficit

For the many participants with whom we held discussions, poverty was discussed as a form of lack or deficit amongst learners, parents or communities. It was associated with hunger, lack of income or absence of schooling. In South Africa interviewees in the provincial education department and the school spoke of poverty in terms of learners or their parents stressing they had inadequate food, income, work or health. They were without possessions, clothes or resources for play, such as a football:

> I was a teacher myself – you find a learner that is gone in high school for [with] that need. And it is not a rural area where I was teaching. . . . You find a learner having gone for two weeks without food. This high rate of unemployment is directly linked to poverty and a hungry mind . . .
>
> (South Africa, Province Official 20/02/09)

> Sometimes if a learner has no school uniform they resist coming to school. At this school there have been some four or five learners like this who were really suffering in poverty. In such cases the principal brings the matter to the attention of the school governing body and requests that they pay for uniforms for these children.
>
> (South Africa, Principal, 12/03/2008)

This emphasis on deficit and want was also evident in observations at the district and school level in Kenya. One of the teachers described poor learners:

> There are children who appear hungry early in the morning. Even uniforms are torn in most cases. . . . You see the nature of the shoes they put on is a sign of poverty.
>
> (Kenya, Teacher 3, February 2008)

Discussing the school feeding programme a district official said:

> There are those honestly who can't afford three meals. They have only the school lunch and in the evening there is nothing. So tomorrow they will come to school because they know they are assured of a meal.
>
> (Kenya, District Official 3, 28/11/2008)

Together with these specific sites of deficit, linked with hunger or lack of clothes, there was also a sense of the pervasiveness and all-encompassing nature of poverty. One senior manager in the province in South Africa said: 'you don't need to articulate it because it's there for everybody to see' (Province Official 2, 04/02/2009). A district Gender Focal Person was more graphic when she said: of poverty 'it's hunger, and I'm telling: chronic hunger! You can even smell hunger when you walk closer to the child' (District Official 1, 16/02/2009).

These evocations, generally spoken with some empathy, were somewhat different to those articulated at official at national, provincial and district levels in Kenya, where particular kinds of phrasing were deployed to distance officials from the poor. Here officials described poor parents not in terms of hardship or the struggle to survive and the indignities of lack of shoes or torn clothes, but in terms of educational, economic or cultural deficits, which made them morally inadequate. The following extracts from officials working in the national Ministry illustrate this:

> [A] percentage of illiterate Kenyans are poor, and thus don't understand the purpose of education. And if a parent does not understand the purpose of education, they are most likely not to take their child to school. And even if they take their children to school, they are not likely to give them higher and continuing education. So that's one factor. Two, it is parents who are not able to afford basic things like pencils and uniforms who are likely not to take their children to school.
>
> (Kenya, National Official 1, 21/05/2008)

> The other parent who is illiterate, can trade off his daughter for a few cows which will die even after a few days because of drought . . . if they are ignorant and illiterate, they marry off their daughters at a very young age.
>
> (Kenya, National Official 3, 07/04/2009)

> So poverty contributes a lot. Ignorance also, and poverty is closely related to ignorance. Where there is poverty there is a lot of ignorance.
>
> (Kenya, National Official 3, 07/04/2009)

In all extracts the discursive pattern works to position a group of parents, who stand at some distance from the boundary of literacy and in deficit on this account. This distance, the argument runs, causes them to fail to cross the line of enrolling children at school. For these officials this is a key marker of deficit. Because the national Ministry and the provinces are audited on the proportions of children enrolling and remaining in school, and these figures are incorporated into national reports relating to the MDGs and EFA, the 'ignorance' of parents is implicitly seen to contribute to failures to get adequate returns. Work place organisation thus appears an aspect of the distance and barely concealed hostility some officials express regarding poor parents who stand at some distance from a line of acceptability. In the first quotation above, the national Ministry official mentions particular areas of social policy support, for example making pencils and uniforms free, but blame is placed on the parent for not being able to afford these essentials for school attendance, rather than on the government for not providing them. In the second extract from the dataset, the official amplifies the social distance associated with illiteracy and ignorance adding a cultural distance regarding the value a poor pastoralist might invest in 'a few cows' or the early marriage of a daughter.

Generally, the implication of the boundary of deficit is that blame rests with parents, and that education officials and teachers are doing their best, but bringing people up to the line stands beyond what they can reasonably be expected to achieve. Only one national official in Kenya expressed some sympathy for poor communities, identifying that although they stood at some distance from the boundary of deficit, there were areas of social policy that were not being enacted to ensure they could cross the line of sufficiency.

> In most of the cases the poor don't get enough support to advance themselves in education.
>
> (Kenya, National Official 11, 13/02/2009)

In the Kenyan school, it was evident that teachers were well aware of the effects of poverty and hunger, and the difficulties that some of their pupils faced. When asked to discuss specific pupils and what might lead to poor performance, they noted how slow learners who could not read were walking 'long distances to school' (Teacher 3, 21/02/2008), staying at school 'without food the whole day' (Deputy Head teacher, 20/02/2008) and experiencing 'poverty at home, peer pressure to do manual work' (Teacher 4, February 2008). However, this understanding sat alongside quite derogatory statements about the children and their parents. The head teacher, for example, in one interview described parents coming from the slum area as 'very lower class people who have received little education'. Meanwhile he also articulated similar ideas to those expressed by government officials about deficit and poor children as a group standing at some distance from a boundary where they could be included in school:

> The parents keep shifting and at times they don't have money. They don't want to pay.
>
> (Kenya, Head Teacher, February 2008)

> [T]he other thing is that [parents'] lack of seriousness and ignorance. Because I don't understand why a parent should not take a child to school.
>
> (Kenya, Head Teacher, 28/05/2008)

In contrast to national and provincial officials who describe the boundary between those inside and outside school in terms of abstractions associated with illiteracy, ignorance and cultural folly, it can be seen that the teachers are much more specific in the way they detail the deficits of poor children. Partly this may be because of their greater openness to members of the research team, partly possibly, because this is a repeated part of their experience. But it is also noticeable that the areas for which teachers are accountable upward to district, provincial or national officials, such as the performance of pupils in exams or the collection of school fees, are the areas in which they locate blame for poor parents, who stand beyond the boundary at which they can provide adequate food to their children or pay the school levies. As the head teacher notes, it is almost impossible for him to understand why parents do not come up to the boundary and cross the line to enrol their children and pay the fees the school requests. In his view this can only be explained by ignorance and 'lack of seriousness', that is deficits that are not merely material. The data suggest that in Kenya the teachers were not confident to share with our research team any insights that came from professional organising, which presented a different perspective on poverty.

There was a contrast in this with the South African school. Here poverty and, in particular, hunger, were identified as a problem by teachers, some of whom described drawing on their own personal funds to assist learners in their classes. However, they also described their frustrations that actions that singled out learners for additional food parcels and uniforms, or attempts to support parents were not well received:

And then some of the kids they are afraid to tell us they don't have. . . . But when you come to class and say [that] those who have nothing, they must come to me, then no, they won't come. [. . .] They are too shy. Yes. They are too shy. [. . .] I said 'somebody who wants food must take'. They didn't. They wait that side. And then I go to him: 'Why don't you take this food because I know your mother is not working?' He didn't say anything. He just take the food. So they are shy to telling us that they are hunger. [. . .] They can't voluntary come and say they are hungry or they have got poverty at home. No.
(South Africa, Teacher 1, 26/07/2010)

When it comes to parents visiting, [the parent of the needy child] won't come. Those who see that they've got a problem and then you call a parents meeting: no; but those who don't have a problem, the parents will come! But for those that we said 'no, we want these parents because . . . , [the learners] are not studying, they are not doing well at school, they have nothing to wear' and then you make these parents visiting, [but] they won't come. [. . .] We don't know why the parent don't come to school! Because they're supposed to come and tell us the problem!
(South Africa, Teacher 1, 26/07/2010)

And then we said when you give the kid a uniform [the learner] must come with his parent. They won't come! 'We've got uniform now, where's your mummy?' The kid says 'mummy's at home'. Why? [She] said 'I mustn't get this uniform'. Why?! One of the teacher principal go and see them and ask why don't you allow your kid to have this because he need this? He said 'no, no, I will try'. He's not working but he said he will try. What's he going to try? Because this thing is free of charge! But they've got that pride. I don't know why they've got the pride.
(South Africa, Teacher 1, 26/07/2010)

In the South African school, such views regarding poor children were expressed with some sympathy and understanding, with participants recognising that some pupils or parents might feel shy about accepting help. In these accounts teachers refer to their colleagues, and there is some depiction of professional engagements with poor parents trying to give support or understand their problems. But these professional and solidaristic notions are mixed with a sense that to some extent poor parents were to blame for their children's lack of food, uniform or attendance, or that their actions were beyond understanding. Here there were echoes of some of the views we had documented in Kenya.

This social distance from the poor was also expressed in a number of interviews with workers in the South African local NGO. One NGO worker blamed girls from poor families for a lack of ambition to pursue further education. She said:

> I was asking [the girls] that in ten years' time what are we going to be. And most of the girls said "I'm going to have a child. I'm going to be married." So few of them was saying that maybe I will be in the university. [. . .] Even the parent do not know if the child finish matric, they do not know what next. They even not prepared that [they] can sell some cows and send [their] child to the university. That's not something that they understand.
>
> (South Africa, Local NGO, staff member 1, 03/06/09)

Meanwhile, although state interventions to reduce poverty through social grants were valued, the NGO worker derided the grants for subtle changes in gender relations:

> In our culture, always men have to take care of the children and the mother, like men have to go to work in order to give money to these people. But now, with most of the child support grant, [it is] the women who are getting the grant. So you might even have that the men say they do not know how much is the money that the caregiver gets for the child support grant. [. . .] The women are getting the power because [they] are the people who are controlling the money . . .
>
> (South Africa, Local NGO, staff member 1, 03/06/09)

But in Kenya the rural-based NGO workers did not speak about local communities with the sense of distance and blame we have documented in Kenyan government departments and in the South African rural NGO selected as a comparison. Possibly this was because the NGO workers shared an ethnic identity with the communities, which government officials did not, but it does not explain the social distance we documented in South Africa, where there was also a shared ethnic identification. The different perspectives might be linked to the different ways in which gender is linked with culture and poverty. In the South African extracts from the discussions, the poor and the social welfare strategies of the government are blamed because gender relations are shifting.

The Kenyan rural NGO workers are critical of the government for pushing too hard and in inappropriate ways to end female genital mutilation (FGM). They reported that parents in the communities in which they worked doubted whether education could achieve what was promised. When discussing why older girls may be kept out of school one NGO worker said:

> The culture is deep rooted in the people down here and changing culture you cannot do it overnight [. . .] if it is the issue of FGM you cannot just go and say stop it today [. . .] it takes a long time. It needs a lot of dedication [. . .] culture turns out to be stronger than the government policy.
> (Kenya, Local NGO, staff member 3, 19/05/2010)

In this response the government is derided for failing to appreciate the conservatism of gender attitudes linked with a poor community. There is still a homogenisation of the community, but not so much social distance or critique.

These data show how components of the blame of the poor include stereotypical assertions that poor people do not read, care about the education of their children, particularly daughters. This has a particular significance in relation to the gender equality and education frameworks. This discursive distancing by Kenyan officials in the national Ministry and provincial and district office was sometimes used to divert attention from the difficulties of achieving gender equality through existing institutions. The teachers and NGO workers with whom we collected data did not use professional or public reflections to consider values about gender equality, intersectional connections, the views of poor communities on gender relationships and marriage and substantive expansion of education provision. The implication is that democratic iterations are not natural or instinctive, but need to be worked for and engaged to build the understanding to help bring about change. As discussed in Chapters 4 and 5, all these groups experienced the MDGs and EFA as coming from very distant places. Little professional education was available to officials, teachers or NGO workers to help them move beyond blaming the poor and connect with the perspectives about rights and equality sketched in the global policy.

Portrayals of cultures of poverty and perspectives on women and girls' lives

This discourse of marginalisation and deficit outlined above share elements with a stigmatisation of particular ethnic groups. Assumptions about inadequate or inappropriate culture was another way in which the poor were depicted, linked with problems where culture, lack of education and a particular location outside the mainstream, which positioned them as 'beyond' or outside inclusion. This was more evident amongst the Kenyan government officials we worked with than the South Africans, which may reflect some of the different histories of the growth of the civil service in each country, as reviewed in Chapters 4 and 5.

In Kenya, at the national Ministry, elisions were often made in describing particular communities, identified by markers of religion, place and negation of the national school policy:

> And then there is also religion, it is coming up. There is cultural and religious factors, like when you go to the North Eastern – their culture. I don't know whether Islamic culture has something to do with not educating the women. So there is a problem. They have negative attitude towards school. . . . You find that very few, less than 20% are accessing school in Ijara, Wajir. Yet education is free and it has something to do with culture and religion of the people.
> (Kenya, National Official 5, 09/05/2008)

> [T]here is also the cultural aspect, some traditions on ladies. I am neighbouring the Kuria and when a girl reaches 13 years that is a woman who should be in her house. So they drop out of school.
> (Kenya, National Official 3, 07/04/2009)

> [I]n some parts of Nyanza particularly the remote sites of Nyanza, the lower sites of Nyanza province you will find that the enrolment there is actually very low. And it could be as a result of cultural practices like where we have maybe the circumcision of the girls (FGM). Once they are through with that initiation, they would want to move to next level and obviously maybe to get married.
> (Kenya, National Official 12, 05/02/2009)

It can be seen that in all three instances a particular place – Wajir, Kuria and 'the lower sites of Nyanza' – are loaded with particular meanings which the interviewees link together with practices around marriage and tradition. Thus, discourse about culture work for these officials to explain girls being out of school and construct meanings as to why rational policies such as Free Primary Education might be failing. In South Africa, there was less overt blaming of particular cultural groups among education officials when discussing reasons that children might be out of school.

For officials in the Kenyan province and district similar meanings concerned with cultural essentialism were deployed, but these went side-by-side with references to marginal groups being out of place to explain why some children may not be in school:

> Poverty has risen into the recent past especially in this district after the post-election violence. There are many street children and families in the town now. If you walk on this street at night you will be shocked at the number of street children. They stay in groups of over 1,000 and light big bonfires. They are a security threat but also an eyesore.
> (Kenya, Province Official 2, 16/09/2008)

When you look on poverty, ok let's go to the slums cause you also have some slums in K & N. . . . They are orphans. . . . And what are they doing? They are building small homes pretending we want to be closer to school which is not true. They are coming there because of poverty. Then they come and start brewing funny liquor and sell it.

(Kenya, District Official 2, 25/11/2008)

Poverty honestly is still an issue here. And it is a major contributing factor to prostitution. . . . We are now seeing a [ethnic group] woman doing prostitution. And you see a mother sending her girl to go for men so that they can have a packet of *unga* at the end of the day. Cause you know you don't have any other source of income.

(Kenya, District Official 4, 28/11/2008)

As the extracts make plain, these officials do not actually know much about the lives of children living on the street, in slums or women engaged in transactional sex. They see them as they pass by and use these images to blame children for not being in the right place, that is in recognisable families or appropriately attending school. Given that officials are required to oversee the enrolment of children in school, these views are hardly surprising. These children evade the meanings that should be attributed to them and officials, in response to this, express hostility and discomfort that children and parents do not fall in line.

Thus, in the face of pessimism about achieving the MDG targets, blame is allocated to communities who appear reluctant to send daughters to school, or who take them out of school early, and what are termed 'cultural values' are blamed by officers for gender inequality. These 'values' are associated with early marriages, female genital mutilation (FGM), initiation rites for young men and child labour. A senior education officer in the province explained how government efforts were being frustrated by entrenched cultural practices saying:

We have tried to withdraw girls from early marriages and take them to rescue centres. These girls sneak out during the holidays and go to live with the men they had been married to. In the process they get pregnant and so when you want to withdraw them they tell you they are now somebody's wife and can't go back to school when they are pregnant. So you realize that the government's efforts do not bear fruit. Again there are even government officials who do not report cases of early marriages even some teachers. People do not want to spoil the names of their relatives who are involved in such cases so you find men protecting others.

(Kenya, Province Official 2, 16/09/2008)

This extract brings out both the sense of blame of communities who practise early marriage, the girls involved, and the teachers or officials, who come from those communities and are complicit with children being taken out of school.

However, these silences and evasions may not be surprising as in some areas very punitive moves were reported to make sure families sent children to school:

> There is a campaign as I speak. Two months ago there was a very good campaign in N division . . . O primary school had 94 children . . . so the provincial administration through the chiefs, DC ordered the chiefs that any-body who does not take the children to schools to be arrested, and they went round. I remember when the educational officer was recently here, he was telling us O primary school now has 180 children. At our last school before you cross to N it has the same problem with 62 pupils with two teachers. And then the chiefs went round. Now they have over two hundred children. So the campaigns are going on. Actually one [man] was arrested and put in the cell for not taking his children to school. He is a very prominent man who had 11 children not going to school. He was held for three days and was given some work like cleaning the waste of other prisoners. He felt humiliated now he is a crusader everywhere the chief goes. He tells others, 'What I have gone through I don't want anybody else to go through.' So the campaigns are paying off.
>
> (Kenya, District Official 1, 24/11/2008)

In other areas there are direct interventions to take girls away from their families if they do not send them to school or are planning an early marriage:

> We are saving girls at two levels. There are those girls who have not gone to school at all. They have been denied that opportunity. So these girls, although they are under aged and are going to be forced to be married and they don't want to be married, so those ones they come to this office and say my father is forcing me to be married and I want to go to school. You see that one has never been to school but she has got an opportunity. So those ones we refer to the children officer we look placement for them our XX Girls Rescue Centre or YY Children Home. That is one level. The other level is, girls are in school but again it might be because of poverty or ignorance of the parents; they try to marry them off. This practice is still common in this district. It is still happening although it has reduced but I cannot say that it has stopped. It is still happening but we are having the support of the provincial administration and there are also very many children's advocates in this district among the organizations that are supporting girls' education. So everybody is shouting.
>
> (Kenya, District Official 1, 24/11/2008)

The prisms of meaning used by teachers and school committee members to construct marginalising boundaries also pivoted on connections between poverty and criminality. They too did not express a sense of the harsh conditions that might have resulted in this form of action. Blame appeared the over-riding attitude. For example, it was alleged that parents were involved in illegal activities, although no detail was given and it is not clear this was based on accurate information. Hunger, a number of teachers said, was associated with theft:

> Especially in our school there are cases of food theft.
>
> (Kenya, Teacher 3, February 2008)

Meanwhile, a number of distancing boundaries were evident in the way some School Governing Body (SGB) members spoke about poor families. The SGB treasurer explained it from her perspective as a parent:

> In our school, most of the students come from the nearby village and they have not been raised up in Christian families. They are brought up in a house that has only one room and the whole family [. . .] share the same room. This in turn affects their interaction with other children in school [. . .] parents should bring them up in the expected manner.
>
> (Kenya, SGB 1, 29/05/2008)

Here overcrowding in slum housing and children's behaviour are associated with them being non-Christian, across a boundary of respectability. The 'blaming the parents' discourse is clearly very closely bound-up with the process of 'distancing' associated with identification of parents as poor as well as illiterate, 'non-Christian' or un-married. Yet there seems to be very little questioning of why poverty is so entrenched in the areas, nor linking of poverty with broader processes of discrimination and exploitation, reflecting the narrow framing of poverty as a deficit and a characteristic of individuals or communities: homogenised and often demonised as the poor.

We saw in the previous chapter how understandings of and policy enactment relating to gender often drew essentialised notions of girls and gender norms and on moralistic views regarding female sexuality, and these were also very apparent in the ways in which participants drew on ideas about moral failings, when discussing the educational performance of children from poor communities. Often blame was laid at the door of single mothers, who, it was suggested, did not make suitable role models. One teacher suggested that single mothers were likely to engage in prostitution:

> Some of the mothers are single and they engage themselves in prostitution or commercial sex.
>
> (Kenya, Teacher 4, February 2008)

Parents' moral failures regarding marriage were linked with the failures of children at school:

> If I'm unmarried, there are those issues that my child will learn from me therefore many children lack discipline . . . in most cases it is parents who are on the wrong.
>
> (Kenya, Parents' FGD, 29/05/2008)

The head teacher in the Kenyan school asserted that the responsibilities girls took on at home, when parents worked long hours, undermine their schooling. But he makes this comment without concern at the nature of the labour market, but in a tone of blame of the parents for their neglect of their daughter:

> But . . . maybe the parents have gone to look for the jobs and maybe the girls are left with the young kids to take care of, or maybe there were some problems at home . . . the mother goes somewhere, the girl is left with the brothers or sisters.
>
> (Kenya, Head teacher, 28/05/2008)

In South Africa, meanwhile, blame was often placed on poor girls themselves. One provincial official, for example, linked the problem of access, dropping out and teenage pregnancy to girls using sex instrumentally:

> . . . girl children [are] opting to have children so that they [can] collect [the child support] grant. In our dialogues it came out a number of times that girl learners – some of them would come out in the open and say it's their parents pressing on them to have babies so that the entire family could receive something to eat, you know. So they are pushed into prostituting and uh you know: "it's ok". The school principal – we've got cases of school principal, school teachers impregnating girl learners and all the parents can say is that he buys us food. . . . Some girl learners feel that it's kind of like you have a child [so the grant] is your reward and then you can live a luxurious life and buy yourself cell phones . . .
>
> (South Africa, Province Official 1, 06/02/2009)

This account was supported in the complaint of one official when she said: 'it's always the girls engaging in affairs with older men for material benefits or so that they could get some money' (Province Official 2, 04/02/2009). She also attributed high levels of teenage pregnancy in rural areas to the cultural practice of *ukuthwala*, whereby a girl is abducted by a man, accompanied by his friends and/or relatives, on the basis of a proposed marriage: 'as a young girl you not going to school [and] by the time you get back to school you have lost two or three weeks of school time and how do you cover that up?' (Province Official 2, 04/02/2009).

In the South African rural NGO, a culture that burdens and blames women and girls was seen as the major impediment to advancing gender equity in schooling. As we saw in the previous chapter, the disruption of teenage girls' schooling due to pregnancy was blamed on girls and their mothers. Boys, meanwhile, were not seen to be carrying responsibility:

> We need to be careful of doing things that perpetuate wrong habits. If the child falls pregnant while doing [Grade 8] and you send that child back to

school, she will do it again because she knows you will look after the baby. [. . .] Today girls start sleeping with boys very early. [. . .] It means we should have a class of young girls where they will be taught about abstinence.
(South Africa, Facilitator 3, Focus Group Discussion, 05/06/2009)

The prisms of meaning concerned with blame for cultures of poverty make it particularly difficult for schools to be established as sites of inclusion, paying particular attention to the needs of all children and valuing their diversity. The way the forms of blame we have identified work homogenise children and adults because of their culture, religion, location or family organisation. Making meanings in this way deflects concern away from inequalities associated with wealth, location, ethnicity or gender. It also does not give particular attention to the ways in which schools, and the national and global relationships which surround them, may reproduce inequalities and exclusions.

Participation and decision-making

A third form of boundary-setting affects the delivery of gender equality policy, undermines democratic iterations and the building of a public sphere for critical reflection and debate. This is associated with the distribution of resources and decision-making, and the ways that the institutions and the organisations of civil society work. In all research sites, we documented few opportunities for the poor and marginalised to participate as equals in discussions concerning the education of their children and reflect on gender equality issues. In Kenya, those interviewed repeatedly delineated the boundaries of policy given by the existing legislation and actions of the government. In the national Ministry this was hardly surprising, but there was little concern to engage in dialogue with parents or include them in assessments about resources. The charge of ignorance was used to distance officials from poor parents, who it was implied were not worthy of inclusion in discussions about rights:

But in many governments, not only in Kenya, the priority perhaps may be where many parents want – the primary school. But it's an issue of ignorance that people just look at children as children, and don't think they have any rights.
(Kenya, National Official 6, 20/05/2008)

Some of the factors could be maybe either the parents are [not] sensitized on the importance of education, or could be some of these children are orphaned and they taking care of the other brother and sisters, despite the free primary education. Or they are just ignorant they are not interested, may be they are in groups [which] belief in getting rich quickly so they don't see the importance of education.
(Kenya, National Official 7, 02/04/2009)

At the provincial and district level officials do work intensively to engage people in discussion, but these appear peculiarly one-sided, where the resolution is always prefigured by those in authority.

> When we explained that what they were doing was wrong [not sending children to school] they were a bit shocked. So what I have been doing it wrong? They were shocked of their own ignorance at that particular time.
>
> (Kenya, National Official 5, 09/05/2008)

> We are showing them also because it is [a] criminal offence and you know before the law ignorance is no defence. We have already told them take your children to school. Education is free; there is no reason why you shouldn't take your children to school. They have no excuse of we don't have school fees. But because they are not, they are still violating the children's rights. . . . So that we use it as lessons for the others – those that are still not taking their children to school so that they can also know that they can face the law.
>
> (Kenya, District Official 5, 18/05/2010)

It can be seen that the discussion at province and district level with marginal groups are highly coloured by a sense that they are outside the law. Although an angle is provided for discussion, it does not provide a space in which power balances are equal and resources can be reviewed together. Similar limits characterise the school governing committee, which has a very limited remit to raise levies, monitor teachers and school performance, but does not see its role as engaging with the poorest. It is the failure of poor parents to pay levies that is seen as a major aspect of blame by the School Governing Body:

> The SGB has long had parents who do not support the school in its running, in that they do not positively guide their children given that the school is in a slum.
>
> (Kenya, SGB Focus Group Discussion, February 2008)

Although some parents participated in the SGB, which enables them to take a more active role in the school, for most parents however opportunities for a deeper engagement with the school appear more limited. While there were reports of parents – usually mothers – coming into school when there were problems with discipline, there did not seem to be efforts to engage the parents on a more ongoing basis. The head teacher felt that the role of parents had been reduced since the introduction of free primary education (suggesting that their involvement was primary considered in financial terms rather than in terms of discussion or engagement with school processes or activities), and explained that they are supposed to provide physical facilities. The SGB does not consider it part of its remit to widen the angle of inclusion in decision-making so that poor parents can contribute to discussion about running the school and supporting children's learning. It is evident that the angle of space for decision-making and reflection on resources is very narrow. The levels of political marginalisation in education are therefore acute.

In the South African school, prior to 2008, there had been a number of pro-active poverty and gender-based initiatives which were somewhat more inclusive. These included committee work and holding workshops to inform parents and care-givers about how to work cooperatively with teachers to support poor and HIV-positive children. Although these mostly ground to a halt when there was a change in school leadership (Deputy Principal, 15/09/2010), some of this work was continuing.

In Kenya, in both NGOs there were efforts to engage poor communities in policy discussions. In the local NGO, some workers were critical of the way in which the government developed policy at a distance from the people. One spoke about the lack of 'involving the local woman at the village level':

> . . . workshops [take place] in towns, talking of this major gender issues [. . .] when you really go to the ground to the village level, you get there is still so much to do, to be able to even make this people aware of what is really their part in development, what is really their rights and how they should fight for their rights [. . .] there is a lot to do.
>
> (Kenya, Local NGO 2, 22/06/2009)

There was a sense that the government did not emphasise participation enough: 'I wish at times when the government is coming up with policies it should always involve the stakeholders of all the Districts and maybe do a piloting project within the rural areas' (Local NGO 2, staff member, 22/06/2009).

The ways in which there was some distance between these rural communities and people in urban areas for whom education might hold out more possibilities, coalesced around experiences of poverty and the reproduction of unequal gender relations. In Kenya, the time of data collection coincided with a major drought and a number of NGO workers spoke about the effects of drought on livelihoods.

> The weather has really changed for the last I think seven years [. . .] this has contributed a lot to the movement of animals from one place to another [. . .] this movement makes people leave development behind, they don't develop back at home, they don't develop their schools, they don't develop their families, they are just moving about and even spend quite a lot of money . . . when there is no water the livestock suffers, so the production of milk becomes low, In fact for the past two years XX women have not been getting milk to sell like other times [. . .] thus the rely on relief food, some are desperate they are selling land because of poverty [. . .] even in making beads there is no market to sell to.
>
> (Kenya, Local NGO 2, staff member, 22/06/2009)

Here there is evidence of a greater understanding of the problems poor communities faced and the challenges that this posed to education, although this was not linked up to an engagement with gender or other forms of inequality.

Strategies for change?

In Kenya in the school where the global NGO was working, there were fewer hostile, stereotyped remarks about poverty, gender and schooling that had been voiced in other sites. The NGO staff themselves articulated the complexity of intersecting inequalities:

> The challenges of the girl child faces could be described in four key areas. First one is cultural, I am sure you are aware that due to patriarchal nature of our society the male dominance, the girl position in the society is challenged. Secondly in the issue of economic challenges you are facing in the country, I would say they co-ordinate. When poverty strikes, lack of food, lack of water, basically the most hit is the woman. Because of the way our division of labour is designed, much of the reproductive work is done by women, because it is the woman who searches for water, who collect water, firewood and process food. So in case of economic challenges, women and girls must face it. Look for example the Maasai who are nomadic pastoralists, during drought they migrate to Tanzania and leave women and children behind.
>
> (Kenya, National NGO, staff member 4, 16/03/2009)

This account links together the complexities of gender inequalities with economic processes. There is not a simple set of statements which articulate a blame of the poor.

While a number of teachers noted, as those in the school research site had done, that poverty exacerbated sexual divisions within families, there was somewhat less of the blame and cultural stereotype than had been expressed in the peri-urban site. A NGO staff member noted:

> . . . I would call education is a privilege because when it comes now to a girl child, preference always goes to the boy child. And that is involved by other issues like economic. If the family is well of they will take both children to school but if there are those economic challenges preferences goes to boy.
>
> (Kenya, National NGO, staff member 5, 19/03/2009)

While there was generally not a clear strategic position with regard to the institutionalisation of gender and poverty reduction initiatives, it was striking that many staff working with global NGOs had more open and inclusive attitudes to poor communities. In this their difference stands out from a number of government officials (particularly in Kenya) and teachers and SMCs in both countries.

Conclusions

Our data suggested that processes of distancing and blame, which draw stereo-typical assertions about the behaviour of the poor, and, in some cases, on particular notions of ethnic identity, is a feature of the everyday discourse of a number of officials charged with developing and delivering on policy at all levels from the national ministry to the school. The active construction of horizontal inequalities, which stigmatise particular cultures or groups, and essentialise what are seen as aspects of moral inadequacy, means that marginality does not just happen, but is part of everyday practices. This has clear implications for the way in which gender issues in education are viewed and addressed. At the school level, a process of distancing and blame plays out particularly clearly in the maintenance of a horizontal disjuncture between the school and the community of parents and pupils and few initiatives to challenge this were being sustained. Similarly, the absence of opportunities for critical interaction and discussion regarding gender and poverty mean that the voices of poor parents were not invited into discussions of policy in the community.

At the national and provincial levels, particularly in Kenya, assumptions were articulated that the poor – and those from particular ethnic groups – do not value education or want to send their daughters to school. Failure of these groups to make progress on improving gender parity in schooling is portrayed simply the result of negative cultural traditions associated with particular ethnic groups in poor areas. Thus, while efforts are made to 'rescue girls' from their communities, there is little attempt to develop more meaningful forms of community engagement. The responsibility for addressing concerns with gender equality more broadly is often allocated by NGOs to marginalised communities themselves, rather than entailing a process of critical reflection on the content of education and the nature of the policy and decision-making process. The global gender frameworks were not used in building professional or political practices to understand processes of change and the connections to be made.

The deep structures that maintain boundaries of exclusion and blame connecting poverty, gender inequality and lack of education are not undone by the administrative fiat of passing a policy package concerning gender parity in schooling, and systems to monitor this up and down a ladder of global, national and local accountability. The gusts of global policy interacting with national and local conditions around gender equality, education and poverty appear to have some perverse effects. The examples documented in this chapter bring to mind Aesop's fable where the wind and sun attempted to have a competition to get a man to take off his travelling cloak. The wind blows powerfully, but the man wraps his cloak even more tightly around him. When the sun beams down on him, however, he takes off his cloak. We have documented many instances of global and national policy blowing through poor communities, with the result that they often turn away from the desired outcome around education. We have fewer instances of kindness, solidarity and participation as strategies to support a different vision of gender equality connecting together those who understand vulnerability, exclusion around global, national and local settings and how to change these inequalities.

Note

1 For example, suveys conducted by the DHS, and analysed by the UNESCO Institute of Statistics for the WIDE database. WIDE [online]. Available at: www.education-inequalities.org/

References

Bourdieu, P., Accardo, A., & Balazs, G. (1999). *The Weight of the World: Social Suffering in Contemporary Society*. Stanford, CA: Stanford University Press.

Caillods, F., & Hallak, J., (2004). *Education and PRSPs: A Review of Experiences*. Paris: UNESCO, International Institute for Educational Planning.

Clark, D. A. (2014). Defining and measuring human well-being. In Freedman, B. ed. *Global Environmental Change*. Dordrecht: Springer, pp. 833–855.

Colclough, C. (2008). Global gender goals and the construction of equality: Conceptual dilemmas and policy practice. In Fennell, S. and Arnot, M. eds. *Gender, Education and Equality in a Global Context: Conceptual Frameworks and Policy Perspectives*. London: Routledge, pp. 51–65.

Davidson-Harden, A. (2006). Extended review: Education, development, and the "re-branding" of structural adjustment. *International Review of Education*, 52(3), pp. 371–376.

de Andreotti, V. O. (2014). *Development Education in Policy and Practice*. London: Palgrave Macmillan.

Dieltiens, V., Letsatsi, S., Unterhalter, E., & North, A. (2009). Gender blind, gender neutral: Bureaucratic screens on gender equity. *Perspectives in Education*, 27(Special issue on Diversity in Education), pp. 365–374.

Farmer, P. (2004). *Pathologies of Power: Health, Human Rights, and the New War on the Poor*. Berkley: University of California Press.

Fukuda-Parr, S., & Orr, A. (2014). The MDG hunger target and the competing frameworks of food security. *Journal of Human Development and Capabilities*, 15(2–3), pp. 147–160.

Hadjar, A., & Gross, C. (2016). *Education Systems and Inequalities: International Comparisons*. Bristol: Policy Press.

Lewin, K. (2009). Access to education in sub-Saharan Africa: Patterns, problems and possibilities. *Comparative Education*, 45, pp. 151–174.

Mbembe, A., & Blomley, N. (2015). The body as placeless: Memorializing colonial power. In Razack, S. ed. *Dying from Improvement: Inquests and Inquiries into Indigenous Deaths in Custody*. Toronto: University of Toronto Press.

Raffo, C. (2013). *Improving Educational Equity in Urban Contexts*. Abingdon: Routledge.

Sen, A. (1999). *Development as Freedom*. Oxford: Oxford University Press.

Slee, R. (1997). Inclusion or assimilation? Sociological explorations of the foundations theories of special education. *The Journal of Educational Foundations*, 11(1), p. 55.

Slee, R. (2001). Social justice and the changing directions in educational research: The case of inclusive education. *International Journal of Inclusive Education*, 5(2), pp. 167–177.

Snilstveit, B., Stevenson, J., Menon, R., Phillips, D., Gallagher, E., Geleen, M., Jobse, H., Schmidt, T., & Jimenez, E. (2016). *The Impact of Education Programmes on Learning and School Participation in Low-and Middle-Income Countries*. London: 3iE.

Unterhalter, E. (2012). Poverty, education, gender and the Millennium Development Goals: Reflections on boundaries and intersectionality. *Theory and Research in Education*, 10(3), pp. 253–274.

Unterhalter, E., Yates, C., Makinda, H., & North, A. (2012). Blaming the poor: Constructions of marginality and poverty in the Kenyan education sector. *Compare: A Journal of Comparative and International Education*, 42(2), pp. 213–233.

Walker, M., & McLean, M. (2013). *Professional Education, Capabilities and the Public Good: The Role of Universities in Promoting Human Development*. Abingdon: Routledge.

Young, I. M. (2011). *Justice and the Politics of Difference*. Princeton, NJ: Princeton University Press.

8 Gender mainstreaming and education policy
Interventions, institutions and interactions

Chapters 6 and 7 showed how ideas about gender equality and addressing poverty, articulated in the global frameworks of the MDGs and EFA, encountered in a range of research sites relationships and discursive forms that refused the processes of inclusion and equality the frameworks had sought to build. In this chapter we look at gender mainstreaming, a key strategy for change, formulated in the Beijing Platform of Action to effect gender equality. We explore whether, when gender mainstreaming was effected within the terrains of a middle space we have sketched, these processes of organisation building and work are able to undo some of the relationships that make effecting gender equality policy change so difficult.

In the decades after the Beijing Conference, as a number of the strategic objectives agreed in the Platform of Action became difficult to achieve, gender mainstreaming was identified as a key focus area. A range of techniques were developed in which women and gender activists, with access to the state or large NGOs, could make significant advances (Macdonald, Sprenger and Dubel, 1997; Miller and Razavi, 1998; Rai, 2003). However, a debate about gender mainstreaming continues to question how transformative this kind of intervention could ever be, given the depth of gender inequalities and the multiple forms of power that were ranged against any change (Eerdewijk and Davids, 2014; Rao, Sandler and Kelleher, 2015; Bock, 2015). In the discussion about whether or not gender mainstreaming was a useful practice for feminist activism, some documentation has started to emerge concerning how gender mainstreaming has been interpreted by groups working on terrains of a middle space, and their experiences of trying or failing to use the approach. In this Chapter we focus attention on some of the analytic debates about gender mainstreaming, before showing how gender mainstreaming was interpreted as a policy-led set of moves in Kenya, and as a practice-led set of engagements in South Africa. We consider what relationships on terrains of a middle space were evident in the two countries, and reflect which form of relationship in which terrain supported gender equality enactments of policy.

Defining gender mainstreaming: some debates

Gender mainstreaming has been the term used for the practices within institutions and organisations developed to give effect to the actions identified in the

Beijing Platform of Action. An often quoted definition of gender mainstreaming, adopted by the Economic and Social Council of the UN was:

> . . . the process of assessing the implications for women and men of any planned action, including legislation, policies or programmes, in all areas and at all levels. It is a strategy for making women's as well as men's concerns and experiences an integral dimension of the design, implementation, monitoring and evaluation of policies and programmes in all political, economic and societal spheres so that women and men benefit equally and inequality is not perpetuated. The ultimate goal is to achieve gender equality.
>
> (UNECOSOC, 1997, p. 28)

The emphasis here is on rationally organised cycles of work within institutions. This was to be an area of much critical comment, which pointed out that the sexism of institutional cultures was as much covert as overt and that gender machineries, or integrating a gender perspective into policies or information, was necessary but not sufficient to change this (Goetz, 1997; Rai, 2003). A number of ironic articles identified the mainstream within organisations as not particularly responsive to gender equality concerns because the mainstream legitimated and routinised practices associated with men and masculinity and could be more appropriately termed a 'malestream' (Alvesson and Billing, 2009; Skaard, 2009). Work on gender mainstreaming was just as frequently ignored and sidestreamed as mainstreamed (Charlesworth, 2005; Kaufman and William, 2015; Mukhopadhyay, 2016).

In an attempt to take account of how difficult it was to change organisations, later definitions of gender mainstreaming within UN organisations became as much concerned with diffuse attitudes as with planning rounds. Hence UNESCO defined gender mainstreaming in 2003 as

> "Mainstreaming" is a process rather than a goal that consists in bringing what can be seen as marginal into the core business and main decision making process of an organization.
>
> (UNESCO, 2003)

This definition acknowledges that gender mainstreaming is not just a matter of identifying and including particular actions regarding women and men within planning cycles. It entails confronting some of the assumptions of what makes some interests and issues marginal, and acknowledging that these categorisations are often themselves the outcome of gender assumptions. In 2009, the WHO defined mainstreaming as primarily associated with attitudes. Institutions bore responsibility for helping to form these:

> The process of creating this knowledge and awareness of – and responsibility for – gender among all health professionals is called "gender mainstreaming".
>
> (WHO, 2009, p. 74)

The formation of the African Union in 2002 was accompanied by a high-level emphasis on gender mainstreaming which found policy expression in the 2003 Maputo Protocol to the *African Charter on Human and People's Rights on the Rights of Women in Africa*. This came into force in 2005, having been ratified by fifteen countries. By December 2009, forty-five of the fifty-three countries of the African Union had signed the Protocol, while twenty-seven, located in all regions of Africa, had ratified it, indicating a commitment to implement its provisions within domestic legislation. The Protocol contains an extensive statement of gender mainstreaming including commitments to Constitutional and legal reforms to ensure equality between women and men. It articulates far-reaching goals to protect women's rights, including action to eliminate violence against women, protect women's property rights, outlaw marriage under eighteen and 'integrate gender sensitisation and human rights education' at all levels of the education system (African Union, 2003).

In 2003 UNESCO published a five-year medium term strategy stating that:

> a gender perspective will be integrated in policy planning, programming, implementation and evaluation activities in all areas of UNESCO's competence with a view to promoting empowerment and achieving gender equality. Women's priorities and vision of development goals and approaches will be addressed and promoted through greater participation of women at all levels and in all areas of UNESCO's action.
>
> (UNESCO, 2003, p. 2)

The strategy proposed established the need to go beyond particular programmes directed to women or men:

> A profound transformation of the structures and systems, which lie at the root of subordination and gender inequality, is required. To do this, we must uncover the hidden biases that limit women's and men's ability to enjoy equal rights and opportunities and find the most effective and culturally appropriate means to support women's and men's capacities to drive social change. For UNESCO this means that we must mainstream gender concerns in all our operations.
>
> (UNESCO, 2003, p. 6)

This transformative vision for gender mainstreaming echoes that of the African Charter. The approach is about transforming institutions and through this undoing 'structures and systems' which constitute and reproduce inequality. UNESCO's vision for gender mainstreaming was somewhat different from that of the World Bank, which has seen the practice in more minimalist terms. For the Bank gender mainstreaming was a key platform for effective poverty reduction because '[there is] evidence that gender plays an important role in determining economic growth, poverty reduction, and development effectiveness' (World Bank, 2001, p. 1). The stress here is on gender mainstreaming as a technique to make particular forms of poverty reduction efficient, while the emphasis in the

African Charter and the UNESCO strategy was for a wider vision of the intrinsic value of gender equality and the complex processes entailed in developing institutions and actions to support this. This tension with regard to whether gender mainstreaming was to be seen as a technical exercise to secure other ends, or as part of a transformatory process to realise values associated with gender equity and equality, was evident in many education and social development settings (Rao, Sandler and Kellehr, 2015).

An extensive debate concerning the definition of gender mainstreaming has been conducted (e.g. Goetz, 1997; Rai, 2003; Squires, 2005). This has considered the extent to which gendered state processes can be changed through the techniques of gender mainstreaming and whether gender mainstreaming has been responsible for a co-optation of feminism, limiting its transformatory politics (Mukhopadhyay, 2016). A persistent question is how, in assessing the usefulness of gender mainstreaming, one takes account of the complexity of local contexts. This issue has been reviewed in relation to a number of South African government departments (Hassim, 2006; Beall, 2005), in Kenya (SID, 2010; Waterhouse and Kamau, 2010; Morgan, 1986, pp. 19–38) and in particular in relation to education departments and specific courses (Dralega et al., 2016; Baily and Holmarsdottir, 2015), and in analysis arising from this project (Unterhalter and North, 2010; Karlsson, 2010). In reflecting on the policy on gender and education for the SDGs, commentators note the ways in which the concepts of gender and policy mainstreaming had been troubled by scholarship and activism over the past decade (DeJaeghere, 2015; Cornwall and Edwards, 2015; Koehler, 2016).

A key question this literature has tended not to address directly is how the relationships within different terrains of a middle space between policy and enactment affect approaches to gender inequities and aspects of gender mainstreaming. The literature has largely focussed on the ways in which gender is or is not brought to the fore. We are interested in how gender is understood and connected with the multi-dimensionality of poverty, and the complexities of delivering education. We are also interested in how the frameworks set by forms of global-national and local relations affect engagements with gender mainstreaming. The academic literature on this theme, has shown how important particular institutional or organisational contexts are for whether or not gender can be mainstreamed, and what interpretations are given to this. One problem, which arises from this insight, is that, as the data in Chapters 6 and 7 show, in a number of contexts the very people who are close to injustices may not easily be able to change these. The perceptions and resources of outsiders, while necessarily always partial because they come from outside, might also be of great importance in supporting insiders to change taken-for-granted relationships of inequality. But how these connections are made between global, national and local levels is a delicate issue.

Interventions, institutions and interactions

The main opposition in the debate concerning gender mainstreaming concerned division between those who saw the approach as a set of technical rationalist moves to be made in organisations, looking inwards, and those who saw it as a set of outward first steps preparing the ground for a more profound transformation of gender inequalities (Kabeer, 1995; Verloo, 2005; Unterhalter and North, 2010). Unterhalter (2007, 2009), in trying to refine some of this discussion, identified three different approaches to the interpretation of global aspirations concerned with gender, poverty and schooling. She distinguished *between interventionist, institutionalising* and *interactive* approaches, each of which positions gender mainstreaming somewhat differently. Interventions are associated with addressing a basic minimum need, for example food or income or enrolling girls in school to ensure efficient economic, political or social development. They tend to involve clear policy messages or precisely defined actions, targeting particular aspects of need, or inequality, often aimed at particular groups. However, they do not seek to address more complex relations of disadvantage or insecurity which might relate to why conditions of want and inequality exist or persist. Thus, interventionist approaches, were they to use gender mainstreaming as one strategy, might interpret gender very narrowly linked to the notions of gender as a noun, addressing some specific needs, for example of poor girls.

An institutionalist approach, Unterhalter argued, is associated with changing the social relations that maintain poverty and gender inequality by establishing legal, organisational, redistributive and regulatory processes for change. The implication here was that gender mainstreaming was not confined to technical and limited interventions, but was considered as a process to change the focus and orientation of the institutions, including those of the education system, that shaped social, economic and political relationships in which gender inequalities were maintained.

Interactions, in Unterhalter's analysis, are associated with linking diverse groups of civil society and state actors to mobilise through participatory processes for gender equality and poverty reduction. This may involve processes of critique as well as collaboration, but they give considerable authority to the lived experience of people who live with poverty, inequality or violence. If gender mainstreaming were interpreted from this perspective, it would make space for documenting the experiences of the poorest, understanding forms of violence and exclusion associated with gender inequalities and marginalisation, and trying to redress some of the cultural, political and social dynamics of constraints on participation and authorisation accorded to these groups.

The terrains of a middle space we have been discussing in this book can be analytically linked with these approaches in different permutations. Interventions are often the work of state bureaucracies or civil society or professional organisations, sometimes working together, but often acting on discrete projects focussed on service delivery. In relation to expanding girls' education they may deliver programmes concerned with conditional cash transfers, building more toilets or employing more women teachers. A key issue to consider in evaluating this form of gender work is whether the technical focus on girls or women associated with these interventions, links with sustainable strategies for gender mainstreaming that go beyond the single intervention.

Building institutions is generally the work of government officials of professional organisations. In considering how much the relationships between these groups take forward some of the more transformative politics of gender mainstreaming we would need to examine whether features of their work are oriented to deep engagements with rights or equality. Questions concern whether changes in organisational cultures and national legislation take forward an institutionalisation of gender mainstreaming to address some of the intersections of inequalities. Professional organisations, civil society and the discussions in the public sphere may contribute to building changed institutions, but, much of the scholarship on the limits of gender mainstreaming, highlights how no single set of relationships associated with terrains of a middle space can realise this alone (Rao, Kelleher and Sandler, 2015).

Interactions may be a feature of all the terrains of a middle space and allow for an engagement with gender mainstreaming that is close to lived experience. These experiences are often documented in relation to the public sphere and civil society. However, a number of critical commentaries on these terrains in the last decade, have pointed out how some of their bottom-up engagements have been reduced under pressures of particular research paradigms, new public management and the enormous reach of highly influential media organisations (Wallace, Porter and Ralph-Bowman, 2013; Hunt, Bond and Ojiambo, 2015; Macdonald, 2016). Sometimes the diversity of voices of poor women or girls become distilled into the experience of a single iconic girl or woman, such as Malala Yousafazi. The challenge this perspective on gender mainstreaming suggests is how to institutionalise around rights and capabilities, perceptions on gender inequality and poverty that may be singular and partial.

The data we collected with groups working on terrains of a middle space concerned with global education policy revealed that the most common approach to the work on gender appears to be either intervention, or intervention with some interaction. We noted limited opportunities for developing processes of debate, discussion and critique across different institutional spaces linked vertically or horizontally. Rarely were there opportunities to take in the full range of possibilities of connection between global, national and local sites of enactment. Sustaining processes of institutionalising work on gender, education and poverty reduction appeared to be a major challenge. We can distinguish broadly between what we have termed a policy-led approach to institutionalisation, largely evident in Kenya, and what we have distinguished as a practice-led approach, documented more in South Africa. This entails policy built up from below. In the concluding section of this chapter we compare and contrast these two approaches and consider their implications for global gender equality and education frameworks.

Interventions: a focus on girls

Examples of interventions in Kenya and South Africa targeting aspects of gender equality or poverty in relation to education were found across all research sites, generally focussed on particular problems associated with girls. Few interventions sought to bring work on poverty together with work on gender or address issues of inequality more holistically. Some interventions were one-off actions, or short term in duration, others were implemented over a much longer time frame, and, in some cases showed signs of starting to be institutionalised within the department, school or organisation. In a number of cases interventions were developed or implemented through collaborations between different groups or organisations. However, the data points to the challenges of sustaining interventions and moving from a targeted focus on mitigating specific forms of disadvantage to addressing wider structures of inequality.

Interventions which focused on issues of poverty included large-scale, country-wide initiatives – in particular the introduction of FPE in Kenya and the child support grants in South Africa – and very localised, small-scale interventions. In Kenya, for example, the rural NGO had undertaken a number of interventions to help build a community dam, boreholes, provide infrastructure for primary schools in remote areas, build two girls' dormitories, providing beds, mattresses, cookers and solar lighting. It had also established a scholarship scheme to support the studies of teachers and health workers. Local interventions were not confined to NGOs. In South Africa, we noted district officials working to support the provision of lunch, school uniforms, school gardens and help with accessing child support grants. At the school level in South Africa, teachers were documented running interventions to help a particular child or family facing a moment of need. The head teacher explained that through participation in the National School Nutrition Programme (NSNP), pupils were able to receive a hot meal and sometimes additional food for other family members:

> I'm happy because that person [who supplies food to the school] has a tendency of giving us more food so now . . . we've got a process of giving . . . to those families that are struggling more.
>
> (South Africa, Principal, 25/03/2008)

In Kenya, there were fewer poverty reduction initiatives noted at the school level. Despite FPE, and the fact that the school could not charge fees, 450 shillings (£3.50) was required from each pupil. This, it was said, was to help the school settle an unpaid electricity bill, but it was clearly deterring very poor parents from sending their children to school. The feeding scheme that had been running at the school had come to an end in 2002, pointing to problems of sustaining interventions in the long term. Staff members expressed disappointment that the scheme had ended. The head teacher explained:

> I think when we re-sit in the meeting they just talk of asking the government to support with food and as I told you the other time, this zone was removed from the feeding program due to some problems here and there. And when we go to the office to ask for the same, their excuse is it's the responsibility of the parents to feed their children. So we hit the rock.
>
> (Kenya, Head teacher, 29/05/2008)

In all these examples of interventions we see how particular groups, NGO workers, teachers, district officials, tend to work on an aspect of poverty or girls' education separated from a wider strategy of addressing the complexities of gender inequalities and poverty. Global, national and local relationships are not part of the way in which these interventions are understood, although links between the local and the national are sometimes evoked.

Interventions targeted at what were termed 'girls' problems' were a feature of work in the national and provincial education departments in both countries. Often these did not address the causes of the problem, although sometimes government officials worked with civil society or the private sector. In Kenya, many of the pilot initiatives implemented under KESSP identified girls as either victims of early marriage or as not being able to attend school during menstruation. With NGOs, the MOE established and supported interventions which focussed on girls. These included Rescue Centres, where girls at risk of early marriage could be taken. With support from a private company, sanitary towels were distributed to girls enrolled in government schools:

we have now a programme where we are providing sanitary towels to 20,000 girls in about 130 schools nationwide for two years. These are girls in class six, seven and eight. That has also seen some of the girls remain in school.
(Kenya, National Official 1, 14/10/2009)

The interventions which focussed on girls did not engage with issues concerning the causes of poverty or the gender discrimination that kept them out of school or forced into early marriage.

The Provincial Education department in South Africa also partnered with the private sector and some NGOs in work that focussed on girls, without any deeper engagement with gender inequalities or the sources of poverty. Bursaries were provided for girls training as teachers in science and technology. A TechnoGirl Project placed girls with a company where, during school holidays, they did job-shadowing and had some mentoring (Province Official 2, 20/02/2009). The Department of Trade and Industry was a partner to the PED on a Technology Women in Business (TWIB) Competition. Girls from rural districts developed business plans for a technology-based venture such as a low-energy cooker. These were entered into a competition and the winners received study scholarships. These were all examples of groups working across some the terrains of a middle space, but the orientation to interventions meant that the potential for addressing the causes of poverty or inequality, as opposed to some effects, was somewhat limited.

However, it was not always the case that all interventions which focussed on poor girls were so narrow in orientation. In South Africa a number of the interventions spearheaded by the Gender Equity Unit (GEU) engaged with building the public sphere to reflect on concerns with teenage pregnancy or Gender Based Violence (GBV). These included the production of resources, such as Genderations, a newspaper supplement, and Speak Out, a resource aimed at young learners on dealing with GBV. At provincial level a peer education programme was being supported in schools for boys and girls working with issues around sexuality, gender relations, teen pregnancy and gender-based violence. There was some civil society involvement with some of these initiatives.

In these interventions there are some attempts to mitigate the problems and forms of inequality identified, and address particular disadvantages faced by girls in terms of their ability to participate in schooling or access particular subject areas. However, the interventions are often quite narrowly conceived. Even though people are working in the terrains of a middle space across organisational boundaries, involving government officials, teachers, civil society and sometimes the building of a public sphere, we can see that often interventions are not connected to broader processes of transformation, to address wider structures of gender inequality or poverty, locally, nationally or globally. The funding for many of these programmes was precarious, reliant on private donors, conditional grants from the National Treasury to provincial departments and discretionary funds, controlled at provincial or district level by senior managers, and sometimes withdrawn, as was the case with the funds for school feeding in Kenya. The resources for interventions were not being institutionalised, and the very approach to interventions as partial and project led worked against this being a strategic engagement for gender mainstreaming change.

Thus the form of action around gender we noted most frequently in all the different research sites were interventions, where there was little attention to mainstreaming, sustainability or building an institutional landscape in which gender equality and women's rights could be supported. However, it was not always the case that all interventions were narrowly conceived and executed to focus only on girls and meanings of poverty linked with income. In some research sites we noted interventions that were coupled with interactions, and processes of changing practice from below.

A practice-led approach: linking interventions and interactions

We have termed a practice-led approach to engaging with gender, education and poverty, an approach which combined aspects of interactions, and attending to voices and perspectives close to the experience of poverty, coupled with interventions that sought to effect some limited change. In South Africa – though not in Kenya – some of the interventions undertaken by the provincial department, were concerned with addressing gender inequalities more broadly beyond a concern with specific issues relating to girls, though not necessarily linking to issues around poverty. For example, the PED supported working with learners outside of their lessons in voluntary clubs, where issues about gender, health and values could be addressed. The clubs included the Boys and Girls Education Movement (B-GEM) clubs initiated by UNICEF, and Soul Buddyz clubs, which focused on public health, especially HIV and AIDS prevention. Workshops and training for teachers and education officials also reviewed gender issues. A special five-day training programme, funded via a large provincial NGO in 2010, had brought together three-person groups from ten schools per district and had been held in seven districts. After the training around a range of health and gender issues the groups held 'dialogues' with other members of their school communities in order to develop school plans. According to research participants, fresh understandings about HIV and AIDS, nutrition, and links between both of these and gender-based violence had led to significant enhancement of understanding at school level. A week long workshop had been held for the PED about gender policies and gender mainstreaming staff (Fieldnotes, 14–15/08/2009; Province Official 2, 30/11/2010). Although PED's senior managers did not attend the workshops and sent administrators (Province Official 1, 30/11/2010), the Provincial Gender Focal Person acknowledged this was very useful:

> The admin staff members realized that they give preference to men in allocating them 'good' and new cars. . . . The men who attended the workshops [said . . .] the workshops were an eye-opener and they now understand that gender was more than merely being about women's issues. [. . .] staff now look at things differently in meetings and they understand that addressing gender inequalities in not a once-off thing and that all can do something about it. Another effect is that now staff members are reporting incidents of sexual abuse and sexual harassment more than was the case in the past.
> (South Africa, Province Official 1, 30/11/2010)

The training workshops for staff and students, although they take the form of interventions, engage a public sphere of discussion and debate, which officials within bureaucracies who are concerned with gender see as an important area of support to their work. Sometimes these workshops draw on aspects of the global currents of debate being channelled by organisations like UNESCO or the large NGO that did the work with the PED on gender mainstreaming in South Africa. Here we see interventions, linking with interactions, and some consideration of how gender mainstreaming work may be institutionalised.

In Kenya, although the national MOE used NGOs to help take forward some of its interventions around girls' education, interactive discussions around gender issues were harder to connect to the terrains of institution building. In a project run by the global NGO in Kenya, girls spoke about some of their anxieties concerning violence, prostitution, rape on the way to or from school, early pregnancy and marriage. Their frankness on these issues suggests the interventions this project supported around latrines may have contributed to building a culture of openness, as other work in Kenya details how difficult girls found it to talk about these issues (Parkes et al., 2016). But limited connections to institutional engagements on these issues was documented. One of the girls said:

> The biggest problem is the sex preference, and you are told you have no right. At times you are married off early to a very old man, whom you don't

want and who cannot satisfy conjugal needs. You will be told to go away. But there is nowhere you can go.

(Kenya, Girls Focus Group Discussion, November 2010)

The NGO was working with some representatives in the communities to argue against early marriage, but this programme had not as yet developed into a full-scale engagement with the complexities of violence against women, or work with the District officials to understand causes and how to support change.

In Kenya, partnership with NGOs or professional organisations was seen by government officials to aid policy dissemination and adoption through decentralisation and to promote top-down policy formulation with bottom-up led implementation. The KESSP was being supported by a NGO network which assisted with, drafting training materials and leading in-service training programmes. While the potential of this approach was eloquently sketched, there was little comment on how capacity within the Education Ministry would be built to support it or where resources to support teachers to work on gender issues would come from. One terrain of a middle space was being used to support another, but without work on gender being understood as transformative across terrains. An official from the national Ministry detailed the piecemeal approach:

You know if we can decentralise the gender using the government policies on decentralisation you remove the gender from the ministry. We don't do too many activities. Let the activities go to the teacher training colleges so that you empower the TTCs. . . . Now we want the effect to trickle down to the teacher trainees so that the effect goes down to the children. . . . I think gender needs to go down towards the people so that when you talking about the school where you visit, let gender be implemented from there so that it doesn't begin from here (MOE). Here begins to do more of the direction, let the SAGAs take up.

(Kenya, National Official 1, 14/10/2009)

In this account, there is very little sense of how work on gender in all these sites could be sustained or resourced.

A focus on collaboration with NGOs in order to implement programmes was also apparent at in the Kenyan district department. In this case, horizontal relationships organised through NGOs, some local and some global, were considered problematic because they gave no indication of how they might be sustained. A field note prepared by a member of our research team that noted district officers consider:

The evidence is overwhelming that school enrolment almost triples when there was school feeding programme. One major challenge is that the school feeding programme is being sponsored by NGOs; the CCF would come in, World Vision and MAAP. When these NGOs withdrew, because these programmes were not going for long, that is when the problem began. Now there was the whole issue of sustainability, and it was agreed that actually communities now, would need to own this school feeding programmes in terms of providing labour for the cooks, in terms of even growing food as we have said. So sustainability was actually the problem. The NGO would not come there start a feeding programme, and run for ten years, they will go for three years then they go to another place, so when they go the children also drop out of school. So ownership and sustainability of programmes is a big challenge.

(Kenya, Fieldnotes, July 2009)

In both cases, although by bringing together different actors – governmental departments and NGOs – the types of collaboration described could be seen to entail some form of interaction. The focus on service delivery and implementation of interventions did not allow for more critical interaction involving discussion, debate. The form of collaboration involved is associated with a strong sense of bureaucratic practices of policy delivery, rather than any sense of discussion, dialogue or accountability. Global NGOs are seen to be part of this mix, but they are associated with some technical strengths relating to work on gender, rather than involvement in helping to analyse the problems and collaborate on change.

The practice-led approach to linking interactions and interventions did not do much to support building an institutional culture to sustain change around gender equality and education policies. Similar criticisms could be made of the work that was more 'purely' an expression of the interactionist approach, was not tied to particular interventions and was often more concerned with process.

Interactions

Much of the work that could be classified as interactive engagements with gender mainstreaming was associated with groups working on the terrain of civil society and did not have a clear programme about how it might link with interventions or institutions, nationally or globally. For example, the national NGO in South Africa, which had direct links to global networks, had begun implementing a Gender Violence programme with community partners. They provided information and handbooks. A next step had been to take the programme into high schools. A lengthy process of getting permission from the district office followed where the true nature of the initiative was left vague:

. . . because we did not want to scare her [the district official] – we said 'it's child sponsorship but we want to do other things, gender training . . . what, what'.

(South Africa, National NGO, staff member 3, 07/12/2010)

The NGO was equivocal about the nature of the project because their interactionist aim of getting girls to talk about GBV in small groups was difficult to link with the work of a PED. The complexity and emotion entailed in working on women's rights and gender issues was frankly acknowledged, but strategies to institutionalise this, and hold this together with supportive interactive work was difficult.

The NGO workers were extremely sensitive to the conditions, experiences and politics in local settings, but lacked a direction on how to build from this to work on gender and poverty at other levels. For girls in schools the NGO anticipated:

> They'll cry, there'll be an emotional outbreak. But because my profession is social work, it's easy – you allow that to happen.
>
> (South Africa, National NGO, staff member 3, 07/12/2010)

According to this NGO worker, the girls reported degrading names and insults but, once the ice was broken, they opened up about harassment, abuse and in one or two instances rape. In some cases, the NGO worker has intervened, visiting the family and providing support when criminal charges were laid. The work was not straight-forward or finished once the workshops were done. Ramifications spread across from school to home to the legal system:

> And I think it's helpful. One of the chiefs was saying to me, that since you've been coming to these schools it's been better, because I've been getting less complaints. And I said, "you should be getting more complaints" because it's happening.
>
> (South Africa, National NGO, staff member 3, 07/12/2010)

There was thus denial of the nature of the problem in official circles. The NGO worker had an astute insight into the problem, but the project she was working on did not give her scope to work further on this. Taking the interactionist approach beyond talking to the girls entailed work to engage community members, raise consciousness amongst men and change attitudes more widely, but this brought out conflicts about power and the difficulties of social change:

> The feeling that is killing people . . . is men think women have got more rights – rights from somewhere. And they can't see women's rights as human rights. That's why I've been saying that in our training on gender sensitivity, men have to be there – so they can understand. Because even if they read a booklet that says: 'women's rights are human rights' they still can't see that sentence – they ignore that sentence. And that makes them feel that they are going to fight for extra rights – beyond human rights – there are these men's rights that they have to have now that women are getting these women's rights. I doubt if they put it bluntly. And I told them: the best weapon – in the name of ownership of the particular programme we are running, we have to have the chiefs, the gatekeepers of the communities to sit in the circles – and understand what we're doing. Because sometimes they think we are gossiping, we're just influencing people negatively. But if they're there they

can see: 'no, this is what is happening. It is a positive thing.' We get a buy-in from them it becomes easy to roll-out the programme.

(South Africa, National NGO, staff member 3, 07/12/2010)

Clearly interactions needed deepening beyond a few workshops. NGO workers were aware of the importance of linking with processes of intervention and institutionalisation, but did not have the time or space to do this. What was needed were considerably beyond the remit of the work of a civil society or public sphere, and required connection with professional organisations and civil servants under a framework of law. This went far beyond the specific projects of this global NGO.

A second form of interaction involved work with local communities. This did not always relate directly to education and gender equality issues. For example, in South Africa the local NGO formed ongoing links with local schools and health services and liaised regularly with village decision-making structures, such as the traditional leaders. These entailed forms of intervention and interaction, but actions were not directed towards gender equality or poverty reduction. The Kenyan local NGO did capacity building work on 'livestock improvement, water resources management, livestock diseases and control, and business development' (Local NGO, staff member 4, 26/05/2010). It also contributed to institution building working with local officials, particularly assisting with training for SMCs and teachers in twenty-one primary schools. It ran programmes to sensitise the community on the importance of education for girls and boys. These local interactions had some focus on improvements for girls and boys, but did not entail in depth work on gender equality or the causes of poverty.

In Kenya, the school head teacher also described efforts to sensitise the local community regarding issues such as early marriage, in order to support girls' education and enable their enrolment in school:

> We have created awareness through the chiefs, local leaders, SMC, the learned and the parents. We are preaching so that the anomaly can stop and I would say it is positive. So for maintenance of those who are here, it is possible. The other issue is when they go to STD 8 we try so that they pass KCPE and go to the next level.
>
> (Kenya, Head Teacher, 29/05/2008)

In these cases, there is recognition of the need to engage local communities in efforts to overcome poverty and forms of discrimination and inequality. However, in relation to concerns regarding gender equality and education, the assumption is that parents need to be "sensitised" or educated in order to send daughters to school, and to prevent harmful practices such as early marriage; there is less concern with eliciting the views of parents and community members themselves and engaging them in discussion and debate regarding the nature of education, or their views on gender equality. In some cases these forms of interaction with local communities, rather than facilitating more participatory processes of planning, discussion and critique, entailed processes of blame and stigmatisation of the poor, as discussed in the previous chapter.

Some more critical forms of interaction could be found among the activities of the national NGOs and the international institutions. In both countries, as well as having some programmes focused on the implementation of specific inventions, the national NGOs were involved in local-level awareness raising in workshops, seminars, non-formal education classes and information exchange, networking horizontally with other community-level organisations and with aims to reach national and international levels, and forms of political mobilisation to lobby and campaign around particular education, gender or poverty reduction provision that the government is failing to fulfil.

In South Africa, the national NGO had taken tentative steps to shift their work away from development projects and into influencing policy (National NGO, staff member 1, 09/12/2010). The idea was to strengthen civil society networks and there was a hope that this would grow into a way of mobilising women around issues that would change public policy. A programme manager explained:

> So there is always been those kinds of challenges . . . how do you provide service delivery projects at the same time not . . . letting the government get away with it because they are the ones who are supposed to be providing some of those requirements that communities need. But at the same time building the capacities of communities to claim those rights from officials themselves without us being in the fore front that actually do that.
>
> (South Africa, National NGO, staff member 4, July 2009)

The NGO's programme work was not just focused on addressing poverty but on finding opportunities for women to have a voice both as an expression of their experiences of poverty and in meeting with others to discuss ways of overcoming poverty. Finding a democratic format for raising issues was also a political act and one which through various communication devises could be escalated into advocacy campaigns:

> It's more on focusing on the root causes of poverty so that then, as we are actually planning and trying to discuss how we deal we that, we are actually involving women to see that they see is important, needs to be so ensuring those voices are heard.
>
> (South Africa, National NGO, staff member 2, 23/07/2009)

In one area, for example, the programme officer had been encouraging the women to fetch condoms (particularly female condoms) from the clinic – but they had been laughed away by the nurses. As a consequence:

> I remember three months back we invited [another NGO] to come and explain this new user-friendly condom to the women. So that those women

could go and campaign and also after campaign they will have access to these kinds of condoms.

(South Africa, National NGO, staff member 5, July 2009)

The linkage the NGO had made with another NGO to develop the computer skills of school girls was partly to respond to a perceived need around lack of computer skills but it mainly the aim was to use the medium as a way for girls to communicate their issues and link to through the internet to a global platform. Explaining the reason behind the ICT project, a programme manager says:

We feel that especially in rural areas young girls are not exposed to a lot of education materials and things like in urban areas but also because of cultural whatever you want to call it . . . but they don't have the space to sit and discuss their issues so this sort of has created that opportunity for them to share amongst themselves . . . seek information and guidance. . . .

(South Africa, National NGO, staff member 4, July 2009)

In the work of this NGO there is an explicit concern to engage programme participants, as well as other stakeholders in discussion and debate about issues that affect them. However, seeking to open up spaces for more critical forms of interaction, and engaging in debate around issues relation to gender, rights and equality did not come without difficulties.

The interactions approach, thus, while concerned with connecting with voices and perspectives from the poor, the most marginalised and excluded, and suggesting some approaches to radical transformation, did not work on sustaining change and building the terrains of a middle space either singly or together to institutionalise change.

Fragile institutions: the policy-led approach

Across all the research sites, sustaining processes of institutionalising work on gender, education and poverty reduction appeared to be a major challenge. Effectively mainstreaming gender within different institutional spaces, and bringing together work on gender, poverty and education to take in interactionist and interventionist approached was a challenge. In both countries, large-scale interventions, implemented over a period of time showed signs of becoming institutionalised, but their work on gender was not always mainstreamed. In Kenya, for example, FPE, while partly conceived as an intervention to encourage children to enrol in school, was moving towards institutionalisation through the enactment of the Constitution and the work of the Commission on Human Rights and Gender equality encouraging reflections on why poor children did not attend or progress through school (Heymann, Raub and Cassola, 2014). The promulgation of the new constitution in 2010 entrenched the right to free and compulsory education (article 53, 1b) and was accompanied by the establishment of the Gender Commission to oversee the work of the government, but the persistence of gender inequalities and their links with poverty were hard to address through joined up strategic work.

In South Africa, the NSNP, originally introduced in 1994 by President Nelson Mandela as a centrally directed poverty-related intervention to provide one free meal daily, was being implemented in 2009 in approximately 3,800 government schools serving the poorest communities, referred to as Quintiles 1 and 2 (Province Official 4, 20/02/2009). The intervention had some potential to address causes of poverty, with food sourced from women's cooperatives in the province:

> [In] the nutrition programme [the MEC] mandated the nutrition supply chain directorates to make sure that the cooperatives should be made out of women, should be women groups that should be doing the nutrition programme in schools.
>
> (South Africa, Province Official 4, 20/02/2009)

This was one of very few interventions documented in any of the research sites that brought together concerns with poverty and gender issues.

While it has been possible to institutionalise interventions designed to address aspects of gender (in)equality or poverty the focus of these on the very poorest were not sustained in the long term. In some cases, as seen in the South African Provincial Department, this was associated with vulnerable funding. This was compounded by issues of capacity: in both countries it was clear that many staff, particularly at district and province level did not have enough training, time for discussion and reflection, or information to develop policy implementation beyond a process of roll out of directives developed elsewhere. This meant that in both countries, poverty reduction and gender equity initiatives at provincial and district level had not been well institutionalised, beyond the provision of low cost education.

However, the lack of success in institutionalising work on gender (or poverty), and the fragile nature of processes of institutionalisation appear to be linked to structures and forms of disjuncture within and between spaces. This was particularly clear in relation to the national education departments in both countries, where concerns with gender equality were seen as the responsibility of a separate – and under resourced – gender unit, and thus officials did not consider that they should be required to take action to mainstream gender through their own work. When field research was being carried out in the Kenya national department, a very common riposte when researchers asked whether a particular IP had a gender plan was to refer them to the gender IP. Although it was quite unrealistic to think that the officer who headed this IP, and who was not a senior figure in the organisation, could mainstream gender, a defensive response to some of the researchers' questions was to say that this was the so far not completed work of the head of the gender IP. For example, one senior official clearly laid responsibility for ensuring gender was mainstreamed through the KESSP activities at the door of the gender office:

> . . . the gender officer is very crucial but you also need the boss, the Director, because under KESSP gender was brought on board. But you know now gender should be a cross cutting issue. But if . . . they have not made gender a cross cutting issue because the gender office should first meet with all the other IPs and they should have imposed on them. In fact they should have done a concept note for them and helped them to infuse gender activities in their programmes.
>
> (Kenya, National Official 8, 17/10/2008)

Meanwhile in the South African national department, some officials considered gender to be a 'special case' to be dealt with by the Gender Equity Unit (GEU), a directorate within the DoE. They saw the GEU as responsible for implementing gender specific policy. Officials recognised the importance of the work of the unit:

> I think there is always a danger for all these areas – gender, race and value, rural education (to a certain extent) – is that you have to explain them all the time. People are always saying these are soft issues, do we really need them, let's absorb them into the curriculum section, whatever. There is always that danger that the unit is in now. Three years ago I might have said well basically there's no reason to argue why but now I would says it's incredibly dangerous to close them down. I think we are going to need to always justify why – it's clear why you need IQMS, or foundation or literacy because that's our biggest challenge in the country.
>
> (South Africa, National Official 6, 04/02/2010)

However, the GEU itself (as well as other directorates in the same chief directorate) had lost personnel after a departmental reorganisation, meaning the extent to which it could realistically be expected to ensure that gender was mainstreamed across the department was limited.

The difficulties associated with mainstreaming concerns around gender appeared to be exacerbated by disjunctures between different teams within departments, and a lack of a culture of collaboration. In the Kenyan national department, Kenyan officials admitted that the sort of collaborative work which might facilitate gender to be mainstreamed across the department was not common. One official, while admitting that they did not have appropriate expertise in gender, explained:

> the linkage aspect and how people are working and the challenges they are facing and how each IP can support complement and so on is not common.
>
> (Kenya, National Official 9, 17/10/2008)

As this official notes, despite a number of cross-cutting themes in the KESSP, the ways of working in the MoE did not support the diffusion of expertise across various IPs. Given the caution and limited expertise concerning gender, it is a tall order to expect officials, whose work environment does not make collaboration very easy, to take on board a whole range of new and challenging ideas and apply them in a context fraught with anxiety about audit, hierarchy and accountability. The lack of a culture of collaborative work made delivering on cross-cutting themes, even in areas that, unlike gender, were relatively uncontroversial, very difficult. In this work environment it is clear that a purposive vision of development handed top-down might be easier to execute.

Similarly, in South Africa, part of the problem with developing strategies to embed gender across the system within the national department was that directorates effectively worked in silos with little cross-pollination. This is reflected clearly in the following extract:

I: Are there directorates that you work closely with on issues of gender?
R: For me, no. Really, no. Why I'm saying that is because we are a branch that deals with social issues – if I can put it in a layman's language – whether you talking gender, rural development, race, values, nutrition programmes, health – so we are that branch. And even within the branch I would say we are not working in the manner in which we are supposed to be. If you talk gender programme, if you touch issues – like curriculum which is outside our branch, another branch. For me it hasn't got to the level as yet.

(South Africa, National Official 7, 17/08/2010)

It was not just in the national education departments that lack of collaboration between teams was a recognised problem. In global organisations, despite explicit commitments to mainstreaming gender, ensuring that gender was embedded in work on education and bringing together concerns with gender and poverty was not always easy. Several participants pointed to the need for coordinated responses that dealt with poverty, gender and education simultaneously, and brought together teams and experts working on each of the three issues. However, they also recognised that these links were not always forthcoming and collaborative work between teams was not the norm. Two participants spoke explicitly about working 'in silos'. One INGO participant explained:

I think we all get accused of working in silos and for sure we do . . . so a lot of it is that poverty is seen as those people's expertise, and education is seen as those. And I think we come from very different routes . . .

(International civil society organisation 5,
staff member, 03/03/2008)

Meanwhile, at national level, difficulties associated with developing institutions for gender equality and poverty also related to vertical forms of disjuncture, and, in particular, the challenges associated with ensuring that concerns with gender expressed in the national departments and written into policy filtered down to provinces, districts and schools. By the second round of data collection in the national MoE in Kenya there was an awareness that the process of working needed to be articulated through wide discussion, training and the overlapping involvement of many parts of the education system. This was a more measured view than that expressed defensively at the project outset, when a senior official had said to the research team that there was little point in conducting the study in multiple sites, as it would be achieved in stages led from the MoE by the gender officer:

> I understand the purpose for you will be to use gender as a cross cutting issue and relate it to the MDGs. Perhaps one MDG. And you should have actually found out from the gender officer what are the anticipations. What I know is that we are even training gender officers from SAGAs now. If you are training people on gender from the SAGAs and the university now, will the information could have reached the school? If our own SAGAs don't know. I don't think we have reached all the districts. If we have not reached all the districts to train and talk with district education officers, how do we expect the schools to access that information? Because we know we might be expecting too much . . .
>
> (Kenya, National Official 8, 17/10/2008)

Similarly, in South Africa, the complication of devising strategies that would filter down vertically compounded the difficulty of mainstreaming gender horizontally across the national department, was:

> But the overall challenge is with regards to the role of national department and the role of provinces. I am sure you know that at national, we are not responsible for implementation, we only get to implement because you find your way around rules and then you find yourself in the school but you are not really supposed to be responsible for implementation that is mainly managed at provincial and district level. And where we are we are expected to help in defining policy and programmes and working with the provinces to capacitate them and that they understand and agree on what the job should be and then they get that done. The issue is although you are national and they are provincial we don't have power over what they do, the Constitution gives them you know they are autonomous, they are their own person, they can do with the money the way they please, they can do with their staff they way they please.
>
> (South Africa, National Official 13, 26/08/2009)

Reaching schools was still a further hurdle. In South Africa participants recognised that if there was consciousness of gender issues within the department, then the disjuncture came with cascading that to schools. So while recognising the problem as one of 'attitudes', there were no clear strategies to overcome this. Senior officials commented on lack of capacity:

> The reality is that part of the reason it is not happening is not about lack of political will and money – it's about lack of capacity to deal with the issues. We can say that about all of us. These are complicated issues that are not simplified easily into policy documents. So these are quite complicated issues. . . . They are political issues in the sense that they are about changing policy, changing the way people think, about power relations. So I think it's a whole combination of things.
>
> (South Africa, National Official 6, 04/02/2010)

Other participants suggested that although there is a statement in policy, the implementation and the effectiveness of the policy falls far short of the stated targets.

> Because I think, I mean the, the world still a male dominated world, our country is still a male dominated country. So you know the whole infra-structure, you know textbooks, culture in schools, culture in institutions and organizations, still tends to be male dominated. So there is a gap between what the policy is expecting schools to do and what actually goes on.
>
> (South Africa, National Official 1, 07/11/2008)

The data suggest that the extent to which concerns with gender equality have reached and been operationalised within the school is limited. There has been more success in embedding concerns with poverty in the school's institutional workings through, for example, a welfare Committee; having a teacher respon-sible for social care and rights matters and; free meal for learners and the employ-ment of local women as cooks; the provision of hygiene bins for older girls. The school governing body has some role in each of these actions and it may be the key ingredient which bodes well for the longevity of these actions. In this, the South African school has gone a very long way towards working on poverty reduc-tion compared to the school in Kenya, where there is no institutional commit-ment to poverty reduction – in fact additional fees and costs are demanded from the poorest – and where the interventions and interactions which were reported were sporadic and un-coordinated. However, despite the achievements of the school in South Africa in establishing and sustaining the feeding scheme, many of its actions too were not able to develop the procedural or processual spaces to take forward work on gender and poverty in part due to the large numbers of orphans and poor children which the school was obliged to assist. Teacher 1 esti-mated that 30% of the learners were single or double orphans and the parents of the other learners were mostly unemployed (Teacher 1, 26/07/2010). The resources distributed to the school from the province were clearly just allowing them to provide a minimal service for these children.

The data suggest that attempts to institutionalise action to address gender inequality and poverty across all sites were fragile, and that concerns with tackling different forms of inequality, which relate both to gender and poverty, together were not well embedded or operationalised either within the formal education system or within NGOs. Within the education department at national and local levels in both countries this was compounded by the lack of a culture of collaborative work across programmes or directorates coupled with the housing of responsibility for gender in a separate, under-resourced, unit. In Kenya, this was to some extent further hindered by the introduction of results based managements across the KESSP: while advocates claim it will lead to greater clarity and transparency and a stronger focus on clearer goal setting and value for money measurements, it allows for little attention to reviewing gender issues, thinking what processes should be institutionalised or considering how critical debate might improve the programme. At local levels many staff in district and provincial departments, as well as teachers in the schools, did not have enough training, time for discussion and reflection, or information and resources to engage in policy implementation beyond a process of roll out of directives developed elsewhere. Meanwhile, despite the active role that NGOs – local, national and global – were playing in mobilising around aspects of poverty and gender inequality, among staff at local levels there was often very little concern or knowledge about gender, although the everyday experiences of poverty were very close at hand. Thus, in both countries the emphasis was primarily on short-term interventions and interactions with communities, and not well focussed on helping build particular institutions to sustain gender equity and poverty reduction work in education.

This chapter indicates how the interpretation of global gender equality policy focussed largely on interventions, or on interventions with some interactions. The very limited attention given to building institutions and terrains of a middle space to support the development of institutions meant that the EFA and MDG frameworks were generally interpreted as limited and partial engagements, which did not in and of themselves generate strategies for sustainability.

References

African Union (2003). *Protocol to the African Charter on Human and Peoples' Rights on the Rights of Women in Africa.* 2nd Ordinary Session of the Assembly of the Union, Maputo , Mozambique, 11 July.
Alvesson, M., & Billing, Y. D. (2009). *Understanding Gender and Organisations.* London: Sage Publications Ltd.
Baily, S., & Holmarsdottir, H. B. (2015). The quality of equity? Reframing gender, development and education in the post-2020 landscape. *Gender and Education*, 27(7), pp. 828–845.
Beall, J. (2005). Decentralizing government and decentering gender: Lessons from local government reform in South Africa. *Politics & Society*, 33(2), pp. 253–276.
Bock, B. B. (2015). Gender mainstreaming and rural development policy: The trivialisation of rural gender issues. *Gender, Place & Culture*, 22(5), pp. 731–745.
Charlesworth, H. (2005). Not waving but drowning: Gender mainstreaming and human rights in the United Nations. *Harvard Human Rights Journal*, 18(1), pp. 1–18.

Cornwall, A., & Edwards, J. (2015). Introduction: Beijing+ 20 – Where now for gender equality? *IDS Bulletin*, 46(4), pp. 1–8.

DeJaeghere, J. (2015). Reframing gender and education for the post-2015 agenda. In MCGrath, Q. G., eds. *Routledge Handbook of International Education and Development*. Abingdon: Routledge, pp. 62–77.

Dralega, C. A., Jemaneh, A., Jjuko, M., & Kantono, R. (2016). Gender mainstreaming in media and journalism education – an audit of media departments in Uganda, Rwanda and Ethiopia. *Journal of African Media Studies*, 8(3), pp. 251–266.

Eerdewijk, A., & Davids, T. (2014). Escaping the mythical beast: Gender mainstreaming reconceptualised. *Journal of International Development*, 26(3), pp. 303–316.

Goetz, A. M. (1997). Getting institutions right for women in development. London: ZED Books.

Grindle, M. S., & Thomas, J. W. (1991). *Public Choices and Policy Change: The Political Economy or Reform in Developing Countries*. Baltimore: The John Hopkins University Press.

Hassim, S. (2006). *Women's Organizations and Democracy in South Africa*. Wisconsin: University of Wisconsin Press.

Heymann, J., Raub, A., & Cassola, A. (2014). Constitutional rights to education and their relationship to national policy and school enrolment. *International Journal of Educational Development*, 39, pp. 121–131.

Hunt, A., Bond, H., & Ojiambo Ochieng, R. (2015). Bridging inequalities through inclusion: Women's rights organisations as the 'missing link'in donor government-led participatory policy development and practice. *Gender & Development*, 23(2), pp. 347–364.

Kabeer, N. (1995). Targeting women or transforming institutions? *Development in Practice*, 5(2), pp. 108–116.

Karlsson, J. (2010). Gender mainstreaming in a South African provincial education department: A transformative shift or technical fix for oppressive gender relations? *Compare: A Journal of Comparative and International Education*, 40(4), pp. 497–514.

Kaufman, J. P., & Williams, K. P. (2015). Women, DDR and post-conflict transformation: Lessons from the cases of Bosnia and South Africa. *Journal of Research in Gender Studies*, 5(2), pp. 11–53.

Koehler, G. (2016). Tapping the Sustainable Development Goals for progressive gender equity and equality policy? *Gender & Development*, 24(1), pp. 53–68.

MacDonald, K. (2016). Calls for educating girls in the Third World: Futurity, girls and the 'Third World Woman'. *Gender, Place & Culture*, 23(1), pp. 1–17.

Macdonald, M., Sprenger, E., & Dubel, I. (1997). *Gender and Organizational Change: Bridging the Gap between Policy and Practice*. Amsterdam: Royal Tropical Institute.

Miller, C., & Razavi, S. (1998). *Missionaries and Mandarins: Feminist Engagement with Development Institutions*. London: Intermediate Technology.

Mukhopadhyay, M. (2016). 'Mainstreaming Gender or "Streaming" Gender Away' Revisited. In Harcourt, W. ed. *The Palgrave Handbook of Gender and Development*. London: Palgrave Macmillan, pp. 132–142.

Parkes, J., Heslop, J., Januario, F., Oando, S., & Sabaa, S. (2016). Between tradition and modernity: Girls' talk about sexual relationships and violence in Kenya, Ghana and Mozambique. *Comparative Education*, 52(2), pp. 157–176.

Rai, S. M. (2003). *Mainstreaming Gender, Democratizing the State: International Mechanisms for the Advancement of Women*. Manchester: Manchester University Press.

Rao, A., Sandler, J., Kelleher, D., & Miller, C. (2015). *Gender at Work: Theory and Practice for 21st Century Organizations*. Abingdon: Routledge.

SID (2010). *Kenya's Vision 2030: An Audit from an Income and Gender Inequalities Perspective*. Nairobi: Society for International Development.

Skaard, T. (2009). Gender in the malestream: Acceptance of women and gender equality in Different United Nations Organisations. *Forum for Development Studies*, 36(1), pp. 155–197.

Squires, J. (2005). Is mainstreaming transformative? Theorizing mainstreaming in the context of diversity and deliberation. *Social Politics*, 12(3), pp. 366–388.

Steiner-Khamsi, G. (2004). *The Global Politics of Educational Borrowing and Lending*. New York: Teachers College Press.

UNESCO (2003). *UNESCO's Gender Mainstreaming Implementation Framework 2002–2007*. Paris: UNESCO. [online]. Available at http://unesdoc.unesco.org/images/0013/001318/131854e.pdf. Accessed 12 February 2017.

Unterhalter, E. (2007). *Gender, Schooling and Global Social Justice*. Abingdon: Routledge.

Unterhalter, E. (2009). Translations and transversal dialogues: An examination of mobilities associated with gender, education and global poverty reduction. *Comparative Education* 45(3), pp. 329–345.

Unterhalter, E., & North, A. (2010). Assessing gender mainstreaming in the education sector: Depoliticised technique of a step towards women's rights and gender equality? *Compare: A Journal of Comparative and International Education*, 40(4), pp. 389–404.

Verloo, M. (2005). Displacement and empowerment: Reflections on the concept and practice of the Council of Europe approach to gender mainstreaming and gender equality. *Social Politics: International Studies in Gender, State & Society*, 12(3), pp. 344–365.

Wallace, T., Porter, F., & Ralph-Bowman, M. (Eds.). (2013). *Aid, NGOs and the Realities of Women's Lives: A Perfect Storm*. Bourton on Dunsmore, Rugby: Practical Action Publishing.

Waterhouse, R., & Kamau, N. (2010). 'Gender mainstreaming in Kenya: Experiences, lessons learned and perspectives for the future' UNIFEM East and Horn of Africa regional office, Social Development Direct.

World Bank (2001). *Engendering Development*. Washington, DC: The World Bank.

World Health Organisation (2009). *Women and Health*. Geneva: World Health Organisation.

9 Perspectives on the SDGs
It's harder than you think

In this book we have examined some of the complex relationships entailed in taking global gender education policy, concerned with equalities and addressing poverty, from the site of agreeing texts, like the MDGs or EFA, to implementation in schools. We have built on literatures which have examined policy transfer (Steiner-Khamsi, 2004; Steiner-Khamsi and Waldow, 2012), policy networks (Vavrus and Bartlett, 2009), the plurality of global education policy making (Mundy et al., 2016), the policy space as a site of negotiation (Grindle and Thomas, 1991), and education policy enactment in local sites (Ball, Maguire and Braun, 2012). We have looked in detail at a small number of global policies – the MDGs, EFA and the Beijing Platform of Action – at a particular historical moment, from 2008–2011.

The issues of concern to us, set out in Chapter 1, were firstly to consider how people, shaped by and shaping social relations under particular historical conditions, inside and outside government, take global gender equality policy and re-make it through practice. We considered the locations and relationships of people an important feature of how policy comes to be realised. We wished to look in detail at how these politico-social locales worked in relation to how global policy on gender equality, education and poverty were understood and enacted. A second issue of interest to us was the fluidity in meanings of gender and poverty, and the challenges entailed, given the lack of precision regarding these terms, in building connections between actors for social development working within and beyond government to support gender equality reform. Thirdly, we wished to investigate whether the critiques of feminist commentators on the MDGs and EFA (Antrobus, 2005; Biccum, 2010; Kabeer, 2015) were justified, and if so, which were the particular sites where substantive visions of transformative gender equality, as outlined at the Beijing Conference of 1995, were being undermined. One aim was to document whether this perception of a dilution of the Beijing Conference vision was shared by people working on gender equality, poverty and education issues in particular global, national and local settings. We set out to investigate the practices and perspectives of reformers and those who refused change.

To undertake this analysis we documented the journey of these global gender equality policy texts between different sites deemed global, national and local. We discussed them with officials working for multilateral organisations and national governments in different locations in Kenya and South Africa. We documented the views of employees of global NGOs, working in the capitals of G8 countries, many of whom were very close to the formulation of the global policy, and their local counterparts in Kenya and South Africa. In each country we also collected the views of employees of rural-based, largely locally funded NGOs, teachers and school management committees, and observed some of the work of NGOs in poor communities, and how schools were situated in settings associated with poverty.

Our analysis worked with conceptual maps that we used to consider global gender equality policy moving to national and local spaces, and some of the forms of relationship that affected how it was interpreted and acted on. We contrasted ways in which global gender equality policy could be seen to travel, and we used three metaphors to consider some of the relationships and discussions we documented. Firstly, the MDGs, EFA and the Beijing Platform of Action, all endorsed by UN organisations, national governments and civil society networks, could be interpreted as a form of policy travelling down a rational ladder of steps of implementation, monitoring and evaluation. Finance, raised from taxes, and aid, supported this progress. According to this model, information clearly formulated was linked with measuring progress. This informed decisions about the next steps to take. Secondly, we suggested, flows of global gender equality policy could be understood as a much more complex set of movements, where global, national and local currents merged, supporting each other sometimes linked with government action within institutions, but sometimes moving through more amorphous spaces of the public sphere, civil society and professional organisation and practice. We used a metaphor of weather systems to convey the potential power of these relationships and the ways in which they were not bounded into a single space or confined to a particular direction. Thirdly, we suggested that global policy concerned with gender, equalities and addressing poverty could be understood as a very personal set of commitments and obligations linked to women's rights, gender equality and feminist activism animating the work of groups of activists connected by concerns with social change and deepening equalities. We used the metaphor of a letter to delineate this process of dedication to meaning making, connection and affiliation.

While much discussion of policy exchange has considered the gap between a text and the site of implementation, we noted the significance of many spaces and relationships that stood between these moments. We termed these, terrains of a middle space and we used our data to investigate four terrains – the institutional relationships within bureaucracies, the public sphere, the professional relationships of teachers and social workers, and the links formed outside the state in NGOs and civil society organisations. We were interested in whether relationships on these terrains shaped or were shaped by flows of global gender equality policies.

Our analysis shows two processes which seem to move in different directions. On the one hand, we point to the complexity of policy negotiation, the fluidity of discursive shifts, particularly concerning gender equality and poverty, and the considerable influence on practice of ideas (whether originating in global policy texts, national or local aspirations) concerning the expansion of education to include all children, features of gender inequality, and the impact of poverty. On the other hand, we note a process of change towards more substantive gender equalities and that addressing the corrosive disadvantages associated with poverty are much harder to effect than the global policy texts suggest or the dreams and aspirations of activists envisage. This is partly because gender inequalities, exclusion and blame of the poor are structured into the political, economic, social and cultural relationships of global, national and local organisations. These do not change under the momentum of policy declaration, but require a work of change that is often difficult to effect. Nonetheless, we documented people working in a range of settings who were committed to make changes in the direction of gender and connected equalities in education, who were not deterred by setbacks, and who had learned a range of strategies to try to effect reform in the sites in which they worked. Thus, relationships within government, in the public sphere, and in civil society do matter and can move in the direction of building gender equality and addressing poverty through education, or can limit the potential of these processes.

The many meanings of gender and poverty may be advantageous to actions to develop connected and substantive equalities, because they can delineate a large terrain on which alliances can be built, and democratic iterations can take place. We showed how the meaning ascribed to gender associated with national contexts could go beyond the limits of monitoring gender parity or confining policy to procedural fairness. But we also showed how, without engaged discussion of gender inequalities and abuses of women's rights, discussion of gender and education could often become blind to the structures of inequality and veer into an essentialised discussion of girls, sexuality and blame. The process of building a common language and solidarities around challenging the structures of inequality that formed poverty was even more difficult. Thus the multiplicities of meanings of gender, poverty and education are a resource, but this appears to be not often enough used to deepen insights into equality polices.

At the level of the policy texts, it is clear that the MDGs and EFA attenuate the vision of the Beijing Platform of Action. But our data show that in places of realisation all three texts were seen as useful in different ways to take forward agendas concerned with gender equalities, poverty and education. Social reformers always went beyond the existing policy text, while those who refused reform were sometimes required by the texts to go beyond practices which reproduced inequalities. The policy texts are clearly in and of themselves not sufficient but we have argued that they can provide some guide to doing gender equality better in expanding education and addressing poverty.

How useful are the conceptual maps we have drawn on? Understanding global gender policy in education as a ladder, we have shown, tended to focus on giving narrow and precise meanings to gender, poverty and education. In understanding the relationships primarily as those of managing policy and information, two substantial areas of disagreement were pushed outside the space of consideration in a range of sites. These were, firstly, difficult questions of different interpretations of concepts, such as gender, poverty or global relationship. Secondly, in this way of interpreting policy and practice, the power between differently located people and how this affected their engagement with the concepts was not considered. This notion of a ladder clearly delineated some relationships with the MDG and EFA agenda at the top of national education bureaucracies, in multilateral organisations and in some NGOs. But lower down the ladder, amongst provincial or district officials, school managers and NGO workers, the sense of connection to a global gender policy project became very attenuated. However, it was not the narrow interpretations of gender as girls, or poverty as income that were lost, but some of the richer notions about equality, rights and global connection. This highlighted the importance of democratic iterations that could open up this space of reflection.

While we have documented some engagements with the ideas of global and national interconnections and currents linked to gender equality work with a strong concern with women's rights, blowing through global NGOs, affecting some of the work of officials in the South African national Department of Education, and some NGO workers, our data suggest that many who took these views found themselves struggling in organisations that did not make it easy to sustain and develop this direction. However, the experience of these relationships built a strong reflexive and political engagement with the issues, which appears to exemplify the process of democratic iteration. For officials, NGO workers or teachers who had these perspectives, the struggle to realise values was a set of practices that could be enacted in many different spaces. Indeed, it appears to us that the notion of gender equality as a letter, posted from one set of activists somewhere in the world and read by others, is a key link connecting these differently situated practitioners. This approach had been sketched through the Beijing process in 1995 and was partly adopted around the civil society mobilisations in support of EFA. This approach linked with some UN organisations and global NGOs but the links of affiliation were imprecise and often hard to sustain. In both Kenya and South Africa, the women's movement and education movement were not well connected, and the links between global and national civil society, and strategies for working with government, had periods of close engagement followed by distance or recalibration of the relationship. We have documented this in the personal affirmations made by some staff working in global organisations, in the South African national and provincial department, and in one global NGO in South Africa. Here this politics of identification and meaning-making around gender and rights was rarely evinced in our two years of data collection, and generally linked with particular relationships of openness to selected members of the research team.

We have documented fragmented ways of engaging relationships across these different terrains of a middle space where global policy is negotiated. The most formal relationships were linked with the MDG framework between multilateral organisations and national governments, but the meanings of these became diluted as we moved from the offices, where the policy was initially formulated, through the different places of negotiation, to implementation.

The three other terrains of a middle space we delineated appear not to have been well used to open up discussions of gender equality, addressing poverty and expanding education provision. Thus, while both Kenya and South Africa have a lively press, with much engagement with politics through discussions on radio, TV and newspaper readership, expanding through the use of the internet, the reporting of issues around gender and poverty did not seem to be growing a public sphere of debate that deepened engagement with equalities or rights. Indeed, some of the incidents associated with an opening of public sphere discussion highlighted the vulnerability of women NGO workers who had advocated for rights, or hostility against poor communities. The data suggest the public sphere does not naturally open up to an examination of equalities and rights, and that much more engaged work to give space to those who have historically been excluded from sharing experiences and insights should be given. More critical examination of the scholarship on these themes is needed and consideration of what democratic iterations look like in practice. A SDG agenda of reflection will not replace top-down MDG directives without considerable work to build the conditions in which local authorship, critique and reflective analysis on global initiatives can take place.

With regard to the third terrain of a middle space we identified, linked with professional practice, we documented how little attention professional education organisations at any level – global, national or local – gave to engaging with gender equality and addressing poverty. There is a huge agenda here around higher education, professional development and support that needs to help build the confidence, insight and space for dialogue of teachers, researchers, NGO workers and officials in government.

The fourth terrain we identified of civil society is amorphous and multi-faceted and we documented close engagement with global gender policy in some sites, and virtually no knowledge or association in others. After the fall of the Berlin Wall huge hopes were placed in global civil society and national organisations to take forward agendas for equality and rights. The women's movement grew under these conditions, and made important connections to governments and multilateral organisations. But our data illustrate how unevenly civil society organisations engage with questions of gender equality in education and poverty. The organisations cannot, merely because of a particular organisational form, do the work of building political membership, affiliation across multiple boundaries, engagement with difficult ideas and implementation of social development. Supporting democratic iterations seems a key task to develop in building a civil society oriented to protecting and advancing education rights and gender equality.

Thus, we have documented that global policy on gender cannot be understood as a train steaming down tracks laid by government structures or civil society towards implementation. In giving global policy form it has to be woven from the fabric of local experiences and relationships, which are sometimes close and supportive, and sometimes highly differentiated, even hostile. Our data show there is little co-ordination or even awareness of the problem of disconnection across different contexts, be these framed nationally, sectorally or around affiliation to gender equality and women's rights. The existence of a space between policy and enactment is rarely acknowledged as itself an important site for reflection, documentation, critique and connection. There is also little delineation of the distinctiveness of different terrains – the institutional, the professional, or civil society and the public sphere – and how histories or concentrations of resources might affect this. Researching democratic iterations would require more detailed attention to these processes.

What does the concept we have used throughout this discussion of terrains of a middle space add to our understanding of these negotiations between people in sites termed global, national and local? We have argued that we cannot understand any of these sites without an appreciation of the complexities of context, and that the terrains of a middle space are features of the context not often commented on. We note education or gender policy and features of its implementation in government or schools, but the reason why these particular forms of enactment occur is linked with layers of work or professional relationships in different kinds of organisations and their interplay with personal and affective relationships. Thus, context is formed both by political economy and the emotive socio-cultural relationships we have sketched associated with the terrains of a middle space. We developed this notion to help explain our data, but the data were not collected to understand how the terrains of a middle space actually work. This will require a further study, to examine what these terrains include and exclude, how their histories form some of the relationships and discourses they deploy, and how actors, differentially situated on terrains of a middle space, debate, negotiate or refuse gender equality policy change, and what the reasons for this are.

Our discussion throughout this book has considered a number of different facets of comparison, between sites of gender equality policy exchange, different formations of policy interpretation and different contextual histories as features of explanation. In standing back from our analysis to reflect on some of its implications for comparative and international education it is evident to us that we have engaged with a number of different ways to think about comparison. In designing our study and organising our analysis we were drawn to forms of analysis about the identity of different sites of policy. We assumed, because the global gender equality policies had been widely adopted, that below apparent differences of size or governance, there would be some marked similarities in how agendas to take these forward were formulated by global organisations, national states and a range of organisations working outside the state. Whatever the particular features of any site of policy realisation, we considered each could be analysed and compared using the same concepts. Thus we have been able to compare where, for example, gender equality reform on education and poverty is most and least evident, how hierarchies of global, local and national affect this and which terrains of a middle space appear most salient.

However, there are two approaches to comparison which question this form of comparing between sites deemed analytically equivalent, and some of these have emerged in the nuance of the data we have analysed. The first derives from De Sousa Santos' denial of a hierarchy (De Sousa Santos, 2015). This entails, for example, that the global, the national and the local are not ranked, as in our metaphor of the ladder, but range in different formations. We show both instances of hierarchies associated with global, national and local being acknowledged and refused.

Derrida (1993) further asserts that any thought is not the same as the thing it is about, and that the thing cannot be contained by the networks of thought that portray it, but will always remain itself. Thus the difference between global organisations, national sites of realisation and the terrains of any middle space will always exceed our attempts to anchor these conceptually and descriptively. Notions of hierarchy or transfer will always be inadequate to convey the things they describe. Thus as Henderson (2015) notes, the concept of gender is heterodox, but does not exhaust the multiplicity of relations associated with gender and education. Vavrus and Bartlett (2009) document how the networks of exchange around education policy exceed in ambition, discourse, or relationships what is realised on the ground. But this does not set limits to what these things are. Our data also suggest multiple meanings of gender, poverty and global relationship and the difficulties of engaging in comparison knowing that it will always be a reflexive move that expresses partial understanding (Unterhalter, 2014).

A third approach to comparison, also drawing on post-structuralism, but this time oriented to the thinking of Deleuze and Guattari (1987) considers the multiplicity of moments of interaction. In this analysis, the global, national and local are endlessly intermingled in exchanges around gender equality policy, poverty and education. Comparison might delineate moments of connection, but these will always branch away into different networks. Our data suggest some of these processes, but also show how distribution of resources or the discursive limits of ideas curtail this multiplicity.

The issue we have tried to discuss in this book concerns how, given different approaches to comparison, we understand the world in which we find ourselves and the actions around gender equality, education and poverty we consider it appropriate to take. The contemporary world is one of staggering inequalities, in which education is implicated both as a cause of injustice and as an approach to equality. Millions of children continue to have no education or schooling that is marked by inequalities of provision. Gender is one key dimension of these inequalities, as gender inequality crosses many formations of social division and is structured by other relationships of class, race, ethnicity and location. Access to high levels of education at elite institutions is a marker of positional advantage for those with incomes and wealth that go way beyond that of majorities in their own countries and the world. Given these injustices, what practices are right and good? The global policy landscape has come to be shaped by histories of experiences with documents that focus on rights, capabilities, equalities, goals, targets and indicators. Under these conditions do the different ways of thinking about comparison help guide an engagement on how to evaluate practice? The post-structuralist inflected critiques are useful because they draw attention to complexity and the limits of conceptual landscapes. But they are generally associated with a denial of ethical precepts. On the other hand, the form of comparison that stresses identity enjoins forms of equal treatment. But this approach confronts the difficulty of the range of diverse actors and sites of realisation this book has mapped, and the salience of the enormous resources needed to realise global gender equality and education aspirations. These are so much harder to achieve in practice than in thought.

Our argument suggests we need a wide range of resources, both material and conceptual, and having more and better connections is preferable to being isolated and having inadequate opportunities for participation and reflection. The MDGs introduced a new element to policy exchange, the notion of indicators and metrics. Gender parity was the metric associated with gender equality in education, and the income level $1.25 the metric associated with measuring poverty. There is an extensive debate on what these metrics were for, and whether they were literal measures of equality or poverty, or just indicators (Fukuda-Parr, Yamin and Greenstein, 2014). What our data show is that the presence of metrics do not seem to, in and of themselves, elicit more engaged work on equalities, although some metrics together with other processes, for example political experiences of work on feminism, or community mobilisation, or even care for the poor (the teachers in the South African school), seem to support some change. But the people talking about this called for a wider set of professional and critical relationships to consider these metrics, and this was not part of the MDG framework. It is not yet clear whether this process will change linked to the SDGs, which have widened the number of indicators linked to the education goals but not suggested more participatory processes for reflecting on these indicators, or what they show (UNESCO, 2016), although some work on gender equality and education indicators is beginning (Unterhalter, 2017).

The rationality or lack of rationality of organisations, and how politics might affect the policy space, was first raised by Grindle and Thomas in 1991 and has been a key issue in driving some of the work on metrics, because these are seen to deliver information, even if the policy space shrinks. However, our data show that organisations can work around rational hierarchies, and report on gender linked to very neutral indicators, but that this has the effect of closing support for the people who work in organisations to deepen the meanings associated with gender, equalities and addressing poverty. The time, money, education, democratic iterations for building understanding of complexity, and the difficulties of engagement are key, and it is these that need to be resourced side-by-side with better indicators of gender equality in education that go beyond gender parity.

The SDGs were adopted after a process on enhanced participation on the goals and targets. The women's movement, after the experience with the MDGs, remains cautious. Our data show the MDG process only patchily supported work on gender equality in education and women's rights. If the SDGs are not to be associated with a repeat of this uneven history, in a time of more unstable economic relations, ever widening global inequalities, war and the threats of climate change, it is clear we need to deepen the participation linked to realisation, and think about how to use the indicators in ways that connect with people's experience, and ways of evaluating and understanding poverty, gender inequality and the space of education.

The period of the 1990s, associated with the Beijing Platform of Action, EFA and the MDGs might have been the *belle epoque* of the 20th century, a moment of possibility, global convening, mobilising political will, the insights of research and translating this into efficient planning. These were all intermixed with the speeded up forms of global economic exchanges and new technologies. It was assumed that advancing global gender equality policy on education and poverty might not be easy, but that it was not impossible. This book has questioned these assumptions. Our conclusion is that the translation of global policy frameworks concerned with gender equality to national and local contexts is harder than anyone thought. The authority, quality of information and opportunities for equitable deliberation given to local actors, concerned with making normative evaluations, is a crucial component of changed practice, as are strategies to sustain the institutions and networks that support equalities and inclusions. This hard work remains ahead of us as we pick up the wider ambition of the SDGs and remember the promises made in the Beijing Platform of Action.

References

Antrobus, P. (2005). MDGs: Most distracting gimmicks? *Convergence*, 38(3), pp. 49–52.

Ball, S., Maguire, M., & Braun, A. (2012). *How Schools Do Policy: Policy Enactments in Secondary Schools*. Oxford: Routledge.

Biccum, A. (2010). *Global Citizenship and the Legacy of Empire: Marketing Development*. Abingdon: Routledge.

Deleuze, G., & Guattari, F. (1987). *A Thousand Plateaus*. Minneapolis: University of Minnesota Press.

Derrida, J. (1993). *Aporias*. Stanford: Stanford University Press.

de Sousa Santos, B. (2015). *Epistemologies of the South: Justice against Epistemicide*. Abingdon: Routledge.

Fukuda-Parr, S., Yamin, A. E., & Greenstein, J. (2014). The power of numbers: A critical review of millennium development goal targets for human development and human rights. *Journal of Human Development and Capabilities*, 15(2–3), pp. 105–117.

Grindle, M. S., & Thomas, J. W. (1991). *Public Choices and Policy Change: The Political Economy or Reform in Developing Countries*. Baltimore: The John Hopkins University Press.

Henderson, E. F. (2015). *Gender Pedagogy: Teaching, Learning and Tracing Gender in Higher Education*. Basingstoke: Palgrave Macmillan.

Kabeer, N. (2015). Tracking the gender politics of the Millennium Development Goals: Struggles for interpretive power in the international development agenda. *Third World Quarterly*, 36(2), pp. 377–395.

Mundy, K., Green, A., Lingard, B., & Verger, A. (2016). The globalisation of education policy: Key approaches and debates. In Mundy, K., Green, A., Lingard, B. and Verger, A. eds. *The Handbook of Global Education Policy*. Oxford: John Wiley, pp. 1–20.

Steiner-Khamsi, G. (2004). *The Global Politics of Educational Borrowing and Lending*. New York: Teachers College Press.

Steiner-Khamsi, G., & Waldow, F. (Eds.). (2012). *World Yearbook of Education 2012: Policy Borrowing and Lending in Education*. Abingdon: Routledge.

UNESCO (2016). *Education for People and Planet: Creating Sustainable Jutures for All*. Paris: UNESCO.

Unterhalter, E. (2014). Walking backwards into the future: A comparative perspective on education and a post-2015 framework. *Compare: A Journal of Comparative and International Education*, 44(6), pp. 852–873.

Unterhalter, E. (2017). Negative capability? Measuring the unmeasurable in education. *Comparative Education*, 53(1), pp. 1–16.

Vavrus, F., & Bartlett, L. (2009). *Critical Approaches to Comparative Education: Vertical Case Studies from Africa, Europe, the Middle East and the Americas*. Basingstoke: Palgrave Macmillan.

Appendices

Appendix 1
Millennium Development Goals

Goal 1: Eradication of extreme poverty and hunger
Goal 2: Achieve universal primary education
Goal 3: Promote gender equality and empower women
Goal 4: Reduce child mortality
Goal 5: Improve maternal health
Goal 6: Combat HIV/AIDS malaria and other diseases
Goal 7: Ensure environmental sustainability
Goal 8: Develop a Global Partnership for Development

Appendix 2
Multi-country research team

Project Director: Elaine Unterhalter, UCL Institute of Education.
Research Officer: Amy North, UCL Institute of Education.
Research Officer: Veerle Dieltiens, University of the Witwatersrand, Education Policy Unit.
Research Officer: Jenni Karlsson, University of KwaZulu-Natal.
Research Officer: Jane Onsongo, Catholic University of Eastern Africa.
Research Assistant: Herbert Makinda, Catholic University of Eastern Africa.
Research Assistant: Setungoane Letsatsi, University of the Witwatersrand, Education Policy Unit.
Research Assistant: Nomanesi Madiya, University of KwaZulu-Natal.
Research Adviser: Chris Yates, UCL Institute of Education.
Interpreters and translators in KwaZulu-Natal: Students from the School of Education, KwaZulu-Natal.

Appendix 3

Members of the Project Advisory Committees

In Kenya the members of the Advisory Committee were Professor Paul Ogula, Professor Mary Getui, Dr. Nyokabi Kamau, Mr. Andiwo Obondoh, Mrs. Edith Wekesa, Mrs. Jedidah Mungai, Mr. Lawrence Waiyaki Kariuki and Mr. Simpiri Sapunyu.

In South Africa, the Advisory Committee comprised Professor Shireen Hassim, Professor Lebo Moletsane, Professor Wayne Hugo, Professor Shirley Pendlebury, Ms. Thandi Lewin, Ms. Alex Kent and Dr. Shermain Mannah.

Appendix 4
Additional project contributions

The following people made short-term contributions to the work of the project:

Dr. Githui Kimamo, Caroline Mani, Rev. Dr. John Lukwata and Dr. Justus Mbae collected some data for the Kenya case studies.

Dr. Fibian Lukalo, Dr. Rosie Peppin Vaughan and Professor Paul Ogula completed some of the analysis of Kenya data.

Clare Thornbury and Holly McGlynn oversaw the financial and organisational aspects of the project.

Charlotte Nussey prepared data for the final report.

Index

Made in the USA
Middletown, DE
06 October 2020